AMERICAN CARS

Pierce-Arrow

Cadillac

Plymouth

Allstate

Packard

Ford

Pont

Ford

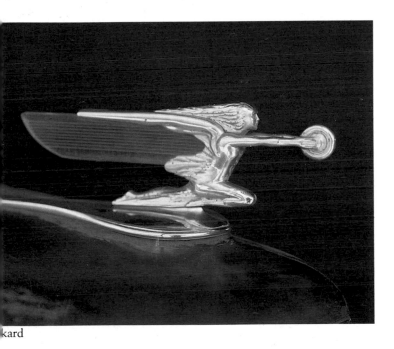

kard

Chevrolet

kard

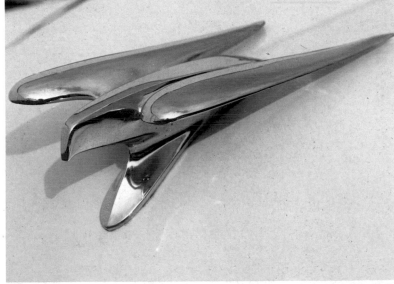

Chrysler

AMERICAN CARS

by LEON MANDEL

Photography by
Baron Wolman and Lucinda Lewis

From Harrah's Automobile Collection

Stewart, Tabori & Chang, Publishers, New York

To Lee and Joe Eskridge,

who were part of all this and part

of the best part at that.

frontispiece:
Hood ornament from a 1933 Pierce-Arrow.
Photo by Joseph Kugielsky

Book design by Nai Y. Chang

Editorial supervision by Leslie Stoker

Library of Congress Cataloging in Publication Data
Mandel, Leon.
    American cars.

    Biblography: p.
    Includes index.
    1. Automobiles—United States—History. I. Title.
TL15.M265   629.2'222'0973   82-5609
ISBN 0-941434-19-2   AACR2

Photographs of Harrah's automobiles copyright ©1982 by
Baron Wolman and Lucinda Lewis.

Distributed by Workman Publishing Company, Inc.,
1 West 39th Street, New York, New York 10018.

Contents

Foreword

The American automobile is a reflection of the pioneers who greeted it — almost full blown—in the New World and devised a way of flooding the nation with it. Americans did not invent the car. American technology, except during the early years of development prior to World War I, took a back seat to overseas refinement and experimentation. In fact, during the Depression and after World War II, it seemed American engineers were sleeping in the back seat.

Nonetheless, the United States contributed mightily to the flowering of auto-mobility. An early pioneer, Eli Ransom Olds, invented subcontracting. Another pioneer, Henry Leland, refined manufacture so that parts were genuinely interchangeable. Walter Flanders of Ford designed auto plants to make manufacture efficient and cheap. Alfred Sloan of GM created the annual model change and boosted installment selling—the two great marketing techniques that put the car in almost every garage in the nation.

In all this, we followed our own course. Our roads and our national mania for movement, combined with the emphasis on mass manufacture, resulted in a car for America that was different from every other automobile manufactured elsewhere except Canada, a virtual subcontracting nation for Detroit. Only now because of world fuel shortages and shortages of strategic metals in the United States are we building cars in the same idiom as those produced elsewhere in the world: same size, same shape, same philosophy of high fuel economy and limited performance.

That Detroit has had to change its course 180 degrees and depart from its huge ocean-liner cars complete with every aid to comfort known to the manufacturing establishment has come as a terrible shock to the industry and the nation. It is costing Detroit as much to change to the world pattern as it cost the United States to send a man to the moon. Car costs have risen enormously as a result of Detroit's forced investment. Because new cars are now so expensive, the market has shrunk—probably permanently.

This suffering by our industry is the inevitable consequence of the excesses of Detroit managers beginning with the founder of GM, Billy Durant, who wanted to flood every segment of the market with a product of some kind. Look into the fenders of a Chevrolet or a Ford or a Chrysler product and you will see the reflections of Durant and Sloan, Henry Ford and his grandson, Henry II, and Walter Chrysler. We had seventy-five years of glorious overproduction of cars appropriate for a profligate country with endless expanses of highway.

Detroit managerial philosophies were not confined to product; the auto industry affected America in many ways. When John J. Raskob accepted the job of chairman of the Democratic party running Governor Al Smith's presidential campaign in 1928, he was a top GM executive doing his political duty, which included exerting influence in behalf of General Motors. Roy Dikeman Chapin founded Hudson Motor Company, and as a member of a variety of commissions and study groups and as Secretary of Commerce under Hoover, he was instrumental in promoting what would become the great interstate highway

Fifth Avenue Bus
The Fifth Avenue bus is used for transportation between Harrah's Automobile Collection and the casinos in Reno, Nevada.

9

system. The pages of American political and economic history are filled with the contributions of (and obstacles put up by) the auto industry chiefs. It is not enough, then, to try to understand our automotive past by examining sheet metal alone.

Although *American Cars* is divided into sections labeled in deference, more or less, to the purists who define the ages of the car by considerations of technology: beginning with the Horseless Carriage (1893-1915), Antique Cars (1916-1931), Classic Cars (1932-1948), Vintage Cars, and so forth, our own sociohistorical tapestry is too rich to be viewed within such a limited framework. If Raskob and Chapin—just two examples of automotive activists—affected the way we lived and worked and voted, it seems appropriate to look first in each section of our automotive history at the state of our society. So, generally, the first chapter in each section does just that. It is followed by a chapter about the technology of the era (here the structure twice follows a slightly different pattern, the result of overlapping automotive genres during the same period); but technology must be interpreted loosely to include, for example, not only the first use of four-wheel brakes but also the introduction of traffic lights and drivers' licenses. The third chapter in each section is a driving impression of a car typical of the epoch. What did it feel like to own and operate a Duesenberg Model SJ Dual Cowl Phaeton? A Model T? A Curved Dash Olds?

In addition, the driving impressions put the car down not only in time but place. Ford's Model B-A, its first real postwar car, probably saved the company as a number 2 power in the industry; its driving impression presents the men who decided to build it and their decisions about its shape and size, the story of its introduction, and finally what it felt like to drive it. Who and where were you if you owned and drove a Javelin in the late 1960s? Perhaps you were an AMC dealer invited to the road races at Lime Rock Park in Connecticut to watch the factory race against its competitors. That is how the Javelin appears in *American Cars*. The Pontiac GTO, the first of the Muscle cars, is set in a drive-in near Detroit, for that is where the whole subculture of street racing flowered.

It is a thesis of *American Cars* that the automobile's ubiquity contributed enormously to the rise of the middle class in our nation, making us equally mobile and almost equally independent in terms of the potential to realize our personal manifest destiny.

It is another thesis that the car has had profound effects on the way we live: from the manner in which it offered escape from the 1930s dust bowl and helped populate California, to the manner in which it pollutes our air, to the 20 percent of employed Americans it encompasses in its primary (car builders and car sellers) and secondary (motel staffs and fast-food cooks) workforces.

Love it or hate it, the car is the central artifact of most lives. We mark our passages by the car we owned at the time of marriage or the birth of a child or a promotion in a job. We have vacationed in our cars, commuted to work or to school in them, raced them, shown them at concours d'élégances, collected them, dragged or cruised Main Street in them. We all have our own particular memories of a specific car or perhaps of several.

We are nearing the end of the Century of the Car; it has been a glorious hundred years in America. Studies by the great think tanks (SRI International, for example) tell us our individual modules of transportation will continue much as they are now through the end of the year 2025, when they will be replaced with . . . something. In the meantime, we have the car and we can look forward to having the car for a little while longer, and we should be delighted about it all. We have built brilliant automotive devices in this country.

I
THE HORSELESS
CARRIAGE
1893–1915

CHAPTER 1

A Nation Unhorsed

Mobility arrived in America a century and a half before the word "auto-mobility" would have been understood. We were a nation of travelers before we were a country with a town named Detroit. We were well on our way to developing a national habit of movement for the sheer sake of movement.

The American historian George Pierson, in the way of historians who give us theses and labels, called this endless circling and shuffling the "M-Factor" ("M" for Mobility). Another historian, Frederick Jackson Turner, decided that with the closing of the frontier in 1889, we had established a national character marked by the push westward.

This great migration, said Turner, forever stamped mobility on the foreheads of Americans. Furthermore, it deified individualism. Turner's "Frontier Thesis" wasn't much loved by his successors, but this didn't prevent at least two of them from sidling around to something of the same opinion. Henry Steele Commager, for example, wrote that "The American rarely expected to stay put," and our present Librarian of Congress, Daniel Boorstin, went even further: "The churning, casual, vagrant, circular motion around and around was as characteristic of the American experience as the movement in a single direction.... Americans were a new kind of Bedouin. More than anything else, they valued the freedom to move."

Little wonder we were ready for the car when Karl Benz and Gottfried Daimler got around to inventing it—though not together, of course. The history of invention is filled with examples of individuals creating the same device at the same time but in different places. The wonder of the invention of the car is that it came together in Germany at a time when the Western world seemed to be impatient for it to arrive.

This is not to say that when Charles E. and J. Frank Duryea's first primitive car chugged across the New England landscape in 1893, we were the same people we are today. We were a nation tied together by railroads financed by some of the great villains of our history: the Railroad Gang. Like their auto manufacturing successors, they had a virtual monopoly on long distance transportation in the United States; unlike them, they showed almost no responsibility to the people they served. At the end of the Civil War the United States embraced 35,000 miles of trackage of varying gauges. Less than a half century later it was criss-crossed by 240,000 interconnected standard gauge miles, and three years before the Duryeas's car ventured timidly out on a September morning in Springfield, Massachusetts, the nation contained one-third of the world's total railroad miles. These railroads were ridden (in lush private railway carriages) by untaxed men of enormous wealth who gazed out of their windows at factories worked by impoverished immigrants or at farms tactically placed near the tracks to facilitate the transportation of produce to market.

In the early years of the automobile, it was nearly as much of a gamble to go driving as it was to put money on red.

13

1893 Duryea
Although the U.S. was advanced in road carriage steam technology, it was behind the Europeans when it came to cars powered by the internal combustion engine. In 1893 the Duryea brothers began to change all that when they put the first successful American gas powered car on the road in Springfield, Massachusetts, on a bright September morning.

Nor did much of American society seem bothered by the enormous gulf separating the men of wealth who profited from the building and operating of the railroads and those who labored in the factories and fields by their rights of way. George W. Vanderbilt, for example, had a little country place in Asheville, North Carolina, named "Biltmore" with 40 master bedrooms that sat on a 203-square-mile plot of land. Said the then Secretary of Agriculture, J. Sterling Morton: "He employs more men than I have in my charge. He is also spending more money than Congress appropriates for this Department." Brother William K. Vanderbilt called his Long Island villa "Idle Hour"; it had 110 rooms, 45 bathrooms, and a garage large enough for 100 automobiles.

This automania by the Vanderbilts was typical of the manner in which the car was greeted when it chugged into the world. It was a toy of the rich man. William K.'s garage contained: DeDion Bouton, Stevens-Duryea, Hispano-Suiza, and later on Duesenberg, Rolls-Royce, Mercedes, and Isotta-Fraschini. He had a twenty-man crew of chauffeurs and mechanics. His ex-wife Alva staged the first private automotive entertainment in Newport, Rhode Island, in 1899, a rally on the lawn of her cottage. Alva's course had obstacles such as dummy servants, police, and babies in carriages spread randomly around the green; the winner "killed" the fewest targets. William K.'s nephew, Reggie Vanderbilt, was often seen leaping and bouncing down backcountry roads in the open cockpit of his car with his dog by his side—driver and dog dressed in matching leggings, coat, and goggles.

14

The contrast to America's lower class was enormous. The average wage of the American worker was not quite $500 a year, and according to the census of 1900, six and a half million were out of work. When they did get jobs, they were grateful for the opportunity to work ten hours a day, six days a week and to work alongside children at that. One contemporary report had 26 percent of boys between 10 and 15 "gainfully employed." We were a society divided by class, no doubt about it. We were rich and mobile or we were poor and not; we lived on farms or we lived in the cities. The automobile would help to change all of this, as we shall see.

And what of that social segment that would most warmly embrace the car and, in turn, be most influenced by it—the middle class? There wasn't much of one as we understand it today. But if a college professor is a representative member of the middle class, then Woodrow Wilson's attempts to lure the very Frederick Jackson Turner of the "Frontier Thesis" to teach at Princeton, where Wilson was then president, may be instructive. Wilson offered Turner an annual salary of $3,500. Mrs. Wilson told Mrs. Turner that a realistic budget would allocate $75 a month for food and light, $42 a month for rent, $3.50 per week each for two servants, $12 for the monthly heating bill (coal) and $4 a month for water.

Two additional factors help explain our readiness for the car. We were strong consumerists, and we had a real pollution problem.

Turn-of-the-century consumerism is not to be confused with late-in-the-

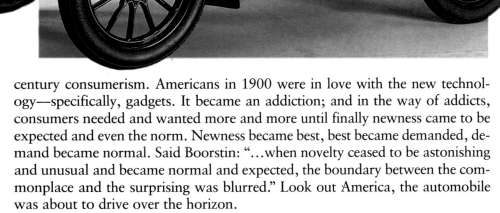

1906 Adams-Farwell Convertible Runabout Model 6A
The Adams company of Dubuque, Iowa, sought innovation at any cost. The Convertible Runabout Model 6A used an engine whose cylinders revolved horizontally around a vertical stationary crankshaft. It also had variable compression control, an automatic spark regulator, and a centrifugal oiling system.

century consumerism. Americans in 1900 were in love with the new technology—specifically, gadgets. It became an addiction; and in the way of addicts, consumers needed and wanted more and more until finally newness came to be expected and even the norm. Newness became best, best became demanded, demand became normal. Said Boorstin: "…when novelty ceased to be astonishing and unusual and became normal and expected, the boundary between the commonplace and the surprising was blurred." Look out America, the automobile was about to drive over the horizon.

As for pollution, it was then, as it is now, especially irksome in the cities. At the turn of the century, New York blossomed under 2.5 million pounds of horse manure and 60,000 gallons of urine deposited on its streets every day. Dead horses littered the streets at the rate of about 15,000 carcasses each year. Clearly, horsepower had its drawbacks.

So the social stage was set. What was the state of transportation at the point when the car was introduced? From our first hesitant steps inland on the new continent until the age of the car, we repeated in the New World the history of movement in the Old. Footpower was useful but slow and its range limited. Domesticated beasts were expensive and contributed to urban pollution. We did carve out canals, which extended our waterborne range inland, but canal building was laborious, expensive, and frequently impossible. But in the same century (the eighteenth) we invented the canal, we discovered an even more important device: the steam engine. It took no great leap of imagination to think of a steam engine reposing in a wheeled box of some kind, and many such were tried—almost all of them failures. The problem was that we had not refined the steam engine to be sufficiently light and small for the carriage that bore it to traverse our primitive roads. Whereupon we rightly concluded that a very special kind of highway would have to be devised, one strong enough to take the weight of a steam-powered vehicle, a highway consisting of parallel iron rails. Harnessing steam was an enormous achievement. What we had not done was offer the average man a means of reaching his own destination, at his own convenience. Enter that extraordinary device, the bicycle.

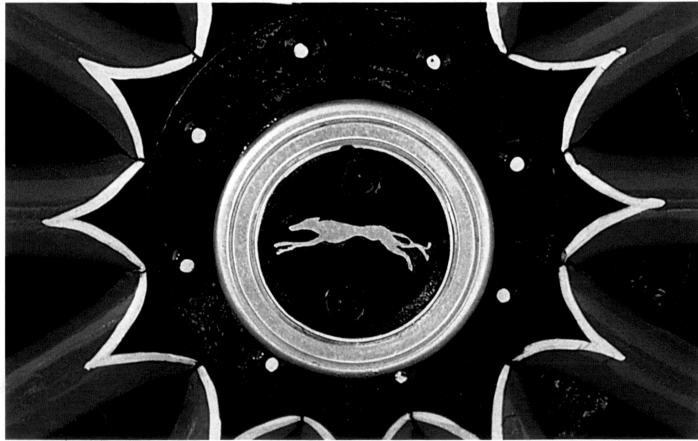

1892 Philion Road Carriage
A two-cylinder, 1-horsepower steamer weighing 550 pounds, this is a one-of-a-kind vehicle. It represents the predawn of the American auto age and an evolutionary dead end.

1907 Success Model B Auto Buggy
For $300, buyers of the Success, made in St. Louis, got an air-cooled, one-cylinder, 4-hp car with solid tires and not much of a future.

"Its principles are so simple, it is at first surprising that no one thought of it before," said B. Bruce-Briggs. "But in fact the technology was not available. To function effectively, a bicycle must be light, well balanced, and easily controlled, and it was not until the late 19th century that metallurgy was developed to the point where lightweight frames, wire-spoked wheels and precision wheels and steering bearings were available."

Contemplate Bruce-Briggs's musings a moment and you will see at what peril you dismiss the bicycle as precursor of the automobile. Extend his thoughts only a little, and you will anticipate how very close the virtues of the bicycle come to the advantages of the car. Principally, the bicycle gave us the notion that it was possible to come and go in our own time at our own pleasure; and once that idea was implanted, Americans became impatient to come and go even further than the bicycle could take them, at an even faster pace, carrying larger loads and more passengers.

But first we needed real roads on which to travel, and again the bicycle played a key role. Its advocates pushed for smooth paths on which to travel, because a bicycle depends on continued forward motion for its stability. Nor was the demand for decent roads the bicycle's only contribution to the development of the automobile. As it became more and more popular, the bicycle drew greater and greater numbers of craftsmen into the arena of its construction, rewarding those builders with money to establish shops and what we would come to call garages.

The curtain was about to rise on the Century of the Car.

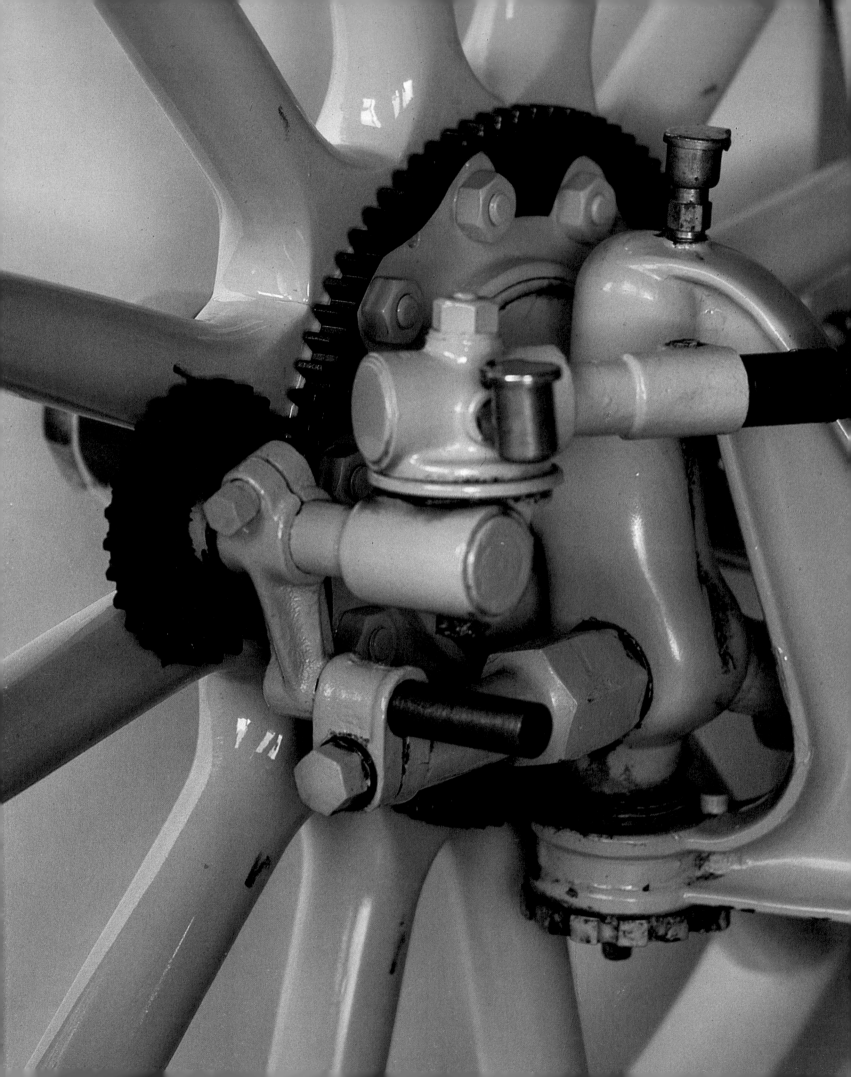

CHAPTER 2

Inventions and Inventors, Pioneers and Plungers

Of course it was Leonardo da Vinci who conceived the idea of the automobile, but he did not stay around to see it work. The real genesis came when Germany's Nikolaus August Otto and Eugene Langen developed an internal combustion engine that ran on coal gas, formed a company in 1864 to sell the things, and had the effrontery to display them at the Paris Exposition of 1867. Eleven years later the engine appeared at the Philadelphia Centennial Exposition. By that time Otto had hit upon the four-cycle notion that still bears his name, and nine years after that, he managed to make an engine run on liquid fuel. So in a manner of speaking, by 1885 things were off and running.

Mainly, they were running in Europe, thanks to Daimler, Benz, Wilhelm Maybach, and Emile Levassor. Germany granted Maybach and Daimler a patent for a V-2 engine in June 1889, and in the same year, the two showed a genuine automobile at the Paris Exposition. No question about it, the Europeans were the inventive pioneers. It remained for Americans to thrash through the problems of production and to plant the automobile as the technological centerpiece of the nation. That they did, but not before a few dozen false starts.

Said one of our principal automotive historians, John Rae: "They [the Americans] had to devise a vehicle that would meet certain rather rigorous technical requirements: it had to be mechanically simple enough to be operated by individuals who knew little or nothing about machinery; at the same time, it had to be well enough constructed to stand up under ordinary usage without frequent and expensive repairs. This vehicle had to be produced at a cost which would permit it to be sold profitably in a highly competitive market, and techniques of production had to be developed to meet a constantly increasing and for a time apparently insatiable demand."

It also had to find a home for its manufacture, people to finance and build it, and decide whether it would be propelled by engines running on steam, liquid fuel, or electricity. Before any of that could happen, it had to work well enough in the New World to be taken seriously. The first internal combustion patent granted in the United States was given to George B. Brayton's engine in 1872. Apart from the fact that today "Brayton Cycle" is the technical name for the turbine, the same kind of engine that propels a jet airplane, it had only one real consequence. Brayton's invention was used to power a kind of trolley that ran between Providence and Cranston, Rhode Island, where it came to the attention of George B. Selden, who decided it belonged not in an interurban at all, but in a horseless carriage. Selden waited until 1879 to file a patent for such a device. Selden's government-granted imprimateur caused mischief for the infant American automobile industry until Henry Ford successfully challenged it in court thirty-two years later.

But we are several laps ahead of ourselves. First, we had to get a horseless carriage (as the automobile was coming to be called) in motion on the North

Inside of the Mercer Raceabout wheel assembly.

1902 Haynes-Apperson Runabout
The Haynes-Apperson saw the light of day in the hands of Jonathan Maxwell on the Pumpkinville Pike in Kokomo, Indiana. There was much argument as to whether this or the Duryea, manufactured in Springfield, Massachusetts, was the first gas-powered production car to appear on our roads.

American continent. The Duryeas's car—the Massachusetts miracle of 1893—was the first gas automobile to run successfully in the Colonies. We had been experimenting—more daringly and with greater rewards than the Europeans—for decades. Then, a year after the Duryeas took their trip in Springfield, Elwood G. Haynes turned over his plans for a one-cylinder internal combustion automobile to Elmer and Edgar Apperson who, with help from Jonathan Maxwell, got the thing to run 6 mph on the nation's 118th birthday over a part of the Pumpkinville Pike in Kokomo, Indiana. By the following year, 1895, the Duryeas had set up in business to make horseless carriages (The Duryea Motor Wagon Company), and Hiram P. Maxim started a "motor carriage" department in the Pope Manufacturing bicycle shops in Hartford, Connecticut.

Already patterns were forming. New England had taken a lead in the sweepstakes to become the auto manufacturing center of the nation, principally because it was already home to the logical progenitors of the car builders: bicycle and wagon constructors. New Englanders were inventive and vigorous; they were blessed or burdened with industrial experience. The very factors contributing to Pope Manufacturing's interest in the horseless carriage eventually identified Flint, Michigan, and then Detroit with the manufacture of cars. New Englanders, including Colonel Albert A. Pope, were not single-minded enough about the car to hold their advantage. (Pope-Hartford experimented—as did many early builders—but the company took its search too far. After early indecision, it built a one-cylinder internal combustion car in 1905—as we're about to see—then a two-cylinder, then a car with double chain drive in 1908, and then switched to electrics.) Pope's adventures with the motor car are illustrative of his understanding of manufacturing but not of automobiles.

Pope took what he had saved from his army pay during the Civil War and started a bicycle company that became the largest in the United States. He discovered very shortly that the real limits to the size of his company and to its sales came from the fact that while he made bicycles, other people were making the parts upon which he relied for their assembly. That would never do. First, he acquired the patents for the building of the parts, then he took over the companies that made them. He bought the Weed Sewing Machine Company and then the Hartford Rubber Works. A year before he agreed to establish a "motor carriage" department at Pope Manufacturing, he built a modern mill for the making of cold drawn steel tubing.

Colonel Pope found Hiram P. Maxim through the people he hired to run his research department and his tube subsidiary. When it came time for Maxim to hoist his boss aboard his mid-engined internal-combustion-powered car for a ride, the results were disastrous for the company. "You cannot get people to sit over an explosion," the Colonel is reported to have said, and he promptly decided to go into the electric car business and be done with trying to make the gas engine smooth and quiet. This, said Rae, was key to the American attitude toward the automobile: "The primary emphasis was [put] on production rather than experimentation."

But back for a moment to that momentous year, 1893. Just as the Europeans were ahead of the Americans in the technical development of the automobile, New Englanders were in front of midwesterners in experimentation. But engineering would not be an early hallmark of our automotive youth. As Rae said, production was the key to growth, and there the midwesterners were making plans to forge ahead. Eighteen ninety-three was the year in which the Flint Road Cart Company was incorporated and capitalized at $150,000 by Josiah Dallas Dort and William Crapo Durant. The company's name was soon changed to the Durant-Dort Carriage Company. It followed Colonel Pope's example of surrounding itself with company-owned subcontractors of axles, paints, wheels, varnishes, and tops, in addition to controlling its source of lumber. The company became the first incarnation of General Motors a decade later. That put the founder, Billy Durant, into the automobile business late, for an honor roll of pioneers had been building cars for years.

Welcome Aboard Henry Ford

Legend has it—and there is more folk tale about the man than perhaps any American in our history—that Henry Ford was a backwoods genius with not much grounding in mechanics. Legend is not to be trusted. He served as an apprentice machinist in Detroit and as a journeyman at the Detroit Drydock Company. He was a watch tinkerer and repairer, and there is some evidence he contemplated manufacturing low-cost watches for the masses. If this is true, it is the first intimation of his later grand achievements in creating and building the Model T.

In 1896, Ford built his first car, the quadricycle, whose virtues were its low weight (500 pounds), and steel-tube, wire-wheel chassis. During the next three years he not only built his second car but found William Murphy, a lumber dealer, who put together a group of Detroit businessmen to manufacture it. Ford was superintendent of a firm formed for the purpose, named the Detroit Automobile Company. It was a failure. But that deterred neither Ford nor Murphy. They founded a second company, this one named for the superintendent. Ford was by this time totally taken with automobile racing, at first with Murphy's approval, later to his disenchantment, which led to the breakup of the partner-

1903 Dyke
It came as a two-, four-, or five-seater; with solid or balloon tires; a 5-horse-power single-cylinder to a 12-horse-power twin engine; and prices from $700 to $1,000—but whichever one you chose, the car came in a box. It was one of the world's first "kit"—do-it-yourself—cars. The company lasted from 1901 to 1904.

ship. But Ford's racing—as we shall discover later—proved an enormous boost to his reputation and his career. It was also something of a sidestep, but enough of one to allow another pioneer, named Ransom Eli Olds, to establish production methods later credited to Ford. These methods were, in fact, the first steps in the beginning of the automobile business.

Ransom Eli Olds's background had given him considerable sophistication in both the understanding of self-powered vehicles and in ways of putting them together. Olds's father owned a machine shop in Lansing, Michigan. By the son's twenty-first birthday he had bought half interest in it; he became sole proprietor in 1890.

Very early on Olds was experimenting with automobiles, if that's what his first effort, a three-wheeled steamer, could be called. He also tried his hand at a four-cornered whistler, but all the while he seemed to have been looking out of the corner of his eye at the internal combustion engine. The consequence of that enchantment was a change of name and purpose for the machine shop. It became the Olds Gasoline Engine Works and, by 1897, the Olds Motor Vehicle Company.

As with Ford's first effort, Olds's company went bust, but two years later he too found a backer and went into business in Detroit as the Olds Motor Works with Samuel L. Smith and Smith's son Frederick L. The company concentrated on engines, but it also built cars, both electric and gasoline—one of which led to a landmark auto. It was a one-cylinder car designed to sell at $650. At this point a piece of disguised good luck descended on Olds and the Smiths: The factory burned down, leaving nothing to be rescued from its ashes but a single example of the gasoline car. Obviously, dramatic measures were required if any of the company's investment was to be recouped, and the drastic measures that were taken would set yet another pattern for the industry. First, subcontracts had to be let for a car somewhat redesigned, since the original plans had gone up in flames with the plant. And then, because it was clear that what was left of the factory, even somewhat reconstituted, would not be up to any kind of real production, another plant had to be found. Enter the good citizens of Flint, who ponied up almost $5,000 to buy a site in the city. Enter then some of the famous names of the infant automobile business to do the outside work: Benjamin Briscoe to do the bodies, Henry Leland and Robert C. Faulconer to manufacture the engines, and John F. and Horace E. Dodge to make transmissions.

Epiphany! What came out of disaster was a system of subcontracting and an absolutely remarkable product—the 1901 Curved Dash Oldsmobile. Rae called it "the first low-priced car to be produced in quantity." By 1904, the company had built 12,100 cars and earned enormous profits, at which point Ransom Eli Olds parted with the Smiths to found another company he called REO—but not until yet another pioneer had demonstrated the quality of the original. Roy D. Chapin drove a Curved Dash Olds from Detroit to New York for the 1901 auto show, a remarkable feat and enough of an encouragement to Chapin that he would go on to create the Hudson Motor Car Company.

Master of Precision

In the meantime, what of Olds's subcontractors, Leland and Faulconer, for example, and Henry Leland in particular?

Leland was a New Englander, brought up through a succession of toolmaker's jobs including employment at Colt Arms and Brown and Sharpe manufacturing, where standards were exacting. Soon enough, he found himself partners with another Brown and Sharpe alumnus in a more prosperous part of the country, Detroit, doing business as Leland and Faulconer. Leland was famous for his insistence on fine tolerances at the new company that made, among other devices, internal combustion engines. When Henry Ford Company, Ford's second venture (after Detroit Automobile but before Ford Motor) went soft, and

LEFT AND OVERLEAF:
1904 Cadillac Touring Model B
When Henry Ford abandoned ship—in the second automobile company he had helped found—to go racing, Henry Leland took over the company and renamed it Cadillac. This touring car exhibits all the expertise Leland brought to early American car manufacture, namely, the fine tolerances of its machined parts.

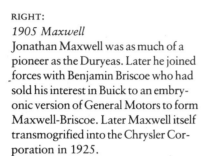

E. Dodge were also Michiganders (Port Huron) and also machinists. Like Ransom Olds, their father owned a machine shop which had been making internal
combustion engines for marine use. Their own success as subcontractors brings
us back to Henry Ford, for he had once again gone to the manufacturing well
with capital from a new partner, Alexander Y. Malcomson, a Detroit coal dealer,
to found the real Ford Motor Company in June of 1903. Ford now contracted
with the Dodges to build engines and transmissions, in fact the whole chassis for
his new car, to his own designs. The Dodge brothers will reappear in the nar-
rative, but first we shall turn to a handful of other automotive pioneers whose
stories are not so intertwined with Ford's and Durant's.

Packard and Marmon

Henry Leland was not the only fanatic on the subject of precision parts in the infant automobile industry. James W. Packard had bought a Winton named for a
Cleveland bicycle manufacturer, Alexander Winton, another immigrant Scots-
man who built his first car in 1896. This was the same Winton who was the first
man to make a long automobile trip—Cleveland to New York in 1898—and for a
time was the largest manufacturer of automobiles in the United States. Packard
had been intrigued enough by Winton's product to buy the twelfth car built by the
Clevelander, but he did not find it very satisfactory. The story goes that Packard's
complaints annoyed Winton sufficiently that he told Packard that if he didn't like
the car he should go off and build one of his own. Packard was not the man to
challenge thus. He had been playing with designs for an automobile for some time
and had brought a French pioneer auto called a DeDion-Bouton back from
Europe. Winton's cranky response to Packard prompted the latter to lure a pair
of Winton's employees away from the company to begin a firm of their own in
partnership with J. W. and his brother William D. Packard.

Now things get a little confusing. The two ex-Winton men and the Packard
brothers joined forces with one Henry B. Joy, whose father had been part of the
Railroad Gang and profited enormously from that association. Joy discovered
one of the first Packards at the New York auto show in 1901. He liked the car,
and he liked the company that was making it enough to invest substantially and
reorganize it as the Packard Motor Car Company. Joy was an educated man,

a piece of disguised good luck descended on Olds and the Smiths: The factory burned down, leaving nothing to be rescued from its ashes but a single example of the gasoline car. Obviously, dramatic measures were required if any of the company's investment was to be recouped, and the drastic measures that were taken would set yet another pattern for the industry. First, subcontracts had to be let for a car somewhat redesigned, since the original plans had gone up in flames with the plant. And then, because it was clear that what was left of the factory, even somewhat reconstituted, would not be up to any kind of real production, another plant had to be found. Enter the good citizens of Flint, who ponied up almost $5,000 to buy a site in the city. Enter then some of the famous names of the infant automobile business to do the outside work: Benjamin Briscoe to do the bodies, Henry Leland and Robert C. Faulconer to manufacture the engines, and John F. and Horace E. Dodge to make transmissions.

Epiphany! What came out of disaster was a system of subcontracting and an absolutely remarkable product—the 1901 Curved Dash Oldsmobile. Rae called it "the first low-priced car to be produced in quantity." By 1904, the company had built 12,100 cars and earned enormous profits, at which point Ransom Eli Olds parted with the Smiths to found another company he called REO—but not until yet another pioneer had demonstrated the quality of the original. Roy D. Chapin drove a Curved Dash Olds from Detroit to New York for the 1901 auto show, a remarkable feat and enough of an encouragement to Chapin that he would go on to create the Hudson Motor Car Company.

Master of Precision

In the meantime, what of Olds's subcontractors, Leland and Faulconer, for example, and Henry Leland in particular?

Leland was a New Englander, brought up through a succession of toolmaker's jobs including employment at Colt Arms and Brown and Sharpe manufacturing, where standards were exacting. Soon enough, he found himself partners with another Brown and Sharpe alumnus in a more prosperous part of the country, Detroit, doing business as Leland and Faulconer. Leland was famous for his insistence on fine tolerances at the new company that made, among other devices, internal combustion engines. When Henry Ford Company, Ford's second venture (after Detroit Automobile but before Ford Motor) went soft, and

LEFT AND OVERLEAF:
1904 Cadillac Touring Model B
When Henry Ford abandoned ship—in the second automobile company he had helped found—to go racing, Henry Leland took over the company and renamed it Cadillac. This touring car exhibits all the expertise Leland brought to early American car manufacture, namely, the fine tolerances of its machined parts.

33

Henry the Original left to go racing, Leland and his son were brought in to save the firm, which was renamed Cadillac.

Given its background, it's not surprising that the first Cadillac had much in common with early Fords. It was called the Model A and it looked every bit as basic as its contemporaries. For example, there was no hood (although after 1906, the company offered the car with a dummy). Its one-cylinder, 91-cubic-inch (1,500 cc) engine was mounted under the floor and sat horizontally beneath the car. It had a two-speed transmission and chain drive. Like its competitors, it had no doors, no windows, and it looked far less comfortable with an engine than it might have with a horse attached to it. By 1904, Cadillac and Leland and Faulconer merged to become the Cadillac Motor Company. Leland and Cadillac brought the second great achievement of the American industry to the manufacture of the automobile: parts so precisely made that they were genuinely interchangeable.

As for Benjamin Briscoe, who had been called in by Olds to manufacture bodies for the curved dash car, he had been a Detroit maker of sheet metal products, particularly radiators, for the new automobile industry. In 1902, Briscoe and his brother Frank received a Scots immigrant engineer named David D. Buick. Buick had been successful first in a business that specialized in mating ceramics to metal for the plumbing industry, but he was far less an achiever when he put the proceeds from the sale of the business into the manufacture of engines. In his second effort, he superintended the design of an overhead valve engine, for his new Buick Manufacturing Company. This engine differed from the then-common L head by introducing the fuel mixture directly into the combustion chamber from above rather than in the cylinder's side via the engine block. It was a worthy achievement but it ran him out of money. Like Henry Ford and Ransom Olds, David Buick had gone looking for backers; he found them in the persons of the Briscoe brothers. They reorganized his company but then became discouraged by the whole thing and sold it to Billy Durant, putting the founder of GM into the car business at last.

Like the first Ford and the first Cadillac, the first Buick (1903–1904) had a horizontal engine (this one a two-cylinder) mounted beneath the driver's seat and a two-speed transmission. For three years, 1906 to 1909, Buick experimented with side valves, but in the years prior and forever thereafter, the marque was distinguished by overhead valve engines—the first of which came from David Buick's drawing board.

The original Buick had a piston displacement of 2,600 cc. This manner of measure was familiar in the early days of the car and is coming back; it signified the combined capacity in volume of the cylinders (how much air would the pistons displace as they moved through the cylinder) and was thought then and now to be a far better gauge of the potential of an engine than horsepower (which could be created by artificial devices like the supercharger or special octane fuel) or number of cylinders, since a single cylinder could be 20 cc or 200 cc or 2,000 cc.

You could buy a Buick for $1,250 in 1903, but David Buick was evidently not much of a production man, for the company was able to build a total of only twenty-two cars in the years 1903 and 1904. Benjamin Briscoe, still enchanted with the idea of the car if disappointed in his experience with Buick, found another automobile enthusiast in the person of Jonathan Maxwell, whom we last noticed motoring down the Pumpkinville Pike in 1893. Together they founded the Maxwell-Briscoe Motor Company in 1903.

What of the third Olds subcontractor, the Dodge brothers, who had been given the transmission contracts for the Curved Dash Olds? John F. and Horace

E. Dodge were also Michiganders (Port Huron) and also machinists. Like Ransom Olds, their father owned a machine shop which had been making internal
combustion engines for marine use. Their own success as subcontractors brings
us back to Henry Ford, for he had once again gone to the manufacturing well
with capital from a new partner, Alexander Y. Malcomson, a Detroit coal dealer,
to found the real Ford Motor Company in June of 1903. Ford now contracted
with the Dodges to build engines and transmissions, in fact the whole chassis for
his new car, to his own designs. The Dodge brothers will reappear in the nar-
rative, but first we shall turn to a handful of other automotive pioneers whose
stories are not so intertwined with Ford's and Durant's.

Packard and Marmon

Henry Leland was not the only fanatic on the subject of precision parts in the infant automobile industry. James W. Packard had bought a Winton named for a
Cleveland bicycle manufacturer, Alexander Winton, another immigrant Scots-
man who built his first car in 1896. This was the same Winton who was the first
man to make a long automobile trip—Cleveland to New York in 1898—and for a
time was the largest manufacturer of automobiles in the United States. Packard
had been intrigued enough by Winton's product to buy the twelfth car built by the
Clevelander, but he did not find it very satisfactory. The story goes that Packard's
complaints annoyed Winton sufficiently that he told Packard that if he didn't like
the car he should go off and build one of his own. Packard was not the man to
challenge thus. He had been playing with designs for an automobile for some time
and had brought a French pioneer auto called a DeDion-Bouton back from
Europe. Winton's cranky response to Packard prompted the latter to lure a pair
of Winton's employees away from the company to begin a firm of their own in
partnership with J. W. and his brother William D. Packard.

Now things get a little confusing. The two ex-Winton men and the Packard
brothers joined forces with one Henry B. Joy, whose father had been part of the
Railroad Gang and profited enormously from that association. Joy discovered
one of the first Packards at the New York auto show in 1901. He liked the car,
and he liked the company that was making it enough to invest substantially and
reorganize it as the Packard Motor Car Company. Joy was an educated man,

knowledgeable in the ways of both machinery and finance. While James Ward Packard was made president of the new enterprise, it was really Joy who was the power behind it. It was not long before Joy became president of Packard and J.W. Packard became an outside consultant.

There was yet another perfectionist pioneer besides Henry Leland and Packard. He was Howard C. Marmon, midwesterner (Richmond, Indiana) and machinist (Nordyke and Marmon Company, manufacturers of flour-milling machinery). By 1903, the Nordyke and Marmon Company had moved to Indianapolis, and its heir had built his own car for much the same reason Packard did: He hadn't found anyone else's product satisfactory. Marmon's story is like the tale of the chocolate chip cookie; his neighbors liked the car Marmon built for himself so much that they began to ask if he would do the same for them. Howard C. Marmon was glad to oblige.

All this experimenting with the horseless carriage would eventually result in almost 3,000 makes and models of cars, and hundreds of constructors. But by the early years of the new century, the imprint of the American industry had been established. Cars were not manufactured so much as assembled. Since the industry was made of assemblers relying on outside contractors, parts had to fit.

1900 Packard
Henry Joy Packard put his name on cars that would represent elegance for more than forty years.

The center of the automobile universe was clearly coalescing in the Midwest, and managers and money men were beginning to become as important as inventors and innovators.

There remain a few other important inventive pioneers to discuss. Some established companies that survived a quarter century of shakeout, and others took daring design steps that may have brought them to evolutionary dead ends, but nonetheless represent technological landmarks.

The Birth of AMC

In addition to Colonel Albert Pope and Alexander Winton, there was a third bicycle manufacturer whose efforts were historic. Thomas B. Jeffery was an English maker of scientific instruments who emigrated first to Chicago then to Kenosha, Wisconsin, where he bought the Sterling Bicycle Company, but not before he had gone into partnership in an earlier bicycle-building company whose product was called Rambler. Inevitably, Jeffery too became intrigued with the automobile, although he did not build one until he arrived in Kenosha. Jeffery shared this with Durant, Chapin, and Ford: The automobile company he founded survives to this day, although through the course of its manufacturing history its name changed—sometimes more than once. Jeffery's company's name was changed to Nash and finally to American Motors.

Two more bicycle builders and one bicycle salesman left their marks. The salesman was John North Willys who took over manufacture of the Overland,

1905 Rambler Surrey
The 1905 and 1906 models of this car were identical, built by the Thomas B. Jeffery Company in Kenosha, Wisconsin. The name survived into the 1970s; the company survives to this day, having undergone a transformation to Nash and then to American Motors Corporation.

originally made in 1902 by the Standard Wheel Company of Terre Haute, Indiana. This was an interesting car. It steered by tiller, as did most of its contemporaries, but unlike them it had its one-cylinder engine mounted in front of the driver. It was also cheap in comparison with its competitors at only $595. In 1905 the car got a steering wheel and a second cylinder; but as with countless other makes, Overland almost disappeared when its first two corporate parents sank out of sight in the panic of 1907. By then, the Overland was being made in Indianapolis, where Willys was able to convince Overland's creditors to convert their $80,000 claim against the company into $80,000 worth of stock and to make him president. When the panic ended, sales took a dramatic upward turn, sufficient to allow him to acquire two more companies that he eventually consolidated into yet another firm he called Willys-Overland.

One of the two bicycle builders, Erwin Thomas, added a motor to his product as an interim step to the manufacture of the Thomas automobile, one model of which, the Thomas Flyer, startled the world and contributed enormous credibility to American manufacture by winning the New York to Paris race in 1908. The other was George Pierce, who began his career building bird cages, went on to bicycles, and then to cars; his were the predecessors of one of the great marques in the American automotive tapestry, the Pierce-Arrow.

Thomas and Pierce created their oeuvres in Buffalo, New York; just east of them, another famous name was at work. The head of a die casting firm in Syracuse, H. H. Franklin, was taken with John Wilkinson's design of an air-cooled internal combustion engine. Franklin called Wilkinson in for a talk in 1901 and the result was the Franklin Automobile Company, which became the

1907 Thomas Flyer
Perhaps the best-known American car in existence, the 1907 Thomas Flyer won the meanest, longest race in history—New York to Paris in 1908—defeating a field of overseas competitors and establishing the engineering worth of the U.S. product. The authenticity of this car was established by its driver, George Schuster, who examined its frame after restoration by the Harrah's Automobile Collection and discovered traces of a repair he had made in Siberia. A 1982 appraisal of the car put its worth at $1.5 million.

leading builder of air-cooled cars in America, many of them classics. By 1903, major changes in the first thirteen cars built included a wheelbase 6 inches longer (from 66 inches to 72 inches) and an increase in horsepower from 7 to 10. This was the first full year of manufacture—the company produced 219 cars in 1903—and the year in which Franklin advertised its Light Roadster with a hint of whimsy: "The Franklin doesn't puff and snort. It's like the hum of an electric motor...and the motor is in front—the only sensible place—no lying on your back to look at it. Having the greater horsepower for its weight than other cars, it is the greatest hill climber."

Air-cooled engines did not survive in America, although they were revived from time to time—the last one as late as 1959 by the Chevrolet Division of General Motors in the Corvair. Steam had an even shorter history.

Freeland O. and Francis E. Stanley (we keep encountering brothers; these two were twins) bought the rights to a steam engine devised by a Rhode Island inventor, and promptly set up business in Newton, Massachusetts. The brothers

1903 Franklin Light Roadster
The 1903 Roadster was built in Franklin's second year, its first full production year and the start of an epoch for America's most successful manufacturer of cars with air-cooled engines. Franklin was bold in its advocacy of the air-cooled engine, proclaiming in an ad for this car: "The Franklin doesn't puff and snort. It's like the hum of an electric motor, steady and strong....In all respects it is properly designed and properly built."

1908/09 Stanley
In 1899, the Stanley twins, Freelan O.
and Francis E., started producing steam
cars. In the summer of that year, with
enough parts on hand to produce about
a hundred cars, they were bought out
by John B. Walker of *Cosmopolitan*
magazine for a quarter of a million dollars. The newly formed company was
called Locomobile. Eighteen months
later, it sold the steam patents back to
the Stanleys and changed over to build
gas-powered cars.

took in partners who split, each taking a Stanley twin with him. One of the partners founded a company that became known as Locomobile, another famous
name in American automotive history; the other went out of business in short
order. After a year, the Stanleys reunited, bought back a plant from Locomobile
(which itself built steam automobiles until 1902 when it converted to internal
combustion cars), and cranked up the famous Steamer, which lasted into the
1920s. This new design had a wood frame with the boiler mounted at its front. By
1903 the Stanley was making 8 horsepower and was rapidly becoming a favorite
among fire and police departments in the East. But it wasn't until 1904 that the
car began to look like the "familiar" Stanley, coffin-nosed hood, steering wheel,
and all.

Two final names remain, one final dead end. Studebaker Brothers had been
building wagons in South Bend, Indiana, since the early 1850s. In 1891, one of
the brothers acquired a son-in-law named Frederick Fish who became fascinated
with the car. Very likely he influenced the company to begin experimentation
with an electric in 1898; they finally produced one three years later. John M.
Studebaker and Frederick Fish soon found themselves so successful in the
automobile business and at the same time so entangled with what had become
scandalous doings in the electric end of propulsion manufacture, that they absorbed a builder of internal combustion cars and were off on a half century and
more in the automobile business. They hung on until after World War II, when
the company acquired Packard, distributed Mercedes-Benz in the United States,
and finally went out of car building forever in 1966.

1912 Baker Electric
As the car developed in the U.S. there was a very real question about the source of propulsion: steam (in which the U.S. was advanced), internal combustion (where the Europeans had an edge), or electric. Walter Baker was an advocate of watts and ohms, and he built one of the most refined and desired of the American electrics, coveted particularly by women, who liked his cars' silence. It was a genteel choice but not a wise one; the technology to propel a car long distances by electricity wasn't there when Baker built his wonderful cars, and it still isn't.

Perhaps the most remembered of the builders of electrics was Baker. In 1898 Walter Baker of Cleveland founded the Baker Motor Vehicle Company, which merged with yet another electric car company seventeen years later, aided by money from General Electric. While the new company turned to building gas cars (The Owen Magnetic), they had electric transmissions. Alas, the device proved expensive and complicated, and the company gave up on the passenger car in 1921 to concentrate on electric trucks.

Although hundreds of other pioneers built automobiles when the horseless carriage arrived upon the scene, only four companies of consequence survived: General Motors, Ford, Chrysler, and American Motors. We have glimpsed the beginnings of GM and Ford in our discussion of the origins of American Motors. For a closer look at GM's beginnings, we must delve into the labyrinth of finance. For Ford's real start, we will plunge into the beginnings of racing. The story of Chrysler's birth is wrapped up in the history of GM.

GM is Born

The story of the founder of General Motors begins with hope, energetic promotion, and riches. It ends with poverty and pathos in a bowling alley.

One automotive writer said of William Crapo Durant, "Beside [him] Henry Ford was a plodding, insignificant, colorless mechanic, utterly lacking in romance or drama, without distinction, without charm—the tortoise beside the hare." Durant himself delighted in this piece of doggerel comparing the two:

> I'm glad I'm not a vacuum
> I'm glad I'm not a myth....
> But most of all I'm glad, O Lord
> You did not make me Henry Ford.

Durant's family was a prominent one in Flint; his grandfather had been governor of Michigan. He was recognized early as a comer; he was recognized at the end almost not at all. One of the automotive pioneers who began as a wagon maker, Durant had a particular genius for salesmanship. Convinced as a young man that he should join a friend in the building and sale of an appealing light carriage, he went forth and sold a year's production almost without otherwise arranging for their financing, much less for a place to build them. In a sense, of course, this was to be the pattern of automobile manufacturing finance: find a dealer to buy the product who would pay in advance, find a subcontractor to build its parts on the come, arrange to have things assembled in somebody else's facility, and discover yourself rich with practically no investment at all.

Durant took his teetering quasi-ponzi scheme to even greater heights by adding another element: He would scout up an investor who didn't know ephemera when he saw it, take his money, and speculate in the stock market with it. It was his good fortune, perhaps his talent, to discover a handful of stunningly competent people to manage his businesses, including Charles Nash and Alfred P. Sloan, Jr. It was Durant's contrariness, his arbitrary manner, and his obsession with speculation in the market that alienated them all and prompted both Nash and Walter Chrysler, who also worked for Durant, to go off and start automobile companies of their own.

You will recall Durant as the owner of the Flint Wagon Works and the Durant-Dort Carriage Company. They were hugely successful enterprises, making Durant a millionaire before he was 40. No wonder then, that he was content to watch others risk their capital and their reputations on the horseless carriage while he spent his energies luring subcontractors to Flint, where he eventually built and owned manufacturing facilities dependent on their products. Through a convoluted deal, however, he became the owner of Buick, which, in the early years of the twentieth century, outsold its two closest competitors combined—Cadillac and Ford.

Durant was pursuaded that the future of the automobile business lay in blanketing the field with every type and kind of mobile device. To accomplish this end, he set up a holding company in New Jersey that he called General Motors and went on a binge of acquisition. These early efforts might have resulted in a company even huger than GM became—he got within a millimeter of inhaling Ford. What happened was this: Durant approached Benjamin Briscoe, who by then was proprietor of Maxwell-Briscoe; together they tried to form a combination including their two firms, as well as REO and Ford. By 1908, however, Henry Ford and Ransom Olds were sufficiently recovered from the financial

panic of the previous year, and also confident enough about their business futures, that they wanted cash. Cash was an anathema to Durant. He offered stock instead of the $3 million Ford and Olds were each asking and the deal fell through.

Durant did buy Cadillac, however, for almost $4.5 million and snapped up Oldsmobile, whose management, having discontinued the curved dash car, no longer saw the rosy future it had expected. He acquired Oakland, which would become Pontiac, and Champion Ignition, both of which would stand GM in good stead. Durant brought Weston-Mott Axle into the fold, another successful acquisition, and tried to buy Ford again (this time the asking price was $8 million), and again failed. The rest of his buying judgments ranged from dreadful to disastrous. He took on Welch, Ewing, Marquette, Ranier, Rapid, and Reliance; all were failures. He bought a company named Elmore Manufacturing, which built a car powered by a two-cycle engine, only to discover that two-cycle engines were neither needed nor wanted. He paid $140,000 for the Carter Car Company, whose product had friction drive, a feature with a predictable tendency to wear out within miles. And then Durant swallowed the Heany Lamp Company, which made a patented incandescent light, and choked on it because its patent was fraudulent.

It was 1910 and Durant's grand scheme had turned into a disaster. Management did not exist for the corporation as an entity. His component companies either did not fit well with one another or were themselves as chaotic as their parent firm. General Motors was the Titanic and her captain was Durant; for-

1909 Welch Model 4-0 Close Coupled Touring
Said the 1909 Welch sales catalogue: "The most luxuriantly upholstered and easiest riding car every produced, especially adapted for the man who wishes to sometimes drive his own car but take his chauffeur along without giving him the best seat in the car (beside the driver) or putting him in with his family. People in the tonneau occupy the best position in the car"—evidence that the rumble seat was first intended for servants.

tunately the corporate ship had a better navigator than skipper. He was none other than that austere perfectionist, Henry Leland, whose son, Wilfred C., was a financial wizard, and whose company, Cadillac, provided General Motors with some semblance of stability, not to mention actual profits.

Leland and his son were able to convince Boston (Lee, Higginson and Company) and New York (J. and W. Seligman) investment firms of the worth of saving GM. The fact that the First National Bank of Boston, to which Buick owed $7 million, also wanted a chance to get its money back didn't hurt. But there were conditions, and one of them was that Durant could keep a title (GM vice-president and president of Buick) but not a job. He was out.

James Storrow, of Lee, Higginson and Company, took control of GM and did a series of helpful things for its future. He liquidated everything but Buick, Cadillac, Olds, Oakland, GM Truck, and the solvent parts builders; but he did these good deeds out of motives other than kindness. GM was lent $15 million of which it actually got only $12.5 million and had to pay back the rest at 6 percent. The banking syndicate also took a big block of stock. Storrow brought in Arthur D. Little, Inc. as consultants; this resulted in the establishment of a research department at GM. Storrow then did the company the best turn of all by promoting Nash and recruiting Walter P. Chrysler to work at Buick. "By 1915, the water that Durant had poured in [to GM stock] had been wrung out again," said Rae, "and most of the indebtedness to the bankers had been paid off. At the same time, the internal administration was greatly improved, with the result that Buick production, for example, increased tenfold."

Meanwhile, Durant could not be expected to sit quietly by. He was 50 years old when he was ushered out of General Motors; a year later he was once again hard at work on an automotive juggling act—this one involving two former employees of GM. One was William Little, a former factory manager at Buick during the Durant regime and the man who had started the Little Motor Car Company, which was building a light, cheap car. The other was A. B. C. Hardy, who worked for Durant-Dort, quit to begin his own company, quit that to go back to GM, and then quit GM when Durant left. Durant, with Hardy by his side, proposed to promote the car built by Little.

Durant also had his eye on another automobile company. This was one founded to produce a car designed by a former Buick racer and wine pump inventor named Louis Chevrolet. Chevrolet had no interest in the company that bore his name but was, instead, president of the Frontenac Motor Company whose products, race cars, were far more to his liking.

Once again, Durant dazzled the automobile world with his financial footwork. The Republic Motor Car Company became his holding company to gain control of Little. It was also the center of gravity for a handful of other companies, including the old Maxwell-Briscoe plant on the Hudson River at Tarrytown. With typical sleight of hand, Republic, Little, and the rest suddenly became Chevrolet in 1913, the whole affair plopped down in—where else? —Flint, but incorporated in Delaware.

At this point, matters become even more conspiratorial. Control of General Motors by the bankers had been limited by agreement to five years, which would be up by 1915. During these five years, Durant had been buying GM stock. Within months of organizing Chevrolet, he quadrupled Chevy's capital through the stroke of a pen and then swapped Chevrolet for GM stock at the ratio of five Chevrolet shares for one of GM's. By 1915, Chevrolet controlled as much of GM as did the bankers, represented by Storrow, and the new GM president, Nash. The balance of ownership was in the hands of an equally fascinating group. All the while Durant was angling to regain control of GM, Pierre S. duPont and the treasurer of the duPont company, John J. Raskob, were also buying General Motors stock. So when elections for the GM board came up in 1915 and Durant was stalemated for control by Storrow and Nash, the choice of Pierre duPont as chairman of the company was a natural solution.

Nash quit as president, Storrow followed, and both scouted around for another car company. Their eyes fell upon the Kenosha, Wisconsin, firm founded by Thomas Jeffery. Thus came the Nash Motor Company into the world. Thus also did Durant reascend to the presidency of General Motors.

But in Durant's absence, as we have seen, changes had occurred. One of them was the arrival of Walter Chrysler, another was the recruitment of perhaps the greatest second-generation automotive inventor of them all, Charles "Boss" Kettering. Durant's resumption of GM's presidency also precipitated change. Henry Leland and his son quarreled with Durant and quit Cadillac. After a disastrous venture into airplane engine manufacture, as we shall see in Chapter 5, the Lelands went back to building cars, and the car they built was the Lincoln.

Meanwhile, Durant was still in the magic business. In 1918 he formed the General Motors Corporation, which included the Chevrolet-owned General Motors Company as well as Chevrolet itself, and one more company whose worth was almost more in one of its managers than in the essential hardware components it manufactured. That company was another Durant combination called United Motors, which included the Hyatt Roller Bearing Company sold to Durant by its owner, Alfred P. Sloan, Jr.

Kettering and Sloan. Despite Durant's wonderful pirouettes, beyond the association of duPont with GM, Kettering and Sloan had far more effect on the modern General Motors than either of the other men.

First came Kettering. Leland had put him to work during the banker's regime at GM solving the problem of having to—literally—crank up the automobile. Crank-starts were difficult (almost requiring the captain of the ship to be male; women were not considered strong enough to start a car) and dangerous. In fact, it was an incident involving a friend's broken arm, which with some complications led to his death, that prompted Leland to call Kettering in to devise an on-board self-starter.

Kettering was just starting Dayton Engineering Laboratories (which became the DELCO name on GM electrical products), after a stint at the National Cash Register Company where he had designed a high-torque electric motor. Such a device, Kettering and Leland agreed, was just the ticket since it delivered its energy in short, powerful spurts. Introduced on the 1912 Cadillac, it became the sensation of that year's New York auto show and a year later won Britain's Dewar Trophy for technical achievement. This, by the way, was the *second* Dewar Trophy for Cadillac. The first had come four years before when the English Cadillac distributor was the only entrant in a challenge to supply three randomly chosen cars, have all of them torn down, and have them reassembled with parts from each to reconstitute three cars created of pieces taken arbitrarily from all of them. The results were spectacular in at least two ways. First, the newly assembled cars were of widely varying colors. Made up as they were from each other's parts, they looked like rolling patchwork quilts. But more importantly, they all ran perfectly, proving to the world that Henry Leland's insistence on perfection in the manufacture of parts was one of the great triumphs of the American industry—particularly given the fact that no other company chose to meet the challenge.

The self-starter was only the first of Kettering's long series of contributions.

1912 Cadillac
The wonder of the 1912 New York Auto Show had the first self-starter on any car in the world, which brought it the Dewar trophy for technological advancement. One of the early industry giants, Charles Kettering, developed the high torque electric motor that made the device possible.

He is credited with the post-World War II "high speed" engine, which wasn't high speed at all, but seemed so in contrast to the low revving engines produced through the late 1930s. This meant reliability and longevity, since a Kettering engine could run all day at 3,600 revolutions per minute without shaking itself to pieces. Obviously too, it meant higher safe cruising speeds. General Motors Research (founded, remember, during the banker's era) is credited with the invention of ethyl gasoline, but that was Kettering's doing really. He also worked with duPont to produce a quick-drying paint called "Duco," which permitted a wide range of colors that would last far better than previous paints, under a variety of harsh weather conditions.

Sloan's great contributions to GM were in the area of management and with the concept of the annual model change, about which more in Chapter 8. Sloan's influence was unquestionably greater than anyone's, other than Henry Ford's, in the way cars were built and sold in America—so much so that Emma Rothschild, the recognized automotive economic writer of the last quarter century, divides the pre-World War II period in the industry into two divergent philosophies. One she calls "Fordism," the other "Sloanism."

But back to Billy Durant, for he had a few things left to do at General Motors.

First, in 1918, he bought the Fisher Body company. Then, although he was not the inventor of the idea nor even the first to apply it to the buying of cars, he founded General Motors Acceptance Corporation, introducing installment sales on what would become a grand scale. It was a logical outgrowth of his own aversion to paying cash perhaps, but Durant also understood that cash on the barrelhead was somehow not the American way of the future. GMAC established installment buying of cars as the accepted manner in which they would be bought in this country from 1919 on. On the other hand, Henry Ford's stubborn insistence on his customers' paying cash meant that his buyers were only allowed to participate in a sort of primitive layaway plan, depositing small, regular amounts of money with his dealers until they had paid the full price, whereupon they could take delivery.

Then Durant did a curious but highly prescient thing. He invested in a strange little company that made awkward and barely effective automatic iceboxes. The device would be perfected, of course, and become the Frigidaire division of GM. It would also fill almost 80 percent of GM's cars with air conditioning by the 1970s.

But for all the wise decisions Durant made during his second stewardship of GM, he made at least an equal number of destructive moves. There was, for example, his decision to compete with Ford's successful Fordson tractor with a farm machine called the "Iron Horse," which was supposed to do the same things as the Fordson but was guided by reins. He also bought two car companies that actually competed with one another—Sheridan and Scripps-Booth. Sloan said about the acquisitions: ". . . where we concentrated with duplication, we did not know what we were trying to do except sell cars which, in a sense, took volume from each other."

By now, it was late in the morning of the industry's day, 1921. Durant's second regime was soon over, but he did not go without one more contribution: the commissioning of the General Motors Building. This imposing structure in Detroit became the scene of what we will discover to be perversions of management as horrifying as any Durant perpetrated. These did not occur for a long while, though.

Alfred P. Sloan, Jr. soon replaced Durant at the helm of GM, and the company's golden age began with his acceptance of crown and sceptre. As for Durant, he ended up trying to put together yet another iteration of GM after his second ouster, failed at it, and spent the end of his life as the proprietor of a bowling alley, which he insisted was only the first of a chain. The chain never materialized, and Durant died in obscurity in 1947, a sad end for a man who may have been often wrong, but was never colorless. Blandness was an affliction that would haunt Detroit managers for two generations after Durant's second reign and would, as well, characterize the engineering personalities of the American industry's main products for almost fifty years.

Ford's Fast Track to Success

When we left Henry Ford, he had parted company with manufacturing in order to go racing.

"The success of what eventually turned into the Ford Motor Company, and its growth into the world's second largest auto maker, with more than 365,000 employees and factories throughout the world, stems from [Ford's] decision" to use racing as a way—and the quickest and surest way—to prove whose product was best. This statement is from Leo Levine's monumental work, *Ford: The Dust*

1903 Ford Rear-Entrance Tonneau Model A

Five years before the Model T was introduced, the third company Henry Ford created, the *real* Ford Motor Company, built this two-cylinder, 8-horsepower car—a very early example of the first Model A. Production started in July 1903, and by November 400 cars had been built. With the serial number 330, this one was probably built in late October.

and the Glory: A Racing History, perhaps the most complete, and certainly the most readable and scholarly, American racing book ever published.

It is not surprising that Levine spent so much time researching and writing his book; racing was key to early acceptance of the automobile both in Europe and in the United States, and Henry Ford played an important role. Once again that fateful year of 1893—the year of the Duryeas's Springfield motoring adventure—appears in the record books. As well as being the year of the first successful American automobile venture, it also saw America's first auto race. The event, held on a snowy Thanksgiving Day, was sponsored by the Chicago *Times-Herald*. The car that won was a Duryea, driven by J. Frank himself at an average speed of 7.5 mph over a 55-mile course. Second was taken by a hybrid car, Mueller-Benz, but only because a race official took over the driving after Oscar Mueller collapsed from exposure. There remains a racing saying to this day, "First is first and second is nowhere," which may be true with the larger fields today but didn't quite do the Mueller-Benz justice, since it was the only other car to finish.

Three years later, J. Frank Duryea was at it again, this time winning an event that was run from New York City to Irvington-on-the-Hudson. Racing was becoming in the United States what it had clearly estabished itself to be in Europe—the best way to prove to the public that the automobile was fast and reliable. That is exactly what Ford had in mind when he entered his first event in Grosse Pointe, Michigan, on October 10, 1901.

The Detroit Driving Club had a one-mile oval on which it had scheduled four

1905 Ford Model C
One of a series of predecessors to the Model T, the Model C was too big, too expensive, and too complicated. Its planetary transmission didn't work, and it set the third incarnation of the Ford Motor Company on the wrong path. The Model C achieved this however: it convinced Henry Ford that he must do things his way or not at all, and consequently, he rid himself of his early partner and cleared the way for the building of the T in 1908.

events, the feature to be a 25-mile race for a $1,000 purse. The event—cut to 10 miles and turned into a *mano a mano* duel between Ford and Alexander Winton as a result of mechanical failures by three other entrants—ended in a win for Ford, to everyone's surprise. Ford was a neophyte. Winton had been so confident he had nodded in approval as he watched his sales manager talk to the organizers about the suitability of the trophy for Winton's collection.

No sooner had Ford won (at an average of 44.8 mph—and this in 1901!) than he announced his retirement as a driver. He had made his point with the car. If the Ford name was to continue to enhance his reputation on the race track, obviously a driver had to be found. He turned out to be Barney Oldfield, who drove his first race in Ford's famous 999.

In the meantime, of course, Ford had been occupied with the Henry Ford Company. Then in March 1902, he left this company forever to go racing full time, taking not quite $1,000 and the plans for his race car with him. It was after this 1902 departure that the company, minus his name on its stationery, was rescued by Henry and Wilfred Leland who neither needed nor wanted Ford's name on envelopes or anything else, as they renamed the company Cadillac.

Ford was far too busy building the 999 (named for a New York Central locomotive) and another racer called the Arrow to be bothered resenting the Leland's nomenclature change. Levine called the 999 race car "the first hot rod."

(Ford did not even bother to put a hood over the engine.) "These primitive monsters...were perhaps the most stripped-down competition cars of all time.

"They were not the best race cars, they were not the most sophisticated race cars and they were not even very good race cars," said Levine. But they had two advantages: They were driven by Oldfield, and they were fast (a land speed record was set in the 999 at 91.4 mph).

By June 1903, Henry Ford was back in the automobile business, his reputation as a designer of sensational cars firmly set in the minds of Americans as a result of the daring of Oldfield and the two fast racers he had built. Now, with $25,000 from Alexander Malcomson, he set out to build a light car that would be reliable and affordable. Associated with him in the new company were two other names of consequence. James S. Couzens had been Malcomson's bookkeeper in the latter's coal business; he became Henry Ford's accounting wizard in the new firm. Recall too that the Dodge brothers, John F. and Horace E., were the subcontractors—to Henry Ford's design—of complete chassis.

In his new effort, Ford was not immediately successful. The criteria Ford had set were four: the car had to be easy to drive; it had to be durable; it must be inexpensive to fix and maintain; it needed to be cheap—that is to say its price had to be less than $500.

The first car from the new Ford Motor Company had its two cylinders opposed with the crankshaft between them—a flat twin—and was called, in anticipation of a much later car, the Model A. Its engine was mounted under the floor, its driver and passengers entered the open body through a back door. The car did not meet the cost criterion Ford had set, however, with its price of $850.

The year after the Model A, Ford built a variation of it called the Model C and then the Model B—the first four-cylinder from the new company. The B was even more expensive than the A at $2,000. Then in 1905, he built a six-liter, six-cylinder car called the Model K, which was yet $500 more expensive. Not only was Ford's whole plan going awry, but the two-speed transmission he had designed for the B, C, and K was unreliable.

Ford's solution was the kind of thing he would do the rest of his manufacturing life. He got rid of Malcomson. According to Rae: "Henry Ford had to make the final decisions. The responsibility was his and his alone." Out the door with Malcomson went the B, the C, and the K; in came the four-cylinder Model N. This was 1906, and Henry Ford was at last on the right road. Not only did the N come close to meeting Ford's four criteria, but, at $600, it undersold the enormously popular Oldsmobile.

Ford made another decision that became a hallmark of his success. He would concentrate on one model and one model only. Over the next two years, Ford worked on his next car, the Model T. It was introduced in 1908, and although its price was even higher than the Model N at $850, it solved the problems of insuring durability and lightness with the first large-scale use of vanadium steel in the manufacture of American cars.

Ah, the Model T. It had an eighteen-year production run during which its price dropped lower and lower until, in 1925, Americans could buy a roadster version for $260. It was a four-cylinder car with an engine of almost 3 liters piston displacement. It had a pedal-controlled two-speed transmission. Top speed was nearly 45 mph in the production version with tinkerers and early hot rodders coaxing far more than that out of it. It delivered almost 30 miles to a gallon of gas. Ford built more than 15 million T's, and he used it as the basis for a tractor in 1916 and a truck in 1917.

To give some sense of what writers of then and today mean when they say the

LEFT AND OVERLEAF:
1909 Ford Model T Touring
The Ford Model T Touring had the longest model run of any car produced in America—from 1909 until 1927. It went through a number of engineering changes in the 1909 model year: The fenders were changed, the transmission went from a two-pedal to a three-pedal version, the headlights and side lamps were changed, and the car went from wooden to metal bodies.

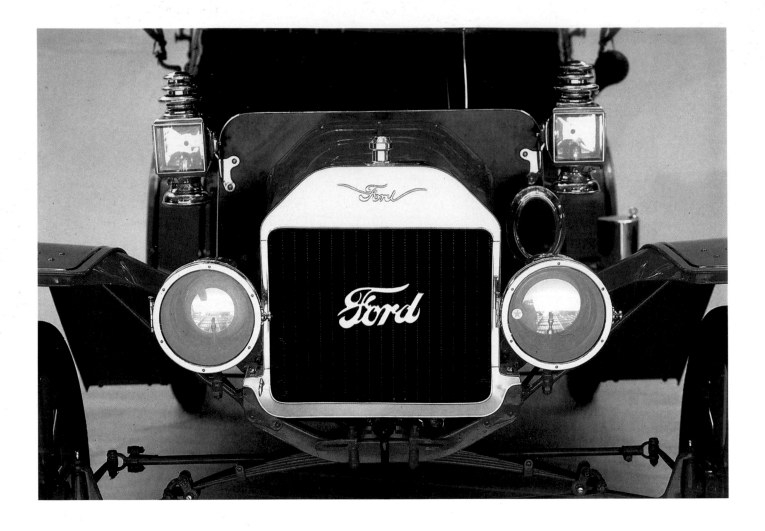

T put America on wheels, let's look at some statistics. There were roughly 8,000 automobiles in the United States in 1900. Thirteen years later, Ford built over 100,000 Model T's and in 1914, 300,000. Ford opened a factory to build Model T's in England in 1911; thereafter, they were built in France and Germany. And yes, they were offered only in black from 1914 until 1925. The T never came with four-wheel brakes, but Henry Ford finally offered an electric starter in 1920. In the company's typical conservative way, the crank-start car was continued for five years thereafter.

Now that the car was developed, it remained for Ford to improve its method of manufacture ("Fordism") and to become independent of outside suppliers. This latter was an obstacle for the entire automotive industry, but one that Henry the Original had taken on as his personal dragon. With a little help from the courts, Ford slayed the Selden patent dragon in 1911.

We last saw George Baldwin Selden watching an internal-combustion-engined trolley in Rhode Island, concluding that such a power unit belonged better in a carriage than a tram, and applying for a patent in 1879. It was granted in 1895. There is much controversy about the whole Selden Patent episode—more accurately, series of episodes—in the history of the development and manufacture of American automobiles. At the same time, there is no arguing that his improvement to the ICE (internal combustion engine) was considerable, that he did design a horseless carriage propelled by it, and that he actually built one—although not until the validity of the patent had gone to law.

1907 Ford Model K Touring
Henry Ford's success came when he decided on a one-model policy—which turned out to be the immortal Model T—but between 1903 and 1908, the year of the first T, Ford Motor Company made a number of false starts. This car was a storm center in the new company. Ford's partner, Alexander Malcomson, wanted a car for the rich. Ford wanted to build for the masses. The Model K was a Malcomson favorite with its six-cylinder engine (Ford would not market a six again until 1941), great weight (2,870 pounds), and high style. It was also a failure, and the internal quarrel over product philosophy engendered by it resulted in Malcomson's departure from the company.

His car did not run well, but after all, Selden's design was obsolete when it was finally built. There was dispute among automotive pioneers about the worth of the car; there was even more about the validity of the patent. Here Rae picks up the story. "The one real champion the patent had was Herman F. Cuntz... who was in charge of patents for the Pope Manufacturing Company. Cuntz called Maxim's attention to the Selden patent in January 1896, and insisted that work on gasoline vehicles must be stopped." In the meantime, Pope Manufacturing had become entranced with the electric and embarked on yet another of those early corporate pyramid schemes that came to involve so many promoters and so many piggyback endeavors that the company eventually tumbled down. Its sole remaining asset was the Selden Patent, which Cuntz had had the foresight to option.

Lawsuits to enforce the patents began in 1900 against Winton, then the largest manufacturer of gas cars in the United States. Before the matter could enter the courtroom, there was a settlement, precipitated by Packard's Henry Joy and F. L. Smith of Oldsmobile. Representatives of the Knox, Pierce, and Locomobile companies joined with Joy and Smith to come to an accommodation with William C. Whitney, who represented the patent owners, to form the Association of Licensed Automobile Manufacturers (A.L.A.M.) The agreed upon royalty was 1.25 percent of the list price of each car manufactured under the patent, divided one fifth to Selden, two fifths to the patent rights owners, and the rest to the Association. Four years later, the Association had thirty members. The successor to the A.L.A.M., called the Automobile Manufacturers Association (and now the Motor Vehicle Manufacturers Association) was forthright about the principal benefit it expected to gain as a result of patent enforcement: "It was at a time when automobiles were being made by almost every large machine shop in New England. Competition was such that many were being made with inferior experience and possible inferior workmanship. The dissatisfaction experienced with such cars was affecting the reputation and progress of the good manufacturers. The Selden patent gave opportunity to exercise a certain amount of con-

trol and was therefore a highly desirable instrument." In other words, the patent offered the opportunity for oligopoly, at the cost of paying the royalties—a hell of a deal.

But not to Henry Ford who went to war against the patent in 1903. The A.L.A.M. bought advertising space to tell prospective buyers, "Don't buy a lawsuit with your car." Ford, by now joined by (among others) Maxwell-Briscoe, REO, and Marmon, offered to bond buyers of his cars against the threatened suits.

At first it looked as though Ford would lose. In 1909, a federal court in the Southern District in New York upheld the patent. Ford appealed and won; the appellate court upheld the patent, but on the basis of a very narrow interpretation of the design that no longer applied to the cars being manufactured by Ford.

The principal results of the court's decision were interesting. First, in the age of strong public support for trust busting, Ford came off as a hero since the A.L.A.M. was seen in the public eye as nothing more than an attempt to form a monopoly within the auto business. Second, the very formation of an industry association proved enormously beneficial, not least because it established a technical branch that led to the formation of the Society of Automotive Engineers (S.A.E.), which in turn pushed successfully for technical standardization. Standardization meant, among other things, lower manufacturing costs and simplified repair for the cars' owners.

There was one more legacy of the Selden War. Manufacturers were made highly conscious of the potential mischief any future brouhaha of the same kind could bring upon their heads, so they instituted a system of cross-licensing to avoid the very thing.

Selden and Ford, unaware and without intending to do so, had brought the industry together and benefited the consumer. Ford came out of the battle with the cloak of legend beginning to wrap around his shoulders. Selden made a few hundred thousand dollars and gained a perhaps undeserved reputation as a troublemaker.

64

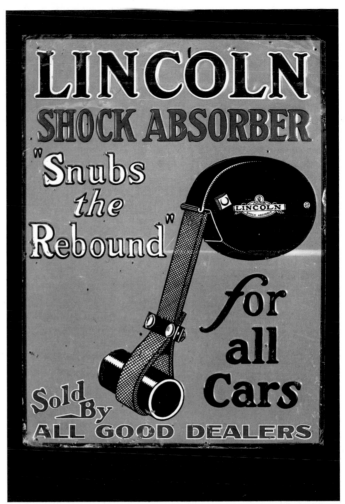

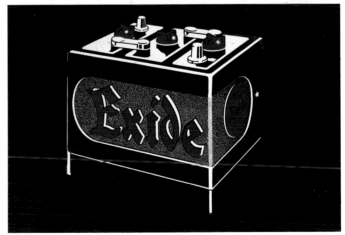

CHAPTER 3

The Curved Dash Olds

You were a rural doctor or more likely a youngish, urban "consumerist" if you owned one of Eli Ransom Olds's little marvels in 1902. Your interest was more probably piqued by an ad in a newspaper than by a friend's car—because not many of your friends had cars. Or perhaps you had picked up *The Automobile* (10 cents a copy) to read about "The Mechanical Problems of High Speed Motors—Part 3."

If you had stopped to look at *Trade News*, you might have discovered an optimistic report about a New York auto dealer: "Another carload of Oldsmobiles will be received this week by the Syracuse Automobile Company, whose management says the demand has been surprising." And then, in the back of the magazine, among the ads for New Process High Duty Steel Balls, you would have found a quarter-page pitch for the 1902 Oldsmobile: "The Best Thing on Wheels. Pretty as a Picture, Speedy as a Race Horse." The ad listed twenty-three dealers from San Francisco to Denver to Atlanta, Detroit, Toronto, and Boston.

Perhaps, in the normal course of your curiosity, you inquired about the local Olds agent, or you even wrote the nearest dealer. And out came a representative. If he were persuasive, you found yourself checking with the freight agent at the railroad station to discover when your car would be coming in. You did not have a dealer unless you lived in town and a big town at that, and your car was not driven to your door; it came by railroad. If an Olds representative did not arrive with the car, it was up to you to decipher its mysteries. If you were fortunate, the agent or dealer rep would be waiting at the depot with your car. You felt a considerable sense of excitement. It was likely one of the first cars in the area. You were a bold buyer, an adventurer. The object standing on the dirt near the station was everything you had hoped for—even today the Curved Dash Olds is an enchantress.

"Curved Dash" is a misleading term, or at least a confusing one. The dash referred to was not at all what we think of now: the instrument panel or fascia. It was the front of the car. And it did not curve around the driver or follow the horizontal axis of the front. It curved up and over from bottom to top, like the front of a sleigh. It was as though someone had seen the first unfinished Olds with the sheet metal flooring continuing out over the front axle a few feet and, instead of cutting it off, decided the driver probably wanted some protection, and just curled it over upon itself.

Between the dash and the seat was a bed of metal covered with a rubber mat that said "Oldsmobile" in tiny letters on the upper-left-hand side, facing forward. Right smack in the middle of the dash was a large steel tiller, hinged just as it joined the front of the car. It went all the way back to the single bench seat, which was covered in leather and, if you were of about average height and were standing on the ground next to the car, was about waist high. (A bolster that ran the length

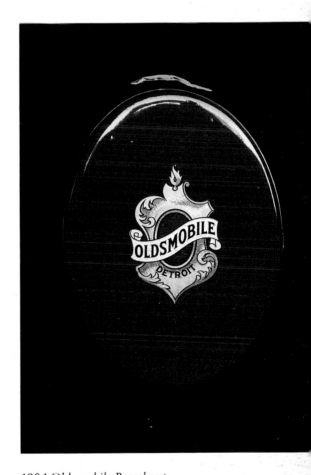

1904 Oldsmobile Runabout
An absolutely remarkable car, the so-called curved dash Olds was last manufactured in 1904 (its first appearance was in 1901). The price was $650, the weight 1,100 pounds. It had a one-cylinder, 7 hp engine. This is the car that established the system of subcontracting by the U.S. auto industry.

of the seat, perpendicular to the bench, was at about shoulder height.) In back of the seat was a sort of rectangle on which you could have a backward-facing second seat (a "dos-à-dos").

Unless you looked underneath the car—or stood somewhat in front and bent over to see cooling fins underneath the midsection of the car—you could detect almost nothing else by way of mechanical contrivances. The engine, built by Leland and Faulconer, was underneath the seat, mounted about where Ferrari would place the engine in its Grand Prix racers seventy-five years later.

The body was minimal. But it was perfectly lovely. It started with the charming shape of the curved dash, and then it was totally open and flat to the midpoint, where it curved upward to accommodate the engine and provide a base for the seat cushion. Then it dropped back down to the rectangular box that was only slightly shorter than the distance between the dash in the front and the seat. Proportions were unconsciously perfect. The body was painted black, of course, but the graceful curves were accented in red, the first stripe outlining the half circle of the dash, then running the length of the front and making a somewhat more abrupt curve upward to outline the engine compartment, which was also topped with a red band about 6 inches deep. The accent stripe then dropped straight down from the back of the box—on which the driver sat—into the black body, ending in a slight curlicue about 2 inches from the bottom. In addition, just at the middle of the box, on the side of the car, was a red oval with Oldsmobile's logo on it. Only after taking all this in might you notice the crank, which came out from the side of the car, bent in a slight "S" shape, with a full knob at the end.

It is almost certain that you would have been surprised at the airiness of the shape. It evoked feelings of the lightest of carriages. It was more than 2½ paces from the back of the rear wheel to the front of the front wheel. The car weighed only 800 pounds. If you had dismantled it and put the parts next to each other, you would have seen some interesting proportions. The wheels were taller than the body was high. The top, erected on its three sets of vertical and one set of "X" bows, was twice the height of the wheels. With the top off, then, the Curved Dash Olds was a mere wisp of a car, a ballet slipper.

Perhaps, at about this moment, you returned your attention to the agent, who was there, after all, to show you how to drive the thing. First, though, you had to go to the local hardware store and, for somewhere between 6 and 18 cents, buy a gallon of highly volatile gasoline—a fifth of a tank for the Olds. Then off came the deck lid, under which sat the engine and gas tank; with gas now poured into the tank in back of the motor, the agent reached in back of the primitive carburetor and primed a kind of pump, a very early choke, feeding raw gas for the mixture.

Since the car was new, and the engine was built to close tolerances, it took some engine break-in time before you could start the car from a perch on the seat. When the car was new, even with the engine's low (5:1) compression, you would need to stand by the right side of the car to crank start it, for the pistons, rings, and cylinders were cast iron and precisely fitted, and it took several hundred miles for them to loosen up.

The agent bent over the side of the car at the front and retarded the spark by moving a small lever attached to a rod that swung a small, flat plate around to make contact with the coil ignition. Then, to draw the mixture, he turned the engine over a couple of times, turned on the ignition, and whipped the crank around two or three more times. The car fired easily. While it sat there turning maybe 200 revolutions per minute, the agent got in at the right, pulling the tiller down on its hinge to rest between his legs, and you got in on the left. There was room on the bench for you both, but it was less awkward if you were friends, for there was not that much room, particularly for two large men.

Once aboard, you could not help noticing that you were far more on than in. Everything except the back of the seat was below you. The curve of the dash was about level with your shin. If you had any trepidations about owning an automobile, surely this sensation of total exposure—and the thought of being so exposed at 25 miles an hour—would have given you a second, and perhaps a third, thought.

The engine was relatively quiet. The Curved Dash Olds had a huge muffler, but you could hear the characteristic sound of the car's one-cylinder 95.4-cubic-inch engine. It chugged. Of course, by now you had paid your $725 in cash, and you could not wait for your first actual ride. The agent switched the spark from full retard to halfway and let the car warm up while you swallowed your impatience.

Finally, he pushed the tiny rectangular left foot pedal down, at the same time pushing the small lever on his right forward into low. The car lurched a little, then took up a smooth chug-a-chug. "One chug per telegraph pole," it was said about the Olds, since its engine turned only 500 rpm at top speed. Up to 8 or 10 mph in low and then the agent moved the lever into high, where the car could get up to its top speed of 25 mph or so. You would not notice, until you drove the car yourself, that you could hear and feel the engine every time it fired in top gear.

That would likely be it for your driving lessons. As for maintenance instruction, the agent left you with a handbook, a small box of tools, and a few precautions. He almost certainly advised you to keep a spare spark plug in the car, to change the plug in the engine every 200 miles or so—at the very least to clean and adjust the tip—and reminded you that unless you drove the car with some regularity not to leave gas in the tank (it turned to varnish). If you lived in a cold climate—that is to say, anywhere in the United States but Florida or Los Angeles—he suggested that driving in the winter was not a good idea. The tires (balloon with tube) were treadless and narrow; they were not useful in the snow or the wet. Oil—which came from Pennsylvania—was usually the equivalent of what is now called SAE #10, relatively low viscosity but impure and with no additives. So if you left the car for any time, the oil had to be drained, taken inside, heated over the stove, and then poured back in before you could start the car.

You were on your own. You were probably somewhat intimidated, but that would go away. *The Automobile* declared that "the Curved Dash was easy to drive. A three-year-old could have driven it; it was used by many women."

Unless you lived in a reasonably well populated community, the roads were dirt and usually not much more than ruts on a path. This did not bother the Olds much because of its light weight. But it did not have very good suspension, so it bothered the driver—although it was likely that he had only a badly sprung buggy to compare it with. So you bounced around a lot. And you bounced out in the open with nothing to hang on to but the tiller.

As for steering, when you wanted to turn the car left, you moved the tiller to the right, as in a boat. The steering, which was very light, was also very fast. The tiller, after all, could only go through a 180-degree arc, so half a turn of the tiller took you from lock to lock of the front wheels.

You were not in a hurry. As a people we had not yet learned about Type A behavior, so we were still leisurely. You probably wouldn't have wanted to go much faster than you could have in a horse-drawn cutter—perhaps 10 mph. Stopping was no problem when the time came. And it didn't come often on the road compared to today's requirements. With very little traffic and no traffic lights, there was not much need to stop and restart. The principal exception came when the automobilist encountered a horse or a child. He and his car were held responsible for frightening human or beast or both, so if you were prudent, you stopped to let either pass by. The car had only two-wheel brakes (on the back), but they were very effective, not because of their excellent design but because of the lightness of the car.

You might have stopped downtown to get the car registered and yourself a license, although the first was not universally required and the second only rarely.

When a license was necessary, you did not have to take a test, you just had to prove you were of "good moral character." But you might have needed a permit to buy gasoline, which was considered as dangerous and explosive as dynamite. (If you had bought a steam car instead of the Olds, you would have had to go to a state agent to get the first of regular boiler inspections.)

Your first trip would end with the car parked outside, since there were no in-side parking places other than stables. Of course, if you had read "The Private Automobile Stable" in the issue of *The Automobile* where you read the Olds ad that caught your attention, you might have decided to build one like it for your new car. If yours followed the specifications in the magazine, it was a white-painted, steep-roofed house, 14 feet by 24 feet, and it cost you about $300. But for that you got not only shelter for the Curved Dash but a workbench, a 2½- by 3-foot pit and, of all things, a 9-foot-in-diameter turntable in the middle of your car stable—although the Olds *had* a reverse gear.

Before setting out on your first real solo, you had to acquire a few accessories. Of course, you had to go back to the hardware store for "spirit"—gasoline. It was kept out back because of its volatility, and unless you were a doctor and used your car regularly (one contemporary Olds collector calculates that only 2 percent of the cars' original owners did that—the rest owned for pure pleasure), you bought only a gallon at a time. Gasoline was too dangerous to keep around, and besides, the car got 25 miles to the gallon—and your longest trip would not be very much over 10 miles. When you bought fuel from the hardware store, you'd drain the stuff into the tank through a chamois or cheesecloth because of its impurities.

You had to buy a few more things besides gasoline and oil and spark plugs. Remember, you were right out there in the middle of nature when you drove your Olds. Without goggles or glasses you'd soon get eyefuls of bees and beetles. And you would always carry a bottle of lotion in the pocket of your duster and stop every few miles to wash out your eyes—goggles or no. You wore a duster closed tight at the neck, or instead of just getting your face covered with muck, you ended up filthy all over. Given the shape of the car and the nature of the roads, driving was really dirty work. If it were hot and dry outside, you got covered with dust. The stuff wouldn't have come from other cars either, since there were precious few of them. No, your own vehicle would swirl the gritty road surface up into a cloud, and given the shape of the car's body, the dust would funnel down right on you. If by chance you lived in a town with roads oiled to keep the grit on the ground, the heat would melt the oil, and the wheels of your car would lift it off the road, covering your head and body with it. Thus a hat was also essential.

But perhaps it was fall or spring, with still a little nip to the air. Now, in addi-tion to hat, duster, and goggles, you had to have a few more items for personal salvation. The first was gloves, since the tiller would get so cold it could pull the skin off your palms. (Blisters were common with or without gloves, and were a source of some pride—a sign of the automobilist.) And then before you climbed into the car, you'd fetch your kidney-shaped portable charcoal heater, fill it with glowing coals, put it on the floor near where your legs would go, climb aboard, and wrap a bearskin robe around you from foot to lap. At least that way your bottom half would stay moderately warm.

Your first few jaunts were probably mildly terrifying, but soon you were en-joying yourself immensely. You could see *everything*: Your pace was leisurely, your vision unobstructed. The car might leap around, certainly the tiller vibrated terribly, but the car's heavy flywheel gave the one-lung engine a kind of stability and momentum. Vagaries of the road surface were not a great problem, the Olds simply leapt over ruts and bumps.

Nor was mechanical reliability a bugaboo. The Olds had a simple, beautifully made engine and a good, two-speed transmission. All the plagues and bothers recounted in a lovely book called *Two Thousand Miles in an Automobile*, which was written under the pseudonym of "A Chauffeur" in 1902, the year you got your car, were more applicable to devices far more complicated than the Olds. A car, the Chauffeur wrote, "possesses the subtle attraction of caprice; it constantly offers something to overcome. The machine is your tricky and resourceful opponent. When you think it conquered and well-broken to harness, submissive and resigned to your will, behold it is as obstinate as a mule—balks, kicks, snorts, puffs, blows, or, what is worse, refuses to kick, snort, puff and blow."

Not so the Olds, particularly if its driver—like the Chauffeur—got used to its peculiar noises and motions: "The real [driver] knows every moment by the sound and 'feel' of his machine exactly what it is doing, the amount of gasoline it is taking, whether the lubrication is perfect, the character and heat of the spark, the condition of every screw, nut and bolt, and he runs his machine accordingly;

at the first indication of anything wrong, he stops and takes the stitch in time that saves ninety and nine later."

That stitch could be the replacement of a blown head gasket with some brown paper or newspaper saturated with oil. If an important nut or bolt had fallen off, there was likely to be another you could use temporarily, which would not impair the car's operation. If a chain (the Olds transmitted power from engine to wheels not through a drive shaft but by a central chain drive) had to be riveted, you could use a wrench as a riveting hammer. And if the most likely thing of all happened, if you got a blowout or a flat, you had a variety of choices. To change a wheel you could use a fence rail as a jack. If you weren't so inclined, you could drive home on the rim, since the Olds's light weight would not ruin the wheel. But most Curved Dash owners brought along rope. The main cause of tire failure was a break in the sidewall or tread, which popped the tube through. To keep the intestine inside the casing, you wrapped the tire with the rope until the tire could be replaced.

It was not always that simple, obviously. When Roy Dikeman Chapin drove

the New York Show car from Detroit to New York in 1901, primarily to establish reliability for the Oldsmobile, he had his problems. He left Detroit in October going via Canada. Since he could not anticipate any repair depots along the way—there were no garages, much less service stations—he took along a large box of spare parts.

Chapin spent the first night in Leamington, Ontario; the second in St. Catherine's, Ontario. Had he wanted to drive at night, it would have been an even more difficult trip since the Olds did not have headlights. An owner could use bicycle lamps, which took carbide crystals to which the owner had to add water to produce an inflammable gas. The result was light about the equivalent in candlepower to a glowworm's. By the third night, Chapin had made Rochester. Western New York roads were worse than those in Canada, so Chapin took the Olds down the Erie Canal towpath. His main problem was tires; often they had to be replaced, but even more often he had to get out of the car and reinflate them with a hand pump. Also, he had to replace a lot of head gaskets, particularly when the car had to strain to go uphill. But the only major catastrophe came when he had to go off the road because a farmer refused to move a hay wagon. He broke a main suspension spring, which forced him to telegraph Detroit and wait for a new one to arrive.

Three more stops and 860 miles and seven days after he started, Chapin arrived in New York City, drove down Broadway and Fifth Avenue to the Waldorf, then located at 34th Street and Fifth Avenue. Olds factory executives awaited him. So did the doorman, who took one look at this filth-covered apparition and almost turned him away.

Two days later the New York *Tribune* recognized the trip as a significant adventure: "Another new machine reached [Madison Square] Garden yesterday for which the owner claims an interesting record. It arrived in the city on Tuesday evening, and was so covered with mud and grime that it will not be placed on exhibition until to-day. The automobile is of the gasoline sort, and was driven from Detroit to this city in seven days and a half…and on the trip covered 860 miles and consumed thirty gallons of gasoline [and 80 of water, which the story did not mention]…the owner says that his experience has showed that the lightweight automobiles are well adapted for such tours."

As countless treks and tours by antique car buffs today testify, they still are.

II
ANTIQUE CARS
1916–1931

1922 Ford Model T Runabout
By 1922 the ubiquitous Model T came in a variety of styles, models, shapes, and sizes. The runabout was the most popular, as well as the cheapest, and was the jumping off point for early California hot rodders who were already beginning to replace the factory body with speedster versions and wildly modifying the engines.

1928 Jordan Blueboy Model R
This car was moderately priced ($1,495) and well built. But Jordan is best known not for its quality cars but for introducing advertising that spoke about the aura of the car.

Buick ad. "There is waiting for you in the Buick more satisfaction than you have ever known." The Jordan approach (Ned Jordan's own copy) outdid everyone's: "Somewhere far beyond the place where men and women and motors race through the canyons of the town—somewhere on the top of the world—there is a peak which dull care has never climbed. You can go there lighthearted in a Jordan Playboy."

In short order, admen abandoned common sense, reason, and restraint. What was the need for truth in advertising when outrage was common? Abuses of decency in national scandals like Teapot Dome, outrageously biased reporting by the country's newspapers in their pursuit of the Red Scare, and the flouting of traditional family behavior chronicled in Robert S. and Helen M. Lynd's *Middletown* were calmly accepted.

This new approach of advertising had profound effects on the ways cars were sold, not to mention the ways in which cars were designed, as a result of the advertising-dulled senses of the consumer. "The public... could be relied upon to regard with complacence the most flagrant assaults upon its credulity," declared Allen. It took Detroit a while to realize that flimflam had lessons for industry product planners; when it did, Alfred P. Sloan, Jr. and General Motors were the first to understand.

Of course the automobile was driving along with all of this change, doing its part to exacerbate upheaval. But by now, the more sober and responsible of its critics understood that it needed some controls, which meant legislation. At the same time, its supporters were also looking to government, not for constraint, but for encouragement in the form of the building of more highways.

The Low Road

Harper's took a look at American roads in 1907 and came away horrified. It found ruts, bumps, gullies, and washouts. It discovered that road builders weren't bothering with drainage (didn't do much preparatory work of any kind, as a matter of fact), and then when the inevitable happened, when the roads crumbled within days or weeks of construction, nobody bothered to repair them.

We have seen that at the turn of the century there were fewer than 8,000 cars in the United States. At the end of the First World War, there were 5 million. Although bicycle clubs had long been pushing for good roads, it was the automobile club that was proving to be the real force. (The country's first auto club, in the sense we understand it today, was the American Motor League, founded in Chicago in 1895. By 1902 the American Automobile Association was organized in the same city.) In fact, the government had anticipated their good-roads campaign by the establishment of an Office of Road Inquiry in 1893, which was principally concerned with the state of railroads but also looked into primitive highways. Then in 1904, the United States Office of Public Roads made its first survey. It discovered 2 million miles of road, but it also discovered that only a little more than 150,000 were "improved." "Paved" would definitely be the wrong word, for "improved" meant covered with gravel or brick or oil or stone.

Pushed by auto clubs and auto owners—now numbering in the millions—the federal government discovered that in its established power to build post offices and post roads, it had precedent for getting into the highway business. The Federal Aid Road Act was passed in July 1916. Congress appropriated $75 million to be spent on construction over a five-year period but there was a kicker; only those states that had established their own highway departments were eligi-

ble for aid. Surprise! By 1920 every state in the union had a highway department. The next year Congress passed the Federal Highway Act to improve interstate travel but also to require the states to share half the costs. This prompted most states to follow Oregon's 1919 gas tax lead, and by 1929 every state was imposing such a levy. Motorists were happy, which made auto clubs happy, and the nation was on its way to being paved over with concrete.

One result of the improved highways was to aid the great migration by auto that had begun after the war. America in the nineteenth century was becoming increasingly urban. Country towns and metropolitan areas each were self-sufficient, tightly woven, and separate communities. Now the gap between them, geographical as well as sociological, was beginning to be filled with suburbs. During the decade of the 1920s Americans (4 million of them) were leaving farms, while the percentage of city dwellers grew by 6 percent (from 51.4 to 57.6); and as cities became larger and congested, the migration of families from cities to the neighboring countryside became more rapid. Here again the automobile played a part.

It also played a part in the way Americans played, and that annoyed a good many people. In 1925 Elizabeth Frazer sat down to let the readers of the *Saturday Evening Post* know just how bad the situation had gotten out there in the lovely countryside as a result of the automobile invasion. Citing the AAA and confronting the club with its own statistics, she said there were 16 million cars in use, the average distance traveled per year by each was 5,000 miles, 10 percent of which was used in "tourist, vacation and weekend activities. It appears therefore that the motorists of the U.S. will travel this year [1925] in their excursions for out-of-door recreation about...eight thousand million miles! And the bulk of that distance will be traveled not by the rich and exclusive with idle time on their hands, but by Mr. Average Man and his family." Frazer took a little time and trouble to break the numbers down into sorts of people and directions of journeys.

There was a north-south traffic ("the great hegira out of the icy Northern farmlands to the South in the effort to abolish winter") made up of "prosperous black-dirt farmers," "retired artisans," and "Down East truckers." The east-west traffic was touristy, vacationing in "luxurious land yachts with their own electrical and refrigerating plant, shower baths and chefs; bungalows on wheels, with chintz curtains, Pullman dining tables, air mattresses, and a canary in the window." She called them "grand moguls of the road," but she added there were occasional sedans and "battered old flivvers" too. And then "another group," of which Frazer obviously approved, "the real lovers of pioneer wilderness.... This particular type of motorist observes the rules of the road with a kind of passionate piety." All of which was to set up the villains of the piece: "The week-end hell-raisers, motor hobos and jazz hounds.... These are the hogs, rooting and snouting and doing their best to reduce all out-of-doors to the squalid filth of a pigsty.

"Only force of authority can reach them."

Poor Elizabeth. Force and authority had been at work almost since the invention of the car, and look what the country had come to. In 1908, *Harper's* ran a piece called "Our Chaotic Automobile Laws" that got right down to it: "If all the evils of which the automobile is accused since its appearance in this country, barely a decade [ago], were to be laid before the bar of justice for impartial adjudication, the list would be nothing less than appalling."

There were court decisions that contradicted one another, state to state, on the subject of whether the automobile was a carriage and therefore entitled to

1917 Winton Custom House Car—"The General"
Built in 1918 by Dr. E. J. Fithian of Grove City, Pennsylvania, on a stretched Winton Big Six Touring car chassis, this early motor home was the doctor's campaign bus in his try for the governorship of the state on the prohibition ticket. The interior shows that Dr. Fithian did not intend to suffer during his campaign: The upholstery is cut velvet, and the fittings include bathroom, storage cabinets, desk, built-in icebox and pure silk spring-rollered window shades. The car came to Harrah's from the collection of the singer and car enthusiast James Melton.

highway-condition safety. There had even been a lawsuit brought in Pennsylvania to determine whether cars were entitled to drive on state roads. By 1908 thirty-six states had enacted one or another kind of law affecting the car or its driver. They were so diverse—ranging from speed limits to the privilege of crossing state lines—that the AAA tried to induce Congress to pass a uniform national law. Its provisions were several: the car owner had to comply with the laws of his own state; there was to be a $5 national registration fee for automobiles, the payment of which would be signified by a license "to be displayed at all times on the machine"; safety would be promoted by a mandate to equip cars with front and rear lights; finally, the proposed legislation would establish a motor vehicle agency within the Department of Commerce and Labor.

If only it had passed. But the various states had already glimpsed the revenue worth of the automobiles owned by their citizens, and they were not about to surrender those dollars to the federal government. Of course they differed on how much to charge. Five years after the Duryeas's first drive, in 1898, Texas was charging a $50 registration fee, while it only cost 25 cents to make ownership acceptable to Alabama. Connecticut followed the European example and charged by horsepower: $3 under 20 hp; $5 for cars with 20 to 30 hp, and $10 for high performers over 30 hp. New York went on the basis of weight. (Such diversity of approach continues, much of it based on the very decisions of 1908.) As for permissible speed, it would remain a problem until passage of a 55 mph national maximum speed limit in 1974, whereupon several western states reneged on even that commitment and threw things into confusion again.

Nor were drivers themselves exempt from legislation. In Kansas City, Kansas, as early as 1904, they were required to be possessed of "skill, experience, capacity and sobriety" and were subject to a $10 fine for "failing to heed the signal of a [rider] whose horse the driver is said to have frightened."

The history of legislation of the automobile is a patchwork of state decisions, beginning with New York's 1901 requirement that a car be registered. The same subjects—safety, taxation (registration), speed limits, driver qualifications—would be addressed again and again and changed as often as they were brought up in various legislatures. Only in 1966, with the National Highway Traffic Safety Act, did the federal government finally enter the arena, and then to the dismay of manufacturers *and* car owners. But by the end of the so-called Antique Epoch of the automobile, 1931, both were concerned about something profoundly more important. On October 24, 1929, post–World War I prosperity came to a brutal end, and what became known as the Great Depression began. It affected the automobile deeply; it changed the nature of the industry even more.

Disaster

With the crash came the Depression and a shakeout in the auto industry. Great automobile names fell by the wayside. Had they wished, they could have looked to their own house—at least to the General Motors house—for the causes. Many of the practices of Billy Durant and his ilk, then taken up by the whole country, contributed to the disaster. When Durant pumped water into Chevrolet, increasing its capitalization from $20 to $80 million so he could swap stock and once again become head of GM, he was engaging in "merger at inflated prices." The piling of holding companies one upon the other had brought down Maxwell-Briscoe and Pope Manufacturing. Flink adds an all-encompassing condemnation of the auto industry. By establishing a manufacturing entity that was capable of producing far more than could be consumed, by shifting social and economic patterns ("What the individual gained from automobile ownership was at the expense of undermining community and family, and it invited anonymity and anomie"), by fueling installment buying and selling, the new automobility "played a key role in creating the most important necessary conditions underlying the Great Depression."

Of course the auto industry did not invent speculative obsessions, and if a single cause could be identified as central to the crash, it was speculation. The use by banks of depositors' funds in ways forbidden by law, such as the creation of "security affiliates," was of the same cloth. So was the swapping among companies of properties inflated at each transaction. Said Allen about these financial dances: "The irresponsible actions of men who did not stop to think that they were constructing a caricature of the capitalist system were paving the way to disaster."

None of the protections and guarantees we have come to expect, even demand, of our federal government existed that fall of 1929. With business booming, business forecasters chanting the hymn of prosperity, advertisers hyping and ballyhooing, and stories abounding of beauticians and hardware salesmen becoming millionaires overnight, a fever of speculation in the market struck the nation. The government allowed it to go on and on, particularly in its virtual ignoring of "margin" requirements. As the market climbed higher, it seemed to make sense to taxi drivers and housewives to buy stocks (if the House of Morgan could do it, why couldn't they?) at 10 percent down. Of course, if the market should drop, they would be called on to pony up not just another 10 percent but 10 percent more than that, and if it dropped even further, the whole thing.

There were ample signals before the crash that disaster was in the making. Charles Nash gave a speech to the annual meeting of the National Automobile Dealers Association in 1925 in which he said the saturation point in car ownership had been reached in 1923. Walter Chrysler is quoted in Flink as having said, "early in 1929 it had seemed to me that I could feel the winds of disaster blowing." Well before the crash Sloan was on record in favor of battening down the financial affairs at GM in preparation for an enormous storm.

Money lent to brokers to carry margin accounts had gone up almost a billion dollars in 1927. The Federal Reserve System responded by easing money rates, which stimulated the market even more. Meanwhile, business was slowing down, an ominous signal. Conservative voices in the financial community were beginning to sound warnings. In early 1928, Moody's Investors Service wondered, "how much of a readjustment may be required to place the stock market in a sound position." The Harvard Economic Society thought, "business is entering upon a period of temporary readjustment." All of this was jargon for "things look bad." Nobody listened. Nobody seemed to be watching either. There was a series of downward swoops in stock prices, one dramatic instance coming late in spring of 1928. It started in the West when bank stocks fell as much as 100 points in one day on the San Francisco Exchange.

That summer Herbert Hoover was nominated by the Republicans, Al Smith by the Democrats. Smith had so many things going against him—Catholicism for one, opposition to prohibition for another—that it seemed Hoover's election was preordained, which meant business as usual. Then Smith did an interesting thing. He hauled in John J. Raskob, vice president and chairman of the finance committee of General Motors and vice president of General Motors Acceptance, to become chairman of the Democratic National Committee. Now even the pessimists were reassured. For if in the unlikely case that Smith were elected, Raskob's commitment to the party was a certain sign that the business of business

88

would be attended to in the White House. In the event, not even Raskob could help Smith. Hoover inundated him at the polls.

That lit off a "Hoover bull market" in November. Stock exchange seats sold for as much as $580,000, a new record. Packard stock hit 145. Then, to the horror of speculators, the market broke again. And again it recovered. One more time it threatened to collapse; one more time it picked itself up off the ticker tape covered floor. Brokers' loans went up from 3.5 billion in 1927 to almost 6 billion as 1929 arrived, representing the money borrowed by brokers to buy stocks for their customers who were paying only 10 percent of the stock's value. That summer *The Ladies Home Journal* published a piece by John J. Raskob of General Motors called "Everybody Ought to be Rich." And the path to riches? Speculation in the market, in "the profit end of wealth production." Frederick Lewis Allen estimates that more than a million Americans actually held stock on margin during the fabulous summer of 1929. Perhaps as many as *three hundred million* shares were being carried on margin.

Summer turned to fall and the market showed signs of cracking again. But not to worry. The president of National City Bank stepped off the ship from Europe radiating confidence: "I know of nothing fundamentally wrong with the stock market or with the underlying business and credit structure. . . . The public is suffering from 'brokers' loanitis.'"

October 22, 1929, was a Tuesday. Wednesday the market plunged. Thursday the bottom fell out. In September, the high price for General Motors stock (adjusted to take into account splits and issues of rights to buy more stock) was listed at 181⅛. In November it was 36.

Frederick Lewis Allen, upon whom we have relied so heavily for a view of post–World War I America, gets the final word: "The Post-war decade had come to its close. An era had ended."

1919 Pan
Samuel Pandolfo launched a company-town enterprise to build this genuinely weird car in St. Cloud, Minnesota, in 1918. It was noted mechanically for its adjustable seats making into a double bed. It lasted, in roadster and touring-car form, until 1922 when authorities caught up with Pandolfo and convicted him of using the mails to defraud the public.

CHAPTER 5

Adolescent Agonies

Bernard Baruch would spend the last years of his life feeding pigeons in Central Park, having seen two world wars and earning a reputation as a man of judgment and foresight. Not many would remember his initial actions prior to the first of those world wars when he became head of the War Industry Board and decided that nothing the auto manufacturers could possibly contribute justified their continuing use of precious resources. The whole idea of allocating steel for the building of cars appalled Baruch. By 1917, in fact, he wanted to forbid the use of steel in the industry altogether. Nor was he alone. Congress put a 50 percent excise tax on automobiles.

It did not take Baruch very long to change his mind, which was fortunate since the War Industry Board had an absolute say in the allocation of strategic metals. After seeing the uses of motor-driven vehicles on French battlefields, Baruch relented to the extent of allowing the industry to use one half of its 1917 consumption in the final quarter of the following year. *Scribner's* noted drily, "For years, [automobilists] have impressed upon the military . . . the indispensability of mechanical locomotion for war purposes. It needed the war to demonstrate the truth of [that] contention to the full."

While fighting Baruch with one hand, the industry was increasing auto production from almost 550,000 units in 1914 to 1.5 million during the following year. It was also making trucks, 215,000 of them in 1916. It is likely the trucks reversed Baruch's antipathy toward the industry to a large degree. Every railroad car was chock-a-block with the materiels and munitions being bought by the Allies, and there was not much additional transport to be found—except the "motor-truck." The squeeze got worse when America entered the war in 1917. Production levels and demand were so great that they significantly altered the car industry. The automobile industry had in fact become an enormous war resource.

A case in point is the contributions of the Lelands to the war effort. It is a curious, ugly story. Leland senior was convinced America would be involved in the war, particularly after a trip to England in 1915. On his return he called on President Wilson urging him with "burning belief" that this country should contribute, more than that should prepare itself for war, and that the automobile industry, and Leland in particular, might be vital in the production of engines. Leland had persuaded the British Air Board to send him a Rolls-Royce engine, which he spent a great deal of time testing. In April of 1917, in fact the day after Congress declared war, Leland went to W. C. Durant of GM to plead his case. Cadillac had just finished a large, new plant where closed bodies were to be built. Closed bodies could be bought out and the plant converted to the manufacture of aircraft engines. Durant was in no mood for patriotism. He was dealing seconds in the market and would have none of Leland's plan. "It is nonsense," he said, "this war should stop tomorrow." Wilfred Leland had gone to see GM's president

1917 Dodge Touring
A 12-volt electric system and nonstandard gear-change pattern characterized this car until 1926. Dodge was a favorite of General John "Black Jack" Pershing, who first used one in his Mexican campaign of 1916. When the United States entered World War I, the Dodge found its way to France as a staff car and ambulance.

along with his father, and at that point he spoke up: "This is our war now," he said, to which a diplomatic Durant replied, "I don't care for your platitudes. This is not our war and I will not permit any GM unit to do work for the government." It was the first time Billy Durant had refused the Lelands freedom to act as they saw fit, and it was the quarrel that set the Lelands off on their own.

The Lelands next went to Washington to initiate a series of negotiations. First they consulted the Signal Corps under which the nascent air corps fell. No, there were no government contracts prepared to be let. There surely would be, though, and one of them would certainly be for engines, came the response. The Lelands were vividly aware that time was short. On their own, then, the two went back to Detroit and bought a patch of houses and a small factory. The name the Lelands chose for the new company was "Lincoln" in honor of the man for whom Henry Leland had built guns as a young man at Colt.

England and France were in desperate need of aircraft engines; their own were not susceptible to the kind of mass manufacture that was the hallmark of the American industry. The Lelands knew they had to develop an aircraft engine that could be built in quantity, if they were to be of any use to the Allies. Development of a new engine was no easy job, nor could it be done overnight. The answer came from Packard, whose Jesse Vincent had a design he had been working on for several years. It made about 1 horsepower per 5 pounds, which was too heavy by more than half. So with the help of E. J. Hall of Hall-Scott Motor in San Francisco, the engine was redesigned in two days: an eight cylinder producing about 300 hp. The first pre-production unit was built in a month and christened the Liberty.

At about this point, Durant realized he had made a terrible mistake. He came to the Lelands and begged them to return to Cadillac. Father and son had gone too far for that. Their project envisioned building twenty, eight-cylinder engines a day (or fourteen twelve-cylinders) in a plant built and financed by the Lelands themselves, "a volunteer contribution to their country for the purpose of ending the war," according to Ottilie Leland and Minie Millbrock, authors of *Master of Precision*, the official biography of Henry Leland.

Others in the the auto business stepped forward to help, including Charles "Boss" Kettering. In August, the government summoned them to discuss General John "Black Jack" Pershing's report that an eight-cylinder would be insufficient in power and that what was needed was a twelve.

Henry Leland had gotten a rough cost estimate from Packard on production costs for the twelve, about $5,000 per unit. But those costs were based on the heavy eight. Now a new, lightweight twelve would have to be built, and obviously it would cost a great deal more. More trying still, the Lelands, who were planning on a maximum output of fourteen motors a day, were suddenly asked to produce seventy instead. Before the contracts had been signed or the final design of the motor determined, their plant had been outgrown.

Lincoln's contract called for 6,000 engines. Leland signed it, knowing it would mean the small factory he had arranged to build would be far too small. On his return to Detroit, he wangled ground, steel, and machine tools for a far larger factory still without knowing how much it would cost to build his engines.

The war was almost over by now. There was not the faintest possibility that the plant would be able to produce the number of engines that could permit the Lelands to recoup their investment. The Lelands were stuck with a huge factory, cancellation of orders for Liberty engines, a recalcitrant government that would not honor its obligations, and debt.

Nonetheless, at war's end, they converted to the building of what they knew

best—automobiles—confident that *some* compensation for their expenditures would be forthcoming, since the secretary of war himself, Newton Baker, had signed a settlement contract.

The motor for the new car was undoubtedly suggested by the Liberty. It was a 60-degree V-8, what the American auto industry would come to agree was the optimum design. The result was an engine of unprecedented quietness and almost no vibration. The 60-degree configuration also permitted the lowering of the center of gravity in the chassis.

Although dealers clamored to sign up (Boston alone had forty-one applicants, Kansas City thirty-six), the car was never intended to be a mass-market vehicle. It was luxurious, quiet, and big. Roadster and touring cars—the least expensive models offered by Lincoln in 1920—were to sell at $4,600; limousine and town cars at $6,600. The first car came out of the plant in April 1920.

In March of that year the United States Treasury Department had presented Lincoln with a bill for $5.7 million, allegedly on the company's war profits. The Lelands were shocked. To begin with, they had gone out to their financial limits even before they had assurances of becoming contractors on aircraft engines. Then they had built a huge factory. After that they had renegotiated a contract without so much as knowing their manufacturing costs. Then, when they had been reassured of authorization to build, they had also been given promises that should the number of engines ordered not allow them to amortize their factory, the government would see that they were left whole. Indeed, when that very thing had happened, the secretary of war had signed a settlement contract. On the basis of all this, the Lelands had spent additional millions to reconvert to peacetime production, only to be told now that Washington had changed its mind.

To top it all off, just as the Lincoln was about to be introduced that spring, the

1913 Pope-Hartford Two-Passenger Roadster Model 29
The Pope-Hartford was a powerful car with enormous stamina. It won many races and hill climbs, including the Oakland Panama-Pacific road race in 1911 and the Davenport, Iowa, and Atlanta, Georgia, Hill Climbs in 1912. This is one of the cars that put the company out of business, not because of its inherent merits or faults, but because it was one of seventeen different models produced by Pope-Hartford that year. Too many models, too much diversification, too far ahead of the marketing strategy of producing a different kind of car for every different geographic and demographic group. In 1914, Pope discontinued car production.

country entered the depression of 1920. They were not the only manufacturers in trouble. The depression of 1920 put an end to Billy Durant at GM (as we shall see); temporarily shut down Nash, Packard, Dodge, and Studebaker; and forced reorganization of Willys by Walter Chrysler.

The depression was full upon the Lelands; Ford was cutting prices to move cars, and Lincoln—even though it was losing money—followed suit. More money would be needed, but a chasm had opened between the company's principal backers and the Lelands. A consulting firm was brought in to mediate the dispute in which the backers insisted the Lelands were up to their ears in mismanagement. The consulting firm, however, reported that "the whole organization . . . is unusually harmonious and uniformly competent." Advertising was excellent; the sales plan was "highly appropriate and skillfully adapted to the marketing of a high-grade motor car"; cost schedules were "as orderly and well arranged as we have recently seen." In fact, by the end of the third quarter of 1921, Lincoln sales had passed those of Chandler, Peerless, Pierce-Arrow, and the combined totals of Cunningham, Daniels, Lafayette, Locomobile, McFarland, and Winton.

The trouble lay with Lincoln's finances. In July, the Lelands' backers made another $1.25 million available, taking a temporary mortgage on all Lincoln's physical assets as security. This was still not enough; the Lelands went to every bank they knew, pleading for money. A financial reorganization was imperative and they knew it. The investors had no faith. The board dismissed the Lelands. Henry Leland's secretary wrote: "It was tragedy; tragedy of trusting investors and more. It was the tragedy of unrealized hopes, the feeling that one experiences at the passing of a young life of promise; or the gashing of a masterpiece by some uncouth vandal." Lincoln was in receivership.

Toward the end of the battle to save Lincoln, Wilfred Leland had gone to Henry Ford who declined to lend a nickel but who answered, when the younger Leland told him things were so desperate that the directors might apply for receivership, "After they do, come and see me." The moment the news was out, Ford called both Lelands in to meet with him and his top executives. During the meeting, Wilfred Leland recalled, Ford took him aside and asked how much would be needed. Leland answered somewhere in the neighborhood of $10 million. Ford didn't blink an eye. Discussions continued at Ford's office and at his house, Fairlane. Wilfred later believed that Ford made up his mind to buy Lincoln in November and that he was prepared to honor the Lelands' terms: dealers' franchise would be honored, creditors and stockholders would be paid in full, the Lelands would continue with the company.

In December, the company's financial status was filed with the court. Late that month, the court-appointed receiver announced that the government, which had *again* pressed a $5.7 million claim against the Lelands, had *again* looked into the matter, found no fraud, and would settle for $500,000. In the same month, Henry Ford announced his decision to buy Lincoln. In a meeting with the Fords and the Lelands before the bankruptcy judge, it was agreed that all the terms the Lelands had made would be honored: The dealers would remain; the stockholders would be paid in full; the Lelands would run the company. Buying price was $5 million.

The Lelands' terms were not honored. Ford took over Lincoln and in short order dismissed the Lelands and refused to pay the stockholders. Henry Leland spent the rest of his life and most of his money trying, unsuccessfully, to force Ford to honor his pledge to Lincoln's stockholders. Worse still, in Wilfred Leland's eyes, Ford built Lincoln the Ford way, depriving it of much of the care and precision of its manufacture.

Henry Leland, who began Cadillac and set a standard for it that Americans came to recognize as representing the finest quality, tried to do the same for Lincoln, only to see it fall into the hands of the same man who had given up on the Cadillac and who never succeeded in making the Lincoln a real competitor. It was not the end of the Lincoln, however. Cars of that marque continued to be built to satisfy extraordinarily demanding tastes and unlimited budgets. But it was the end of the Lelands in the auto industry. It was also the end of a great number of their contemporaries, for what was coming to be known as "Detroit" was undergoing shakeout.

Some Shapes of Things to Come

Part of the reason for the diminution of the numbers of manufacturers was the beginning of standardization of the automobile. We will climb inside the Model T in the next chapter. But as the 1920s advanced, another car began to represent what the industry was coming to. What, for example, was the Chevrolet of the middle of the decade like? In the first place, there was nothing horseless carriage about it. The industry had long since abandoned the notion that because the car replaced the barouche or brougham, it still had to look like one.

Engines had been moved from under the passenger seats to under a front bonnet. Cars were now likely to be sedans, at least to have hard tops, unlike their predecessors, which were almost all open. They had windshields, electric starters, and roll-up windows. Almost all cars on American highways had left-hand drive. Except for the Model T, most cars came in a choice of colors. Chevrolet, like Ford, was following a one-model policy. The 1925 Superior coach had disc wheels (although artillery spokes were still seen, wire wheels had become very popular in other makes and models) and the duPont/Kettering Duco paint. Chevrolet was still using an overhead valve four-cylinder engine; and it would not offer front-wheel brakes until three years later. The price of a Chevrolet in 1925 was $650.

Clearly we are beginning to see familiar automotive outlines. Since the end of the war, a number of features we take for granted had been introduced. In 1919, the Wescott touring introduced front and rear bumpers as standard equipment. Indirect lighting on the dash had arrived the same year. At the 1919 New York auto show, about 90 percent of the cars shown were open. In 1920 the ratio was reversed. Chauffeur-driven cars were on the decline. Heaters had become standard equipment. Mack had rubber engine mountings and rubber spring shackles. Two years later, cars with automatic backup lights and air cleaners were displayed in New York. A year after that some cars were showing gas gauges as standard, and in 1923, Packard introduced the first mass-produced straight eight L-head engine, while a number of manufacturers had gone to four-wheel brakes, power-operated windshield wipers (vacuum assisted), and the foot-controlled headlight dimmer switch.

A year before the Superior coach appeared, not a single steamer, nor even one electric, was shown at the twenty-fourth National Automobile Show. It was the first U.S. show exhibiting 100 percent gas-powered automobiles. In its year of introduction, the Superior coach was surrounded by cars with straight eight engines (Packard, Duesenberg, Auburn, Hupmobile, Jordan, and Rickenbacker), cars with rumble seats, one-piece windshields, crank-up windows, tire jacks, locking radiator caps, trunk racks, mirrors inside and out, ashtrays, cigar lighters, and

Engines:

1913 Pierce-Arrow: A monster of a motor, 824.7-cubic-inch piston displacement or almost three times the size of most 1982 passenger-car engines. TOP RIGHT

1925 Doble: The ultimate steamer—75-horsepower, 213 cubic inches, working pressure 1,250 pounds per square inch, a four-cylinder double expansion steamer that could propel the 3,900-pound coupe in which it sat to 90 miles an hour. MIDDLE RIGHT

1914 Chalmers: A six-cylinder engine with a long stroke (5½ inches compared to its 4-inch bore) that made 50 horsepower—not bad for 1914. BOTTOM RIGHT

1925 Julian: An example of experimentation almost for its own sake, the Julian engine was air-cooled, six-cylinder radial—good configuration for an airplane, bad for a car. BELOW: photo by Joseph Kugielsky

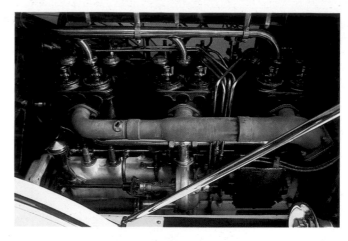

OPPOSITE:
1926 Chevrolet Superior Deluxe Depot Hack
This very early station wagon differs from its sedan relative in its stamped steel dash and firewall instead of the more elaborate piece on the passenger car. Also, the throttle and spark controls are just under the steering wheel, not on the dash or steering wheel as in the sedan.

temperature indicators. Oldsmobile introduced chrome plating.

During this six-year span (1919 to 1925), the industry itself saw major changes. A new marque, Essex, appeared from the Hudson Motor Car company. "[Roy D. Chapin] introduced the first closed car to sell at almost the same price as the open touring cars in an era when a sedan body was a luxury," wrote his biographer, J. C. Long. "This innovation, as Chapin's friend . . . Edsel Ford observed, vastly enlarged the scope of motoring in America and made the automobile industry a stabilized, all-year business instead of a seasonal one." A significant claim, for here was the first cheap sedan, tall and ungainly perhaps (its body was built by Fisher), but a bold experiment that succeeded brilliantly. More than 20,000 pieces were shipped during the 1919 calendar year, which made

1929 Hudson Four-Passenger Sport Phaeton
Under President Roy Dikeman Chapin, Hudson was known as an innovative company and Chapin the tasteful aristocrat of Detroit manufacturers. This car's official model designation was the "Greater Hudson." It had a Biddle and Smart custom body, weighed 3,795 pounds, and had a 92-horsepower, six-cylinder engine. Price: $2,200.

Essex one of the auto establishment's most successful first-year cars. It had a four-cylinder long stroke engine that developed about 50 hp, mounted in a chassis with a 108½-inch wheel base (some 10 inches longer than today's MGB). The car, a strong seller for Hudson, was made from 1919 until 1932; a total of 1.3 million were built during its years of manufacture.

There were other changes in the industry as well. Flat rate repair had been introduced; Duesenberg had appeared; Maxwell had gone into receivership; total Ford Motor production since the company's founding passed 5 million (in 1921); Durant was once more out of GM but would go on to found Durant Motor. Auto insurance was revised to cover the actual value of the automobile instead of the purchase price, in consequence of a belief by insurance companies that owners were deliberately destroying their cars after a year or so of ownership to cover depreciation. Traffic light systems were being introduced, and Ford was lowering prices, as we have seen. Nineteen twenty-three saw a 4-million-car sales year; "Ethyl" gas came on the market; Ford swallowed Lincoln; Chrysler appeared; Cannonball Baker crossed the country in twelve and a half days; and Alfred P. Sloan, Jr., became president of GM. In the following two years, Winton went out of business, Nash bought Lafayette, and Maxwell-Chalmers was reorganized as Chrysler Corporation.

Of all these things—and they are only a representative sampling of what was happening during the 1920s—the three most significant developments were the triumph of the Model T, the departure of Durant and the ascension of Sloan at GM, and the appearance of Chrysler.

Trial of the Giants

To give some sense of the growth of the Model T, and the utter dominance of both the industry and the market by Ford Motor Company, contemplate the figures in the following table. Even before the war, from 1909 to 1916–1917, the car dropped in price and rose in numbers astonishingly.

Year	Number of Model T's	Price
1909–1910	18,665	$950
1911	34,528	780
1912	78,440	690
1913	168,220	600
1914	248,307	550
1915	308,213	490
1916	553,921	440
1917	785,432	360

By the end of the 1920s depression, banks were no longer reluctant to lend money to prospective buyers of cars. Said *Harper's,* "With the finance companies reaping a golden harvest and calling themselves 'the nation's transportation bankers,' people were urged to borrow." Ford sales grew and grew during the era of the great boom. By 1924, Ford had produced its 10 millionth car, and you will recall that the year before, the industry had its first 4-million-car year with Ford capturing 55 percent market share. Obviously, Henry the Original's decision to concentrate on one had been the right one—at the time.

All of this had been made possible by the contributions of others. Historian John Rae points out that Hayden Eames at Pope was the first to organize work gangs and assign specific jobs to each, that Henry Leland was the genius behind truly precision-made parts, and that Ransom Olds (however inadvertently) was the inventor of the subcontract system that stamped the American industry as assemblers. Walter E. Flanders, perhaps the original "production man," was the first to take enormous pains with plant layout for optimum manufacture. Thus, as Rae said, "the claim that Henry Ford 'invented' mass production must be dismissed as absurd. The introduction of the moving assembly line at Highland Park in 1913 was a momentous and epochal innovation, but it was essentially the capstone of an edifice that had been rising for over a century."

We will rejoin Ford in a later chapter to watch the Model T eclipsed, primarily as a result of Ford's own intransigence, but also because of the remarkable marketing skills of Alfred Sloan at GM. To bring about the historical confrontation between Ford and Sloan, Durant would have to do himself in at GM, paving the way for the once-owner of Hyatt Roller Bearing to climb into the ring with the champ.

Durant had lost the Lelands. Next he was to lose Walter Chrysler and then his own grip on General Motors. The Chrysler blowup was precipitated by Durant's attempts to override Chrysler and run the Buick Company as he saw fit—echoes of Durant versus Leland. Chrysler seems to have been a far less patient man than Henry Leland. Durant, preoccupied with his stock market maneuverings, was forever on the telephone. Chrysler's reaction to being called by Durant and then put off while he spent hours on the phone was one of increasing rage. But this, really, was only the touch-off to the penultimate argument.

This occurred because Chrysler was bypassed by Durant when he informed the Chamber of Commerce in Flint that GM would build a new plant for Buick there, never once mentioning the fact to Buick's president. Add to this violation of

1924 Chrysler Phaeton Model B
Triumphant in creating a car bearing his name at last, Walter B. Chrysler introduced this to very considerable acclaim. It was a high-performance car for its time and in its price range ($1,495).

protocol that Chrysler was negotiating to buy elsewhere the frames that the new Flint plant was to build. Then, within the year, Durant embarked on his famous tractor-guided-by-reins program on which he proposed to spend $30 million. That did it. It was 1920; business was rotten; Buick under Walter Chrysler was providing half of GM's earnings; and Durant wouldn't listen to a word of advice from anyone, much less Buick's president.

Finally, Durant's speculation caught up with him. There is argument—at least difference of opinion—about whether he acted in good faith, but as it turned out he was telling his chairman, Pierre duPont, as well as Alfred Sloan, one thing while he was doing another. They confronted Durant with the charge that he was manipulating GM stock; he denied it; they called in auditors who confirmed their suspicion that Durant was way overextended. DuPont and Raskob were not inclined to allow Durant to go down, fearing (probably correctly) that it would have drastic consequences for GM. They bailed him out through the duPont company, which bought up Durant's stock, and then bade him good-bye. Pierre duPont assumed the role of chief executive officer with Sloan as his adjutant and the real operating power of the company. In short order duPont, who didn't want the job anyway, stepped aside, and Sloan took over. His reorganization is the subject for another chapter in which we will compare what was happening at the two giants, GM and Ford.

Walter Chrysler went on to Willys at the insistence of the company's bankers, where he discovered he had signed on with another incarnation of Billy Durant.

Even though he was given authority to run the corporation, and John North Willys retreated to lick his wounds, there was no rescuing a company that had been run in an even more disorganized fashion than GM had been. Willys went into receivership.

Walter Chrysler seems to have been a glutton for punishment. Not only had he stayed with Durant despite Durant's abominable management, leaving only when he simply couldn't tolerate it any longer, not only had he taken on the same kind of job at Willys, but he then agreed to try to reorganize Maxwell-Chalmers.

The story gets even more complicated in consequence of that decision. While at Willys, Chrylser had brought in a group of men who designed a six-cylinder car that he hoped would save John North Willys's company. As we discovered, nothing could help. When Chrysler took over Maxwell-Chalmers, he tried to buy a Willys factory where the six-cylinder was to have been built. He was outbid by Billy Durant (he had by this time started his new company), who wanted the place as the manufacturing facility for a car called the Flint.

Now we turn to Chrysler's efforts to straighten out the tangled affairs of the Maxwell-Chalmers firm. Maxwell was a recognized name, but in debt $26 million worth. Again, creditors who appreciated his organizational talents were responsible for Chrysler's hiring. Chrysler discovered disaster at every hand. He decided on a fresh start and put both Maxwell and Chalmers into receivership. With the sale of their assets and an infusion of $15 million from creditors, Chrysler formed a new company called the Maxwell Motor Corporation of which he became president in 1923.

Meanwhile, Chrysler put the trio who designed the six-cylinder car at Willys to work at Maxwell Motor. Their assignment was to devise a car to be named after Chrysler himself. It was shown in New York in 1924, and reaction to it was sensational. The car virtually created Chrysler Corporation. Chase Securities agreed to lend Maxwell $50 million for its production, and Chrysler Corporation (still to be called Maxwell for the moment) was off and running.

For the survivors of the depression of the 1920s there was to be success. A good number of independents, however, did not live to see it. Lafayette, built by Charles Nash, went down; so did Cole. Durant's old partner, Dallas Dort, had gone into car manufacturing with the Dort. It too failed. Away went the Wills Sainte Claire, although not without a fight. Among the great names to go as well were Locomobile, Simplex, and Mercer. It was a bloody episode in the industry, but a bloodier one was still to come.

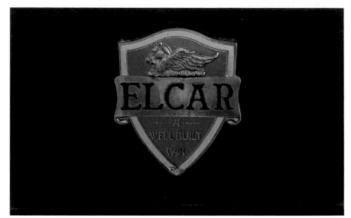

CHAPTER 6
The One That Did It

The Ford [Model T]... has a tank for father, a hood for mother, and a rattle for baby.

On October 1, 1908, the world was introduced to the Model T. Soon wherever you looked there was a T. In the year of its glory (circa 1923), then, what was the personality, the sense, the feel of this marvel that captured the heart of an auto-mobile nation?

It came in an absolutely bewildering choice of personalities from truck to town car to four-passenger touring (the most popular) to runabout. Its speed-crazed drivers performed operations that converted it from honest journeyman to high-speed traveler by use of special speedster body, overhead multivalve per cylinder head, and apparatus to enhance the engine's breathing including huge carburetor, special manifolding, and pressure fuel system. The T would have seemed terribly primitive to the grandchildren of its owners. A Runabout (base price $295 in 1923) stood plain and innocent before the world: It was black, of course, weighed 1,620 pounds, stood 5 feet 10 inches tall with the top up, was just over 11 feet long (with a wheelbase of 8 feet 4½ inches) and 5½ feet wide (track was nearly equal front and back: 4 feet 9 inches in front, 4 feet 9¼ inches in back), and had ground clearance of 9½ inches.

Its L-head engine had four cylinders, making 20 horsepower at about 1,800 revolutions per minute from its 176.6-cubic-inch piston displacement (2,896.7 cc). It was almost "square" with a 3¾-inch bore and a 4-inch stroke. It had a Holley carburetor and magneto ignition—a kind of self-contained permanent-magnet electric generator that provided current before the invention of the more modern and familiar battery, coil, and distributor—with coils for starting. It had no shock absorbers. Suspension was by transverse leaf front and rear, solid bar springs that ran crosswise about at the same position as the axles.

The T was as straightforward-looking a device as you would encounter, particularly given that the automobile was already beginning to appear in a variety of wonderful shapes and sizes. It had a short hood that came up about to the top of its front fenders and then tumbled inward on a 45-degree angle for about 6 inches, where it flattened off to form the top. The Runabout sat a pair of people in a single bench seat 37 inches wide and 19 inches deep. The seat was indeed a bench, but it wrapped around both passenger and driver, supporting one thigh each and providing an armrest for the driver's left elbow, for the passenger's right.

The wheels were large and light. They were twelve-spoked artillery 30 x 3s and most probably mounted Firestones (Henry made a deal with Harvey Firestone to supply tires for new Model T's in 1908), which were treaded, narrow, and came with tubes. There were no lug nuts, in fact, no standard demountable tires on a rim. You took off the wheel and then worried about replacing the tire on

LEFT, AND PP. 106–108 AND 113.
1923 Ford Model T Runabout
With its L-head engine and base price of $295, it "stood plain and innocent before the world." This is the car that put America on wheels.

it. The car had a steel running board on which you could have a variety of options including a tool box and an accordion X-frame luggage rack.

The brass radiator of earlier T's was gone by 1923; instead, the whole car was black-painted steel. There were headlights prominently displayed between the front fender openings, a crank that had a permanent home on the bottom front of the car, and coach lamps on both sides of the passenger compartment. The top, when raised (or the back of the passenger compartment with the top down) came to an abrupt halt right behind the seat, and from there the car trailed off in a low, flat rear deck to the rear of its conventional fender.

It was fairly difficult to mount. To get from the running board (a sizable step up) to the floor of the passenger compartment took about the same contemplation and daring as climbing aboard today's high-boy pickup truck. The door was just over 17 inches wide—not very wide. But once you were inside, the T was surprisingly comfortable to sit in. The seat provided far better support than it looked like it would. The driver had a big plastic four-spoke, thick-rimmed wheel to hang on to; it came close to his lap, but it was at a convenient angle. The passenger had ample leg room.

There were no standard instruments. The driver sat at the wheel beneath which was a finned metal half-collar attached to the steering column. Two levers, one on the right the other on the left, traversed the corresponding 90 degrees of the collar. When the levers were in the downward position, they almost touched; when they were at their uppermost slots, they stuck out from the steering column like ears. One lever advanced or retarded the spark; the other was the throttle. Sticking up at the driver's right was a handbrake lever. At the driver's feet were

three pedals, the center one slightly to the rear of the others; reading left to right: gear change forward, reverse pedal, and brake. The car had a tall (5-foot) two-piece windshield, giving the driver and the passenger a view of the world not equaled for half a century, until GMC built a bus whose whole front end seemed to be made of glass. With the top up, however, vision out the back was perfectly dreadful. The top, by the way, was useful to keep birds from strafing the car's occupants, but was otherwise not terribly reassuring. The car did not have roll-up windows; the top was attached to the windshield pillars by bungee cord—a stretch rope with hooks at both ends. You couldn't lock yourself out of the T because it didn't have outside locks; it didn't even have door handles.

Driving was easy once you got the hang of it, but the trouble was getting the hang of it. The driver used both feet and hands, and some coordination between them was required. Mainly, he used his left foot and his right hand. His right limbs he reserved for the far right pedal, a brake that worked on the transmission, and the middle pedal, reverse. The left lever on the quadrant was the ignition control, a spark advance that determined the moment after the intake stroke when the plugs would fire. Once the thing was in motion, it required the use of the left foot and right hand only.

Pay attention now; the way the car worked is very different from the familiar pattern of today. The left pedal was clutch and gear operator. Well, the left foot and leg operated the thing, but pushing in the left pedal halfway put the car in neutral. Pushing it in all the way put it in low. Letting it out full put the car in the higher of its two speeds (the reverse pedal had only one speed—reached by pressing all the way down on the floor.) You could also get into neutral by releasing the hand brake halfway. So once the motor was running, you got in, pushed the left-hand lever on the quadrant to advance the spark, let off the hand brake to halfway forward, pushed the left pedal to the floor to put the car in low, at the same time moving the throttle forward, which was done by moving the left lever on the quadrant. Whew! No wonder some states had two licenses, one for T's, the other for everything else.

The car was lively. You could get from a stop to 20 mph in just over 8 seconds, to 30 mph in 7 seconds more, and to a reasonable cruising speed of 40 mph in a total of 35 seconds. The standing quarter mile could be done in 33 seconds flat. For comparison, a good American Ford of the middle sixties with a medium-sized engine and automatic transmission could do 0 to 40 in perhaps 10 seconds and the standing quarter in 20.

Even without shocks, the car rode decently. Like the Curved Dash, it leapt over things because of its light weight. The driver felt some fore and aft pitching because he sat so high on such a short chassis. His steering was very fast: He had only 1.25 turns from lock to lock, and the turning circle was 37 feet. Another comparison: A Porsche 911 coupe, which we think of as agile and quick to respond when the wheel is turned, uses 3.1 turns from lock to lock and has a 35.1-foot turning circle.

Cornering—going around a bend—was not to be done without concentration. The tires, pumped up to high pressure, maybe 50 pounds per square inch, were mounted on 3-inch rims (today's Volkswagen Rabbit gives half again the rim width, and the "footprint" its tire makes is almost three times as wide), so particularly when it was raining you e-a-s-e-d the car around the curve.

Driving in the rain was no fun at all. Wipers did not come with the car—hand wipers were an option—and if the rain came with dark clouds or at night, it was not easy to see. The bicycle lamps on the Curved Dash had been discovered lacking; as we've seen, by 1915 the T finally came with headlamps, but they ran off the magneto, which meant the slower you drove—which would be pretty slow in the dark and the rain—the dimmer they were.

Braking was a thrill. The car did have internal expanding rear-wheel brakes (front-wheel brakes were not offered), but the foot brake applied a kind of vice to the transmission band. On long down grades this meant you had to let up on the brakes frequently to allow a little oil to get back between the brake and the band so the lining would not get dry. On the other hand, if you really wanted to stop, you just pushed down on the reverse pedal. That was one of the marvels of the transmission, which has been called the "first American automatic."

If you had bought a car in its peak sales year, 1923, you would more than likely have been male and middle class. You would *not* have been making anywhere near Henry Ford's reported $264,000 a day (he was sole proprietor, don't forget), nor would you have been, as the AP reported of Ford, a billionaire.

OVERLEAF:

Ford Town Car, Couplet, Speedster, Mail Truck, and Touring. All Ts except Mail Truck and Town Car.

109

Perhaps you lived in one of the growing towns of the West, Sacramento, for example, then a city of about 100,000 souls. You might have been an independent contractor—an electrician, say—or a hotel manager. Your car was probably on the edge of being a luxury and you took it very seriously. You had bought it from a franchised dealer, whose salesman had shown you how to cope with its mechanical peculiarities. You might have paid cash, or you might have participated in Ford's layaway plan, so much a month until you had the price of the car deposited with the dealer. With the car you got a small tool kit containing a monkey wrench, pliers, and a hammer.

You had to register the car with the state of California and get license plates almost the moment it became yours, but first you had to start it so you could go down to get the piece of paper that said you were legal. This you did very much as you might have twenty-one years earlier with the 1902 Curved Dash. With the hand brake on halfway (neutral, remember), you reached over to the right side of the steering column and retarded the spark. Then you walked forward to find the crank in the six o'clock position. If it wasn't there, you put it there; you jerked toward you and up on the handle, not away, for fear the car would backfire and the handle would come whirling back to break your arm. You had already pulled out a wire sticking out from the front of the car, which activated the choke. These things done, you walked around and turned the ignition from magneto to coil then walked back and gave the crank a few upward jerks. If you were a small woman, this was not easy to do. If it were cold out and you were a large man, it was not easy to do either unless you first jacked up the rear wheel, since starting the car also meant turning the transmission and engine, and the oil in both was close to the consistency of jelly. You'd let the thing run for a while until the oil got warm and less viscous, then off you'd go.

You'd set out on a trip familiar to today's driver: to the store, to a business appointment. And parked your car right out at the curb. Even though some cities were beginning to experience congestion, Sacramento wasn't one of them. Mainly, you'd go for a drive on Sunday to see a relative or to have a picnic. But not before the ritual. Every Sunday, if you cared about your car, you'd get it down to the service station. You'd wash it there (or you would have washed it at home), and you'd fill it with gas. The stuff came in three grades: low, regular, and the new ethyl, at about 16 cents a gallon for the regular, 2 cents less for the low grade, 2 cents more for the ethyl. It would come in a two-wheeled cart right to your car, and it would be pumped by the gallon. If you needed oil, you could, by this time, choose among grades: 10, 20, 30, or 40 weight. About 90 percent of the oil sold to motorists was bulk, but it was possible (and if you were a strict and careful owner, you took advantage of this) to buy brands. Possibly you'd specify Quaker State. This was an age of brand loyalty; you used the same oil all the time, the same gas, bought the same kind of car, and waxed it three times a year with your own very carefully chosen brand of paste, likely Simonize.

If you needed further maintenance at the service station, your family would wait at home (after church, which you went to in your T), perhaps reading about the plague of grasshoppers in Montana, or Hitler's Beer Hall Putsch in Munich, or the Yankees in their new stadium beating the Giants 4 games to 2 in the World Series. Meanwhile, you might be overseeing the service station owner replenishing the grease in the rear axle (every 500 miles) or greasing the steering gear (every 5,000 miles). Every 200 miles, he had to apply oil to twelve oilers and screw down six grease cups one turn. The front hubs needed regreasing at the same time that the rear end had to be checked, and the ignition needed to be looked over as well.

Then you would return home to pick up the family and drive out past the macadam roads of the city to the dirt or gravel roads of the country. You'd have a spare coil in the car and at least two spare wheels.

The children, if there were any, would be in back; your wife would be riding shotgun. She might be nicely dressed, but you would have to have chosen clothes you were willing to get dirty, for it was a frequent adventure to have to get out and change a wheel. You'd also want to be warm, even in the Sacramento Valley. The T had no heater and it had no windows.

You'd head north or south or west from Sacramento if you had a choice. East lay Rocklin and then Auburn and the mountains, and you absolutely, positively did not want to climb up the western side of the Sierra. Not because the Ford wasn't able to sail on up, *you* weren't. To climb any kind of grade at all, it was necessary to drop into low. Low, recall, was engaged by pushing in the left foot pedal, which required some effort. It required still more to keep it there, so that after twenty minutes or so you'd begin to get calf cramps and you'd have to stop.

Just as well. If you had gone east, or in almost any other direction for that matter, you'd have encountered some pretty rutty roads outside Sacramento. The Ford took every ounce of your attention under those conditions, for with its narrow rims and light weight, it would follow every corner, depression, crack, and ridge on the surface, leaping about like a frog on fire. So really, no matter where you went, you'd get home tired. Still you'd likely calculate the fuel mileage (probably close to 23 mph) in order to brag about it the next day at work.

The trip would have been an adventure. In 1923, we were still very much in the middle of our national love affair with the auto—particularly that quintessential American car, the Model T.

III
VINTAGE CARS
1932–1948

CHAPTER 7
The Walls Come Tumbling Down

The stock market collapsed in the fall of 1929. Prosperity disappeared and with it a large part of the automobile market. As a result, a number of auto manufacturers crashed as well. The first three quarters of 1929 were encouraging to the car builders; they built and sold 5.3 million units, a high-water mark for the industry and a record that would not be matched until 1949. The 1929 New York Auto Show, which was held before the collapse, seemed a triumph to the manufacturers' association, which said, "Public interest in new automobiles reached such heights that most Manhattan hotel lobbies [the show was held in a field artillery armory] were packed with displays." A year later the association confessed "confusion was apparent" at the show, reflecting the effects of the first year of the Depression.

By 1930 a quarter of a million auto workers were on the street and the auto companies were drawing their wagons into a circle. They cut costs, increased productivity, standardized low-line models into what would become known as The Big Three—Ford, Chevrolet, and Plymouth—and didn't lose a dime all during the Depression.

The new range of low-priced cars was created to appeal to Americans who managed to keep their jobs. But while millions eked out a living and hundreds of thousands stood in bread lines and sold apples on the streets, a far smaller number still lived in great stone mansions in Newport or Manhattan, and they constituted a market too. Thus the Depression industry was schizoid; it made cheap cars for poor people and it made enormously expensive cars for the rich.

LEFT:
1933 Chevrolet Five-Passenger Phaeton Series CA Master
These were the days of fierce warfare between Ford and Chevrolet for industry sales leader. Ford was cheaper, but the 1933 Chevrolet Phaeton at $515 offered body by Fisher, a six-cylinder engine (which Ford did not have), an honest 70 mph top speed, and free-wheeling. Only 543 phaetons were built in 1933 by Chevrolet.

BELOW:
1932 Plymouth Sport Roadster Model PB
By the middle of the Depression, Walter Chrysler's company had a good lineup of cars, including the equivalent of Ford's Model A and the best from Chevrolet. Joining the Ford and the Chevrolet, the Plymouth became part of a triumvirate known (interchangeably with their manufacturers) as the Big Three. Cost for this car was $595.

The continued romance with the automobile during a time of national deprivation had some social advantages. American motorists paid taxes and the money went not just to the building and maintenance of highways but also to finance relief programs. More than that, what strength there was in the economy came from auto and auto-related industries, however curtailed their profits. *Harper's* noticed in 1939 that during a good part of the Depression, "Petroleum and auto manufacture led all industries in sales...Beyond this there were thousands of businesses of all sorts that depended on the auto in one way or another."

This last was an early indication of how deeply the automobile had penetrated the American fabric, but it was not the only one. In fact, it seemed *everybody* was noticing the effects of the car on America and not only the economic effects. In 1926, just one year after Elizabeth Frazer had bemoaned the cheapening of America in the *Saturday Evening Post* and blamed it on the car, the *Literary Digest* applauded the automobile's promotion of outdoor activities: "It carries tens of thousands touring, camping, picnicking, hunting, fishing, sailing, hiking, mountain climbing, golfing and outdoorsing in every conceivable way." *Newsweek* estimated tourist expenditures to be as high as $5 billion in 1937. *Harper's* said that with the Depression and the need to save money came a boom in tourist camps. "By 1940, there were 20,000 of them in the country." The 1935 census had already listed 9,848.

The *Literary Digest* celebrated the car in terms of public health. In 1933, it reported, 16 million Americans living in rural areas now had "whole-time" health officers. *Newsweek* decided that we had become a national village in consequence of the car: "To a great extent the motor age has erased the distinction between country yokel and city slicker." It estimated the farm family car ownership at 85 percent—"up-to-date citizens," it called them with slight condescension, "buzzing to town and city for shopping, movies, cooperative meetings, community sales, home economics demonstrations and what not."

Then the *Literary Digest* reconsidered the effects of the car and decided that in addition to improving the nation's health, it also promoted education. It cited

the consolidated school as one result of auto-mobility and applauded busing as a device that allowed farm children to attend school in "up-to-date buildings" where classes were taught by "modern methods." The magazine even credited the automobile with promoting electricity and electrical devices. Housewives, it said, were able to travel around to see how watts and ohms had contributed to "relief from drudgery. . . . The farm woman saw her friends plugging in toaster, percolator, flat-iron, vacuum cleaner, washing machine and refrigerator."

As with the original post-1908 boom in the passenger-car population, this Depression era travel and use of the car prompted legislatures in most states to put their energies into efforts to control auto-mobility. An estimated 4,000 bills were introduced yearly on one matter or another, of which perhaps 600 to 700 became law. Some of the bills were on the same old subjects, of course: registration, speed limits, taxation. But new ones had been added, the results of increasing congestion. They regulated, at least attempted to regulate, the use of commercial vehicles, the boom in installment selling, and the startling rise in accidents resulting in injury and fatality. For the years 1913 to 1917, highway fatalities averaged 6,800. That average rose to 12,700 for the years 1918 to 1922, to 21,800 for the years 1923 to 1927, and to a startling 36,313 during the middle of the Depression (1933–1937).

A particular legislative concern was the increasing parking problem. Most municipalities had zoning or planning commissions. Parking meters were beginning to appear, municipal car parks were sprouting up. All this legislation was an indication of the increasing problems being brought by the car, despite the bows to its blessings by the likes of *Newsweek*, the *Literary Digest*, and *Harper's*.

The nation was still in a depression, although Franklin Roosevelt had saluted the industry as being "in the vanguard of recovery" as early as 1935. It was the war—in the form of defense spending—that finally came to the rescue. Clear threats in Germany, Japan, and Italy prompted massive rearmament—which meant reemployment.

Two final automotive landmarks of the Depression era, although we would not pay much attention to them for quite some time. In 1935, Toyoda Automatic Loom Works introduced a prototype automobile in Japan called the Toyota. It was inspired by lessons learned by Kiichiro Toyoda, the company's heir, who had sent one of his engineers to Detroit as a "tourist" to bring back a complete description of Packard's assembly methods.

Two years later, the cornerstone was laid for Volkswagenwerk AG in Wolfsburg, 40 miles east of Hanover, Germany. Cornerstone indeed.

1929 Ford Model A Mail Truck
Durability, operating economy, and low cost ($675) made the Model A a wonderful all-around work horse.

CHAPTER 8

Despite Depression

The Depression scarred the auto industry as it scarred the nation. Still, automobiles were here to stay. So, if there were as many as fifty independent manufacturers before the Depression, and only nine afterward, that was the dark side. As Frederick Lewis Allen described it: "Villages on Route 61 bloomed with garages, filling stations, hot-dog stands, chicken-dinner restaurants, tearooms, tourists' rests, camping sites and affluence [affluence?]." The small, intercity railroads began to disappear, and in their place, "mammoth interurban busses and trucks snorted along concrete highways." We gave up what we called "light rail," the trolley. It was a trade we were quite willing to make, although nobody asked us our opinion. In its place we got "red lights and green lights, blinkers, one-way streets, boulevard stops, stringent and yet more stringent parking ordinances—slowly but surely the age of steam was yielding to the gasoline age."

Surely, yes, slowly, perhaps not. Stand back and watch the panorama unfold: 1926 was the year that Pontiac replaced Oakland in somewhat more than name, that the Chrysler Imperial was introduced, that E. L. Cord acquired Duesenberg, and that Chevrolet sales came close to displacing the Model T. A year later, Ford shut down to prepare for the introduction of the Model A. In 1928, Chrysler came out with DeSoto and completed the Big Three triad with the introduction of Plymouth. Cord's new company introduced a boattail Auburn Speedster with an eight-cylinder engine that made 115 hp and went 108.6 mph on the sands at Daytona.

Just in time for the crash of '29, Duesenberg, Inc., gave the world the stunning Model J. It had 265 hp and was 8 miles an hour faster than the Auburn. GM bought Adam Opel in Germany, and at home they stuffed a six-cylinder engine into the Chevy at the same price as the old four-cylinder. Ford built the first station wagon off the Model A platform. And Hudson gave the world its first mobile trailer.

Nineteen-thirty was a grim year. Model A sales went from 2 million to 1 million, but Cadillac nonetheless decided that what America needed was a sixteen-cylinder engine. Grim year or not, let's put it in perspective: We had 23 million cars registered; Japan had 50,000. We upped our thirst for gasoline, consuming almost 16 billion gallons compared to the 2.5 billion we had swallowed in 1919. We used the gas to drive ourselves over almost 700,000 miles of paved road, and we still had 2.3 million miles of road that remained unimproved.

Things got worse later, in the last year of the Hoover administration (1932–1933). But in 1931, Auburn sales shot upward (a little over 28,000), and Cord's company signed 1,000 new Auburn dealers and made as much money as it had in 1929. Sameness was beginning to descend on the Big Three, although there were still visible differences. The Plymouth and the Ford were both four-cylinder cars, but the Plymouth had a 110-inch wheelbase and a motor that made 56 hp; the Ford's wheelbase was 103.5 inches, and its motor churned out 40 hp.

1929 Ford Model A Station Wagon
After World War I, the station wagon became important as people began to move to the suburbs. Ford provided one off the Model A platform—the first mass-produced station wagon (previously they had been produced by custom body shops). Bodies were assembled at Murray Body from wood subassemblies supplied by Ford. Price: $650.

LEFT:
1926 Oakland Sport Roadster Model 6-54
Predecessor of the Pontiac, the Oakland was a six-cylinder car with middle-class aspirations, a Fisher body, and a price of $1,175.

1934 Chrysler Five-Passenger Coupe
Body by Budd, the Airflow is a famous flop in American automotive history. It was an attempt to sell streamlining to a public not ready for aerodynamic cars, much less deco grilles. Like other Chrysler products, it had remarkable engineering features, including unitized body and frame construction.

The Chevy's six-cylinder engine had 50 hp. Prices compared closely: Ford at $430 to $595, Chevy from $475 to $635 (although you could get a somewhat more expensive model), Plymouth at $535 to $645.

In 1932, the year of Franklin Roosevelt's election, total sales dropped to what Ford alone had sold the year before, 1 million. (Two years before that, in 1929, total sales had been 5 million.) The savior of the Ford Motor Company, the Model A, was being redesigned in-house as a V-8, and Hudson introduced the Terraplane. (In this year, also, GM formed its subsidiary to suck up streetcar companies and convert them to GM bus operations. This is what finally led to the criminal conspiracy consent decree sixteen years later.) Frederick Lewis Allen got the inspiration for his hymn to the concreting of America with the 1932 opening of Route 66—Chicago to Los Angeles, via St. Louis and Oklahoma City, Flagstaff and San Bernardino—route of the Okies, route of the great westward migration from drought to palm trees.

In 1933, the city of Detroit defaulted on $400 million worth of debt brought about by welfare payments to a sick automobile business.

The next year, 1934, Chrysler made its first big mistake with the Airflow, an attempt at streamlining to reduce frontal area. It bombed. Just over 11,000 pieces were sold. Three years later, it and its sister, DeSoto, were discontinued.

Nineteen thirty-six saw sitdown strikes at GM, and the introduction of the Coffin-Nosed Cord 810, designed by Gordon Buehrig. It had front-wheel drive, preselector gear change, disappearing headlights. Like almost all the other cars from Auburn-Cord-Duesenberg, this classic was a wonderful car with a limited lifetime. At last, in 1936, Ford introduced the V-8.

In 1937, there were more mixed signals from the industry. Packard had record-breaking sales, having brought forth the "120," which represented a

1939 Mercury Town Sedan Model 99A
Ford competitors, principally Chrysler and GM, had already identified buyers striving to own something better than the least, but not quite so expensive as the best, with De Soto and Dodge for Chrysler, and Pontiac, Oldsmobile, and Buick for GM. In 1939, Ford introduced the Mercury, created to capture a part of the middle-class market. It cost $916, had a 95-horsepower engine and Bendix hydraulic brakes, and weighed 2,900 pounds.

retreat from the premium segment of the market. And three companies, Pierce-Arrow, Stutz, and Auburn-Cord-Duesenberg went out of business.

The Depression was still upon us in 1939 when Ford Motor Company introduced the Mercury (the same year in which Connecticut's Merritt Parkway opened). The federal government, increasingly activist so far as the industry was concerned, indicted the Big Three for their dealers' supposed coercion of buyers to use corporate-owned finance companies, General Motors Acceptance, Chrysler, and Ford Finance. It was a futile effort, and the government admitted it, dropping the case against the smaller two (Ford and Chrysler) and waiting two years to see the action against GM technically successful but requiring no divestiture by the company.

In 1940, the year before Pearl Harbor, defense spending on research and development gave birth to the jeep (it became Jeep with a capital "J" when it went civilian after the war), designed by Willys. Ford's competitive effort was rejected by the government, but the company got contracts for the manufacture of the Willys design. Prices in 1940 were not very different from what they had been all decade. A Chevy cost $659, a Studebaker Champion $1 more, a Nash, $795 (all sedans or coupes). Pontiac's station wagon was just over $1,000. And Packard had dipped into the common man's segment with a car for $867, but it also continued to serve the John O'Hara people, with a car priced at $6,300.

Except for the high-priced cars from Auburn-Cord-Duesenberg, some special coachwork Packards, Lincolns, and Cadillacs, and the likes of Stutz, not much was happening in the engineering departments during the Depression. Heavier crankshafts and shorter strokes characterized higher-revving engines. The six-cylinder, the eight-cylinder, the V-12, and the V-16 all joined the four-cylinder (which would not return in force until the seventies). Hot-water car

1937 Airomobile Sedan Experimental
As suggested by its name, the 1937
Airomobile Experimental never saw
the light of air much less day. It was
designed by a pair of ex-Franklin
engineers as a three-wheeler with an
air-cooled engine. The combination
was too bizarre, and the Airomobile
never got off the ground.

*1934 Dymaxion Four-Door
Transport*
In designing the Dymaxion, inventor
and architect R. Buckminster Fuller
meant to bring the principles of his
geodesic dome to the automobile. It
was never put into production.

heaters and four-wheel brakes became standard equipment. The first synchro-mesh system appeared, designed to eliminate clash when gears were meshed, followed by automatic transmissions, shatterproof glass, streamlining, down-draft carburetors, hydraulic tappets, which used oil pressure to keep metal from touching metal in opening and closing intake and exhaust valves, freewheeling, and the 90-day, 4,000-mile warranty. Cars got fender skirts (which changed gender as they aged; initially they were called pants), automatic chokes, and power brakes. The shifter climbed from the floor to the steering column ("three on the tree"). Side windows sloped; defrosters were built in; seats became ad-justable, and windshield washers arrived (they first became standard in Europe). Coil springs replaced elliptical leafs at the rear of some cars, and others were go-ing to the new overdrive. Sealed beams appeared, new car colors became available, and air conditioning pointed the way of the future as the industry turned to gimmickry. A very real improvement was the monocoque, "unit" con-struction, which followed aircraft practice in relying for structural integrity on the strength of a frameless body—the same principal as the egg. Running boards were called inside from the rain. Grilles got wider (taking on a look that would be called the "Dollar Grin" by postwar Europeans who could scarcely contain their laughter at what had become the symbol of American automotive obesity), bumpers got heavier, and front fenders began to fair into front doors.

This seems like a long list of changes and improvements, and it is. But con-sidering what had come before—and, what would come when the industry was challenged by overseas manufacturers in the last quarter of the century—it was thin.

Our real accomplishments—and they too were mixed—came not so much in hardware as in organization and marketing. For those, we go to the stories of three men we have already met: Henry Ford the Original, Alfred P. Sloan, Jr., and Walter P. Chrysler. These men ruled the industry in its palmy days, however odd that may seem as a label for the years of the Depression. They established institu-tions of sale and construction of cars, not just here, but all over the world. For good or bad, they affected everything they touched.

Ford Unadorned

"American industrial history does not record a more stubborn egotist or better public relations expert than Henry Ford." We can find no better source than John J. Flink, author of *The Car Culture*, to trace Ford's path through the first half of the Century of the Automobile. An early hero when the car arrived, Ford is a myth today. But the history of the man, the techniques of assembly, the company, and the cars offer a far different view from the conventional one. We have already seen him at work as an apprentice machinist off the farm (and discovered the first Ford myth, that he was just a simple country boy, untutored in his trade). We remember his first two companies and his shrewd appraisal that racing would establish his reputation. We were there at the birth of the Model T, and we gave him full marks for its contribution. Then, in his dealings with the Lelands, we began to get a better look at the legend. It is time to push aside the mists of memory. Who was Henry Ford? What was he up to? How and what did he think?

Flink called him "our first, and probably our last, millionaire folk hero." Will Rogers thought that in his time Ford influenced more lives than any other man. It was said that he got 2,000 letters a day; it was thought he might have become president. He was idolized not only in the United States but, strangely enough, in

1936 DeSoto Taxi Cab
The DeSoto Cab often appeared in Hollywood movies, and this particular car was acquired from Paramount studios. DeSoto dominated the taxi cab fleets in major U.S. cities during the 1930s.

OVERLEAF:

1926 Ford Triple Combination Pumper Model TT
Another of the infinite variants built from the passenger car (Model A) platform, the triple pumper was popular with small-town fire departments because it cost far less than its rivals—American La France and Ahrens-Fox—and was highly efficient. This model—only two of them still exist—has two chemical tanks, which made firefighting possible even when water pressure was low or water was unavailable.

1936 DeSoto Taxi Cab
The DeSoto Cab often appeared in
Hollywood movies, and this particular
car was acquired from Paramount
studios. DeSoto dominated the taxi
cab fleets in major U.S. cities during
the 1930s.

OVERLEAF·

*1926 Ford Triple Combination
Pumper Model TT*
Another of the infinite variants built
from the passenger car (Model A)
platform, the triple pumper was
popular with small-town fire departments because it cost far less than its
rivals—American La France and
Ahrens-Fox—and was highly efficient. This model—only two of them
still exist—has two chemical tanks,
which made firefighting possible even
when water pressure was low or water
was unavailable.

121

Germany ("I am a great admirer of Ford," said Adolf Hitler. "I shall do my best to put his theories into practice in Germany") and in the Soviet Union ("The Russians . . . viewed Henry Ford not as a capitalist but as a revolutionary economic innovator," said Flink). Woodrow Wilson, who was a Democrat and a pacifist, and wanted a sympathetic senator from solidly Republican Michigan, persuaded him to run. Ford allowed his name to go on the ballot and then made absolutely no effort to campaign. He lost by a bare 5,000 votes of half a million cast.

Henry Ford had seriously eccentric views of the world, the first evidence of which was his dispatching of the World War I Peace Ship to Europe (on which he sailed), in the naive belief that Fordist reason would douse the fires of war on half a continent. When the Chicago *Tribune* labeled Ford an anarchist in response to his criticism of Wilson for sending troops into Mexico against Pancho Villa, Ford sued for libel. There was a famous trial, with an infamous cross-examination by the *Tribune*'s lawyer, which revealed that Ford was almost totally ignorant of history and during which Ford's ringing statement "History is more or less bunk" truly issued from his lips. (But there is contradiction here, for Henry Ford also created Dearborn Village, in Michigan, a museum/town filled with American hardware achievements—tangible history—to "give people a true picture of the development of the country," Ford told his secretary.) In explaining Ford's embarrassing performance at the *Tribune* trial, Flink admitted that while Ford may not have known history's "esoteric facts," he did have a sound position: He believed that "history was a bastion of tradition rather than a force for change." Indeed,

LEFT:
1938 Phantom Corsair
Designed by Rust Heinz, of the H. J. Heinz family, the Phantom Corsair was based on a Cord 810 chassis. Its body was done by Maurice Schwartz in Pasadena. The Lycoming V-8 engine had a semiracing camshaft designed by Andy Granatelli. This car was the automotive centerpiece of the movie *The Young at Heart,* in which it was called "The Flying Wombat." Heinz wanted to start limited production of the car but was killed in an auto accident before it could be gotten under way. Projected price was $12,500.

BELOW:
1929 Ford Brewster Model A Town Car
Although the basic Model A was an inexpensive car, the addition of a Brewster coachwork body gave it an understated sophistication. This, and its beauty, made it a popular car in the urban Northeast.

Ford's own words supported that view. "That's the trouble with the world," he said. "We're living in books and history and tradition. We've done too much looking back. What we want to do, and do it quick, is to make just history right now. The men . . . responsible for the . . . war in Europe knew all about history. Yet they brought on the worst war in the world's history." Technically, the *Tribune* lost the case—principally because it was dead wrong in printing that Ford employees who were called up for border duty were fired. But the court's award of 6 cents was a

slap in the face to Henry Ford.

This was only the beginning of Ford's demythification. He had a newspaper of his own, the Dearborn *Independent*. In the early 1920s—when America was wallowing in what became known as the Red Scare—his newspaper printed what E. Digby Baltzell calls, "the most infamous anti-Semitic document of the twentieth century—*The Protocols of the Elders of Zion*—brought to New York by Czarist army officers." An immigration law had just been passed (in 1921) that

Family Portrait of the Model A
Of course all Model A's ran four-cylinder engines (Henry the Original was stubborn about that) of 200.5-cubic-inch piston displacement making 40 horsepower. The A was a four-year model-run car of great popularity.

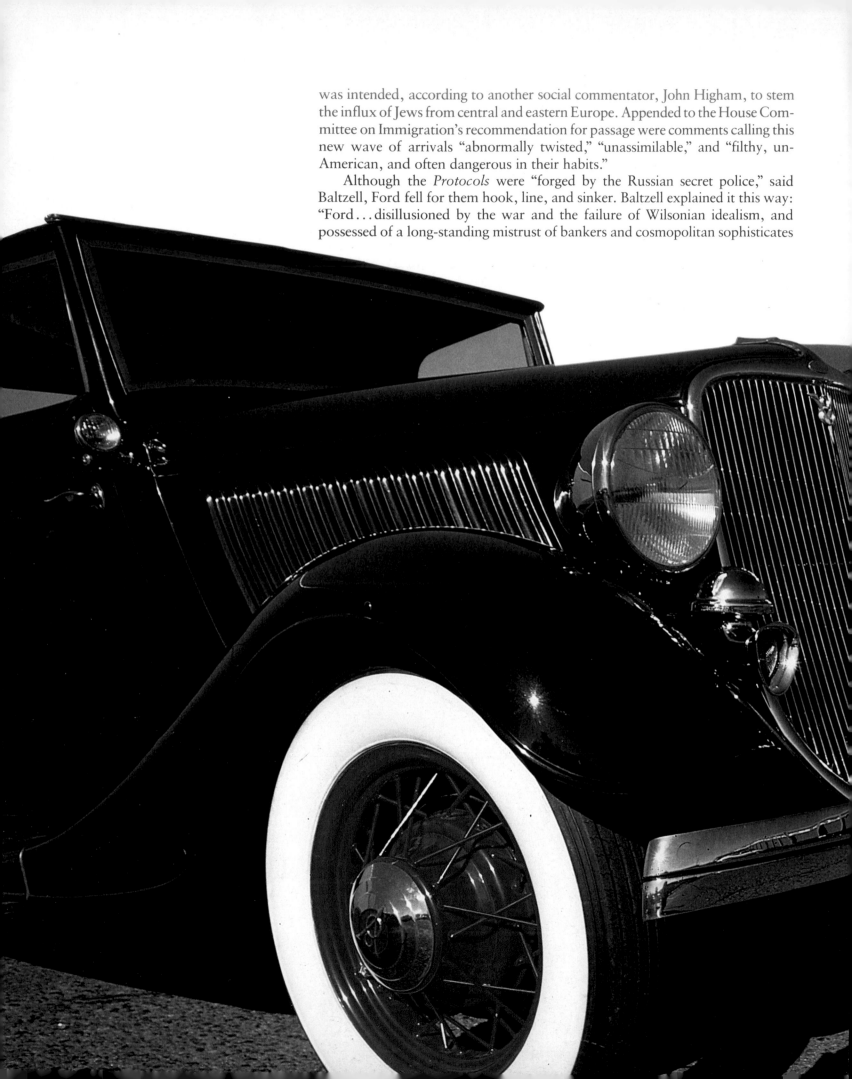

was intended, according to another social commentator, John Higham, to stem the influx of Jews from central and eastern Europe. Appended to the House Committee on Immigration's recommendation for passage were comments calling this new wave of arrivals "abnormally twisted," "unassimilable," and "filthy, un-American, and often dangerous in their habits."

Although the *Protocols* were "forged by the Russian secret police," said Baltzell, Ford fell for them hook, line, and sinker. Baltzell explained it this way: "Ford...disillusioned by the war and the failure of Wilsonian idealism, and possessed of a long-standing mistrust of bankers and cosmopolitan sophisticates [accepted the notion] of a Jewish conspiracy to rule the world." In fact, Ford had said it himself: "I know who makes wars. The international Jewish bankers arrange them so that they can make money. . . . I know it because a Jew on the Peace Ship told me so."

Ford later printed an abject apology. Charity demands that it be accepted at face value; other views have not been so kind. Sales were falling; Chevrolet was threatening to surpass Ford in the market; Jews bought cars.

Perhaps Ford's anti-Semitism was a natural accompaniment to his passionate antilabor views and totalitarian administration of his company. In 1932, there were bitter and bloody battles with the newly born United Auto Workers at the Ford Motor Company with police firing into a crowd outside the gates, killing 4 and wounding 100. Henry Ford brought in two men, Charles E. Sorensen, in charge of production, and Harry Bennett, a kind of enforcer, both of who terrified everyone, "Prussianized" the company, and forced the resignation of what executive talent was left. Said Flink: "A complete list of the Ford executives who

In the 1930s Ford was an evolutionary, rather than a revolutionary, company.

were arbitrarily fired or who resigned in disgust between 1919 and Henry Ford's retirement in 1945 would add up to a small town's telephone directory." Ford bought out the man credited with his early financial success in 1915, business genius James Couzens. "After [Couzens,] the most significant losses were probably William S. 'Big Bill' Knudsen and Norval A. Hawkins. Both went to GM and were instrumental in Chevrolet's sales' surpassing Ford's by 1927."

Ultimately Sorensen, "Ford's chief hatchet man," left too, only a year before Ford's own retirement, but at Ford's insistence. The old man had become senile and was terrified that Sorensen wanted to take over the company.

All of this is not a very nice picture. But surely Henry Ford's insistence on lowering the price of the Model T and then lowering it again and again are to his credit. Flink called it "the only progressive move that Ford made." Alfred Sloan was not so sure. He wrote in his autobiography (*My Years with General Motors*) that at first Ford was indeed progressive, but it was the growth of the used-car market that prompted Ford to lower the prices of his products. Citing the years covering the last production of Model T's, when their price was lowest, Sloan said: "While the total market, including used cars, expanded, the new-car market leveled off... the role of the new car was to cover scrappage and growth in car ownership. Meanwhile the used cars at much lower prices dropped down to fill the demand at various levels for basic transportation.... On this basis alone Mr. Ford's concept of the American market did not adequately fit the realities after 1923."

There is still another innovation attributed to Henry Ford, one that made headlines and that he was given enormous credit for as an altruistic friend of the working man: the introduction of the $5, eight-hour day in 1914. However, Flink said it was a self-serving decision. He presented Ford's own words: "The payment of high wages fortunately contributes to the low costs [of production] because the men become steadily more efficient on account of being relieved of outside worries. The payment of five dollars a day for an eight-hour day was one of the finest cost cutting moves we ever made." Flink thought it was also a splendid advertising and public relations gesture and as such "alone was worth more than the $5.8 million [it] cost."

There is absolutely no question that Ford did not implement the plan out of his regard for his workers. Well-paid labor was consuming labor. Increased purchasing-power meant more sales of Model T's. Furthermore, the wage reduced turnover, a significant problem at the time. But the experiment in benevolent paternalism did not last longer than a few years at Ford. As Flink noted, "By 1918 the inflation of the WWI years had reduced the $5 minimum daily wage to only $2.80 in 1914 purchasing power."

As for Ford's hiring practices, Flink gave him great credit: "Except for the outspokenly anti-Semitic articles . . . for which [he] apologized, no employer was more immune than Henry Ford from the prevailing ethnic, racial, and social prejudices of the day. . . . By 1919 the Ford Motor Company employed hundreds of ex-convicts and 9,563 so-called 'substandard men'—a group that included amputees, the blind, the deaf and dumb, epileptics and about 1,000 tuberculars.

"By 1923 Ford employed about 5,000 blacks, more than any other large American corporation and roughly half the number employed in the entire automobile industry.

"As at all automobile factories, however, the bulk of the Ford labor force . . . consisted of immigrants from southern and eastern Europe."

Ford's and the Ford Motor Company's definitive biographers are Allan

Nevins and Frank E. Hill. In their three-volume work, they described these assembly-line workers: "At the Ford plant the foundry workers, common laborers, drill press men, grinder operators and other unskilled and semi-skilled hands were likely to be Russians, Poles, Croats, Hungarians, or Italians; only the skilled employees were American, British or German stock."

And how were these unskilled and semiskilled workers actually treated? Dreadfully. They were shunned by the Anglo-Saxon preferred employees; they were hired young and fired early. Past the age of thirty-five, "experienced hands, if they did not possess some indispensable skill were the first to be dismissed," wrote Nevins and Hill. By the time Harry Bennett ascended to his Himmler-like gestapo position in Ford's "Service Department," early firing was the best thing that could happen. In 1928, the *New York Times* called Ford "an industrial fascist." One Ford critic wrote that Ford was the worst among the worst. Said he, "Over the Ford plant hangs the menace of the 'Service Department,' the spies and stool pigeons who report every action, every remark, every expression. . . . No one who works for Ford is safe from spies—from the superintendents down to the poor creature who must clean a certain number of toilets in an hour."

It all added up to mismanagement, and it all came home to roost. When Ford finally stepped down in 1945, his grandson, Henry II, took over a company with a bank account of $685 million, but a company in shambles. He brought in a GM man and a group of highly competent managers known as the "Whiz Kids" and made the company efficient, working conditions at Ford humane, and, ultimately, Ford products contemporary. But what was once the world's greatest auto company was clearly on the brink of collapse when "Deuce," Henry II, arrived.

So what are we to think of the man who put America on wheels? As an industrialist, he was an early genius and a final failure. John Kenneth Galbraith said of him as a businessman, "If there is any uncertainty as to what a businessman is, he is assuredly the things Ford was not." As a manufacturer, according to Nevins and Hill, talking about Ford's crediting himself with the invention of the assembly line in his autobiography *(My Life and Work)*, "It is clear that the key ideas of mass production percolated [not] from the top of the factory downward . . . ; rather seminal ideas moved from the bottom upward." Flink said, "The image of Henry Ford as a progressive industrial leader and champion of the common people that Americans clung to during the 1920s was incredibly incongruent with much of the philosophy of industry expounded by Ford himself."

Ford is long gone. The social legacy of the Model T is with us still. If we are in large measure what the automobile made us, we owe this strange, eccentric, willful, purposeful, achieving man a very great deal indeed.

Alfred P. Sloan, Jr., and the Rise of GM

To the extent that Henry Ford can be criticized for authoritarianism, arbitrariness, repressive behavior, and shortsightedness, Alfred P. Sloan, Jr., can be praised for the opposite traits and behavior. Yet if the critics of the effects of the automobile on America want to settle on a villain, it isn't Ford, it's Sloan.

"GM produced some of the most memorable men in American business history [including] Alfred P. Sloan, Jr.," said another memorable man, John Zachary DeLorean, a defrocked GM vice president who would found his own car company some fifty years after Sloan became president of General Motors. "Alfred Sloan was the major prophet of GM's . . . sales policy," Emma Rothschild, no friend of the car, wrote forty-six years after Chevy captured the

1929 Buick
In 1927 Harley Earl came to GM from the coachbuilding arm of Don Lee Cadillac in California and revolutionized the concept in American cars with his first GM styling exercise, the La Salle. By 1929, his influence was being felt in all GM divisions including Buick, as can be seen from this convertible.

sales lead from Ford for the first time. "Sloan's was the engineering approach to management at its best," said John Rae. With all this praise, can Sloan really have been a villain?

It depends on your point of view. If you believe the car has wrought evil, not good, upon the American landscape, Sloan was indeed a villain. If your opinion of the car is a more positive one, your opinion of Sloan must rise accordingly.

Sloan took over GM when it was on its feet but still wobbly. He reorganized the company, a Harvard Business School textbook case of how to make bigness work. And then he introduced marketing techniques that Rothschild said "became a worldwide model for the selling of expensive consumer goods, showing businesses how to create and nourish demand."

Sloan last appeared in our story taking over from Pierre duPont after Billy Durant's second reign at GM, when duPont admitted that he had never wanted the job of running the company in the first place. As commander-in-chief, Sloan immediately set about solving many of the problems that Durant had created.

The very first problem to be tackled involved structure, the way the company was managed—or mismanaged. This shortcoming as much as anything else had kept GM from realizing the potential of its component companies: Chevrolet, Oakland (soon to be Pontiac), Buick, Olds, and Cadillac (the same car divisions it has today). Durant had lost Charles Nash to the consequences of his own (Durant's) mismanagement; Walter P. Chrysler had departed for the same reason. Both had been president of Buick, the most profitable of the GM companies. Both had quarreled with Durant over his incessant interference. Each

went on to build a successful auto company of his own. When Durant had been caught in the stock market turmoil of 1920, the DuPont company bailed him out but on the condition that Durant leave GM once and for all.

Clearly, Sloan was set up either for a total disaster or for a stunning success. GM wanted only for someone to come and make sense of the company. It wanted—and it got—Alfred P. Sloan, Jr.

Sloan learned management as a very young man when he took over the failing Hyatt Roller Bearing Company and put it on its feet. He learned the value of care and precision from one of his customers, Henry Leland. Sloan sold Hyatt to GM as part of what became United Motors; another part was Dayton Research Laboratories, which belonged to Charles Kettering, with whom Sloan got along splendidly, and from whom he learned the uses of mechanical creativity. His lessons in what not to do came from the master of mismanagement himself, Billy Durant.

Sloan took over the presidency of an organization that had not merely disparate divisions but, indeed, separate companies. This is where Sloan began—with the integration of the company. He "created" what became known as the line and staff principle of management. It was, in fact, taken straight from the military. There are field, or operating, officers; and there are headquarters, or planning, officers. Sloan applied this notion to the companies within GM. To manufacture cars, clearly there needed to be operating people: engineers, production men, factory managers. But to integrate their efforts required overall planners.

1929 Chevrolet
Alfred P. Sloan, Jr., was at the helm of General Motors, of which Chevrolet was a part, when this car was built. His marketing strategy was to build at the high end of each market segment, to manufacture a car just a little bit better than its competitors.

143

1926 Oakland Sport Roadster
Model 6-54

Sloan set up central committees for finance, planning, and marketing. He left up to the heads of the companies, soon to be divisions, how those plans were to be carried out. This kind of reordering process was obviously dear to Sloan's heart and very much central to the man himself. In his autobiography, *My Years with General Motors,* Sloan wrote lovingly—and exhaustively—about the years of restructure. Every moment of every plan, what seems to be every memorandum of consequence that he ever wrote on the subject, is reprinted. The book was on the best-seller list for twenty-two weeks when it appeared in 1963. *Fortune* called it "the last word on how to run a company." *Time* said it had "revelations for every executive—and everyone who aspires to be an executive." No less a pundit than Joseph Alsop said of Sloan's book, "Every so often . . . the United States produces a book of such interest . . . it ought to be regarded as news."

It was written by a man who showed himself—and whose photos showed him—to be austere, dry, methodical, and very, very sure of himself. There is no question that he was all of these things. There is little warmth in Sloan's words, but there seems to have been enough in his style that he got on splendidly with his adjutants. In contrast to Ford, in utter distinction to Durant, Sloan set an impeccable example for his managers. His life was exemplary, his manner absolutely correct, his leadership—whether or not by iron hand—was inspirational. Sloan knew what he wanted, but he anticipated the Japanese style of management by consensus. He may have had some of the autocratic instincts that characterized Henry Ford. If so, his reason told him to subdue them, and his enormous discipline allowed him to. He worked in concert with the likes of Boss Kettering, who was called "thorny" by many of the people who knew him. If Durant had not returned to GM when Nash and Chrysler worked there, perhaps Sloan would have become president of the company far earlier, in which case both of those formidable men, Walter Chrysler and Charles Nash, would surely have devoted their extraordinary talents to making GM even more successful than it became, and neither American Motors nor Chrysler Corporation would exist today.

By the time Sloan got GM's house in order, he had long been yearning to get on to the business of selling cars. One of his most famous statements was "Our operation is to cut metal and in doing so add value to it."

It was a credo that took GM along an almost preordained path. First Sloan (in committee, of course) set marketing principles. The unspoken premise (later articulated in his autobiography) was that "the first purpose in making a capital investment is the establishment of a business that will both pay satisfactory dividends and preserve and increase its capital value." In following that premise, an executive committee that included Norval Hawkins (former Ford sales chief) and Charles Kettering, not to mention Sloan himself, set what Sloan called GM's "product policy." Sloan wrote in his autobiography: "We said first the corporation should produce a line of cars in each price area, from the lowest . . . to one for a strictly high-grade quantity-production car, but we would not get into the fancy-price field with small production.

"Second, that the price steps should not be such as to leave wide gaps in the line and yet should be great enough to leave their number within reason so that the greatest advantage of quantity production could be secured." (Today's jargon is "economy of scale.")

"Third, that there should be no duplication by the corporation in the price fields or steps."

All this made great sense, but Sloan (and his committee) enunciated another pair of tenets that formed the basis for Rothchild's outrage, for much of today's consumerist criticism of GM, and for many of what we will discover to be post–World War II GM management perversions. "The policy was valid," said Sloan, "if our cars were at least equal in design to the best of our competitors in a grade, so that it was not *necessary* [Sloan's italics] to lead in design or run the risk of untried experiments."

And just exactly how would GM lure customers into showrooms to buy, for openers, a car at the top of the lowest price segment, keep them coming back, and *then* keep them in the GM car family as customer affluence grew and a more luxurious car was aspired to? Why, the annual model change, of course. This idea brought GM's Art and Color section into existence. (Sloan had said in a letter to one of his executives in 1926, "I am sure we realize . . . how much appearance has to do with sales.") Given that conviction, what reason could a customer be expected to have to buy a new car? Change in appearance. "The changes in the new model should be so novel and attractive as to create demand for the new value and, so to speak, create a certain amount of dissatisfaction with past models as compared with the new one," wrote Sloan.

In 1926, Sloan came upon the chief designer (Harley J. Earl) of a California Cadillac distributor (Don Lee) who had a shop specializing in "special bodies . . . for Hollywood movie stars and wealthy people." In short order Earl was summoned to Detroit as consultant to the Fisher (of "Body by . . .") and Cadillac Divisions. Cadillac was in the process of designing a new car to fit a market segment it had decided existed just under Cadillac itself. "The car, named the La Salle, made a sensational debut in March 1927, and it was a significant car in American automotive history. [It] was the first stylist's car to achieve success in mass production," Sloan wrote.

Sloan compared it to its contemporary Buick: "The La Salle looked longer

BELOW, OVERLEAF, AND PP. 148–149:
1932 La Salle Two-Passenger Convertible Coupe
A GM effort at placing a product just below Cadillac, La Salle was not a marketing success although it was a splendid car. This convertible had a Fisher body, a large eight-cylinder engine of 353.4-cubic-inch displacement that made 115 horsepower. List price was $2,540, which worked out to about 50 cents a pound.

and lower; the 'Flying Wing' fenders were drawn deeper than their predecessors; side windows had been reproportioned; the belt line had a new type of molding; sharp corners had been rounded off. . . ."

In 1954, Earl uttered the ultimate GM styling premise: "My primary purpose for 28 years has been to lengthen and lower the American automobile, at times in reality and always at least in appearance."

During Sloan's last years, GM built some of the handsomest and some of the ugliest cars ever seen. Perhaps Art and Color's (very soon changed to "styling") ultimate moment was the discovery of the tailfin. The reader can almost see Sloan swallowing that one hard: "New styling features were introduced that were far removed from utility, yet they seemed demonstratively effective in capturing public taste. One of the most striking of these features of the postwar car was the 'tail fin' which first appeared on the Cadillac in 1948," Sloan wrote in his autobiography.

Line and staff organization and the annual model change—these are Sloan's remembered contributions. But he also set the dealer organization in order, launched GM overseas, pushed GMAC into prominence as part of his marketing plans, embraced and encouraged the advertising of cars (emphasizing his overall philosophy of selling the sizzle not the steak), and left his company the model of the industry for not only Detroit but the world.

Toyoda Loom Works, the very company that sent an engineer over to look at Packard's assembly methods in 1936, would later return to take its lessons in marketing Toyotas from General Motors. If today GM is agonized over the successes of Toyota and its Japanese fellows, it has only Sloan to thank.

The Success of Walter P. Chrysler

In the late 1800s when he was a boy in Kansas, Walter P. Chrysler hid in the basement of his house when a local hysteric shouted that Indians were coming. This seems to have been the last time in his life that he backed away from anything.

In 1912, just as Chrysler had been offered a raise to $12,000 at American Locomotive in Pittsburgh, GM Chairman James J. Storrow hired him for GM President Charles Nash as works manager at Buick. The starting wage at GM was $6,000 ("We've never paid anyone that much in our lives," said Nash when Chrysler brought up American Locomotive's offer). It is a measure of the lure of the automobile business that a man such as Chrysler would take such a huge pay cut to become a part of it.

Nash wanted Chrysler as a production man, and Nash was right. It didn't take Chrysler long to adapt methods developed in the manufacture of locomotives to the building of cars. The first thing he wanted to see when he arrived at Buick was the production schedule. There wasn't one. In his walks through the Buick plant he noticed a second problem: "I was looking at workmen trained to handle wood. The bodies were being made of wood. In a big carpenter shop, long wide poplar boards were being bent and shaped in steam kilns. With wood [the workmen] were admirably skillful, for most of them had been carriage builders, but wherever they were handling metal, it seemed to me there was an opportunity for big improvements. I saw a hundred such opportunities."

By way of comparison, in late 1912, Ford was making hundreds of cars a day (by the next year, Ford was up to 1,000 a day) and Buick only about 45. Each Buick chassis took as long as four days to move through the shops; each was laboriously—even lovingly—put together, then painted, then sanded. Each was left to dry overnight, and the next day a coat of liquid primary (Chrysler's word)

1938 Buick Special Business Coupe Series 40
An odd type, the business coupe—a two-passenger car with the entire rear seating area given over to storage. It was meant mainly for traveling salesmen with sample cases. Detroit marketers were recognizing that traveling salesmen wanted to work in cars with higher status than Plymouth, Ford, and Chevy. The price in 1938 was $945.

was put on. This took another night to dry and was followed by a careful sanding and then a coat of varnish, with still another day to dry. In applying a philosophy of manufacture that would be enormously helpful to Buick and to the industry, Chrysler put an end to all this craftsmanship in short order. At the time the philosophy was probably appropriate. Half a century later, it would come back to haunt Detroit.

"Listen," said Chrysler to Nash, "what is the use of finishing up the hidden parts of the chassis as if you were going to put it in the parlor? This stuff is caked with road mud on the first day it is used." True enough and a sensible decision at the time. But when the Great Foreign Invasion of the sixties started, buyers of cars competitive with Buick and Cadillac in particular would notice that as much care was taken with the "hidden parts," and decide if that was the case, the same degree of care had been lavished on everything else. By this time, Chrysler's "hidden part in the parlor" philosophy had so permeated the domestic industry that it was suf-fering a crisis of quality control. Manufacturing costs had been cut, thanks to Chrysler; it took less time to build each piece, but the consumer was beginning to doubt the commitment of the industry to high quality. Perhaps the shoddiness of the American product can't be traced exactly to the instant Walter Chrysler walked through the Buick shops that day in 1912, but the moment will do.

Soon enough, Chrysler had upped Buick production tenfold, to Nash's ab-solute delight. And Nash had upped Chrysler's salary more than fourfold in the process. By the time Billy Durant walked into the 1915 GM stockholders' meeting to announce that he was again taking over, Chrysler had become recognized as one of the top production men in Detroit. Nash and Storrow liked and admired Chrysler, and so when they went off to find a car company of their own, they tried hard to take Chrysler with them. Before acquiring the Thomas B. Jeffery Co. and changing the name to Nash, both Storrow and Nash had come close to buying Packard, and Chrysler was going to go with them. At almost the very moment the Packard deal was together, Durant walked into Chrysler's office and offered him the presidency of Buick. "If [the Packard deal] goes

through . . . I'm committed," answered Chrysler. It didn't, and Walter P. Chrysler became president of Buick in 1916.

We saw Chrysler's career skyrocket from there; we heard his fury at Durant's interference in his affairs. It is all the more interesting that Chrysler wrote many years later that the Durant style was enormously engaging: "I cannot find words to express the charm of the man. He [had] the most winning personality of anyone I've ever known." But he couldn't keep his hands out of Buick, so in 1920, Chrysler accepted a two-year, $1 million a year offer to become executive vice president of Willys-Overland and rescue the company from both John North Willys's mismanagement and its creditors. Chrysler got Willys-Overland on its feet by 1922 by putting the company in receivership, selling its assets, and convincing the creditors to back a smaller entity called Willys.

Now comes the fascinating story of the first Chrysler car and the beginnings of Chrysler Corporation. At the same time Walter Chrysler went to Willys-Overland, he somehow obtained permission from its creditors to try to reorganize Maxwell-Chalmers in his spare time—a very early case of top management moonlighting. He was successful using many of the same devices with Maxwell-Chalmers he employed at Willys-Overland, this time emerging in 1924 as president of another phoenix company called simply "Maxwell."

All the while he was juggling books, Chrysler was remembering the design for a new car he had initiated at Willys-Overland but whose plans had been sold in the receivership proceedings. He had put together a three-man team of engineers, Fred Zeder, Owen Skelton, and Carl Breer, and they had done him proud. Now, as president of Maxwell, he pushed a variation of the Zeder/Skelton/Breer design. For the moment, the car had the Maxwell nameplate on it, but Chrysler made clear it would become the first car named for him *if* it was well enough received at the '24 New York Auto Show for the bankers to give him money to turn Maxwell into his own company based on its sales promise.

While the car was undergoing development, Chrysler and his engineers drove much disguised versions on the streets of Detroit. In his autobiography, Chrysler talked about those adventures. "Under an old car's shabby hood we had hidden the unsuspected power of our high-compression engine. Zeder and his boys had outdone themselves. At the whistle's sound [traffic police used whistles to indicate "stop" and "go"] we would be past the cop and on our way, while behind us, open-mouthed, our chance rivals would just be getting into second gear. What flexibility we had! The Chrysler car? Nobody had [yet] heard about a Chrysler car. But we had dreamed about it until, as if we had been its lovers, it was work to think about anything else."

Since the car was not actually in production, the New York Auto Show would not allow it to be displayed. Undismayed, Chrysler rented the lobby of the Commodore Hotel. Reaction was highly favorable, and Chrysler was able to convince the New York banking establishment that the car—and a company created to build and sell it—was worth investing in. Maxwell became Chrysler Corporation; Zeder, Skelton, and Breer's updated design became the first Chrysler car in 1925.

To bet your future on one showing of one car was Durant-like, but it was also Fordist. Chrysler did it, and what's more, he pulled it off.

This made Chrysler a discrete company, but not a very large discrete company. This was soon to change. Swallowing Dodge Brothers in July 1928 put Walter Chrysler squarely in competition with GM and Ford. John and Horace Dodge had died, and their widows were not inclined to become manufacturers.

1931 Chrysler Custom Roadster Imperial Eight
From the 1926 Imperial 80's more-or-less modest beginning, Chrysler went on with the model to build some of its greatest cars ever. This one has a body by Le Baron. It is the first year of production for the car, called "one of the most distinguished models ever developed by Chrysler." The chassis frame of 8-inch-deep pressed steel is further strengthened by six cross members. A nine-bearing crankshaft, counterweighted at eight points, almost completely eliminated engine vibration.

They sold the company to the banking house of Dillon, Read. Dillon, Read did not want to be in the business of making cars any more than the Dodge widows did. They had paid $146 million for Dodge and they wanted out. The negotiations were a classic in American financial flirtation, with the courtship consummated when, after months of bluff and counterbluff, the principals—Dillon, Read, and Chrysler—took a suite at the Ritz and spent the final five days head to head.

Finally, the deal was set. Finally, Chrysler was one of the big boys. He already had a top-line car in the Chrysler. Now he would bring out a low-priced car, Plymouth, and a second medium-priced car, DeSoto, to go along with Dodge. From the first, then, Chrysler was known as an engineering company; and the acquisition of Dodge did not hurt that image, for Dodge Brothers had been in the car business from the beginning. Chrysler was strong and healthy, its products admired. But it was a company that seemed to depend as much on Walter Chrysler as Ford depended on its founder. For all Chrysler's management genius, he did not leave Sloan's impregnable fortress behind. He had brought in designers of distinction, and managers too, including B. E. Hutchison and K. T. Keller. But when Chrysler died in 1940, the Chrysler Corporation seemed to sit still in the water, buoyed only by the rush of postwar demand. When that was gone, Chrysler began, imperceptibly, to sink.

Roy Chapin: The Independent Statesman

Of the nine out of fifty independents to survive the Depression, Hudson stands as the ideal symbol, not only because it was successful but because it could trace its roots to the very beginnings of the car business. Equally important, during the Depression the company advanced the cause of auto-mobility, not only in its products but as a result of the civic-mindedness of its chief, Roy D. Chapin.

The only other company to live to see the last quarter of this century, Nash, we have watched. Indeed, its current incarnation, American Motors Corporation, is far more Nash than it is Hudson (the two merged to form AMC in 1954). But the lesser partner, Hudson, was far more innovative, interesting, and promising than its devourer. It is to the history of Hudson, then, that we turn to find out how the lesser lights in the great Detroit galaxy fared, particularly during the Depression.

Hudson was a company born in the way of many early Detroit manufacturers, out of dissatisfaction with others and out of the efforts of young men of various backgrounds, all with great energy and all hypnotized by the car. Hudson's central figure, Roy Dikeman Chapin, was the pioneer who drove the Curved Dash Olds from Detroit to New York for the 1901 Auto Show. He became Olds's sales manager; later and more important, he became friends with the company's chief engineer, Howard E. Coffin, its purchasing agent, F. O. Bezner, and the man who saved the one car from the ashes of the Olds plant, James J. Brady.

All four became unhappy with Olds, took up the typical hunt for a backer, and found one in the owner of the Thomas Motor Company. The first result was a firm called Thomas-Detroit, which built a car designed by Coffin (that Olds had refused to build) to be distributed through the Thomas organization. This was good, but not good enough for the four who wanted to do their own selling. Chapin went looking again. This time he discovered Hugh Chalmers. Chalmers ponied up enough capital to buy half of Thomas's stock in Thomas-Detroit on the condition that he market the car. Chapin's group accepted the condition.

When Coffin designed a second car (at about the same time two more Olds men, G. W. Dunham and R. B. Jackson, joined the company), Chapin and partners—still bent on total control from design to sales—went looking for another source of outside financing. They found it—as well as a substantial, well-known name—in the person of J. L. Hudson, who not only owned a Detroit department store but was also Jackson's wife's uncle. In 1909, then, the Hudson Motor Car Company came into being as a subsidiary of Chalmers-Detroit to build and sell the Hudson Model 20. It was a sturdy, open car with a number of virtues, trumpeted loudly in an ad in the *Saturday Evening Post:* "Strong, Speedy, Roomy, Stylish." Single rumble seat, oil lamps, tools, horns, gas lamps, and generator were standard equipment. For an additional $150, the buyer could order a Bosch magneto, a Prestolite acetylene tank, a double rumble seat, and a top. But the most appealing aspect was that the car sold for $900.

At this point, with the Model 20 well received by the public, Chalmers and the Chapin group parted ways. Chapin became president of Hudson.

Roy Chapin had enormously wide interests and a clear sense of responsibility not only to the automobile community but to the nation. After Hudson was on its feet, he was in and out of its management, in mainly when the company was tripping on its own products. Often, his hiatuses were for trips abroad or to Florida; more frequently they were in pursuit of forming a highway lobby and then pushing for what became—although he did not live to see it—the interstate highway system. His war work was extraordinary. The consummate diplomat, he cajoled and flattered the federal government into using trucks to carry war materiel, an innovation, relieving enormous railroad congestion of goods (including the trucks themselves, which at the beginning of the war were shipped on flatcars).

He took great delight in his family. His elder son, Roy, Jr., later became chairman of American Motors in very bad times for the company and did as well for it as his father had done for Hudson. He was active in the National Automobile Chamber of Commerce; he became Secretary of Commerce under Hoover.

But, aside from his initial founding of Hudson Motor, his principal contributions to the automobile business were the closed car at a low price (the Essex)

and the introduction of a bright, inexpensive car in the middle of the Depression (the Terraplane). The Terraplane was meant not only to bolster his company (it did) but also, and perhaps equally, to reassure the Depression consumer that Detroit was still a vital manufacturing community, to which attitude its lively sales contributed.

Chapin's figure does not rise as high on the historical landscape of Detroit as Ford's or Durant's or Chrysler's or Sloan's; the contemporary Detroit manager would be hard put to call his contributions to mind. But he was a major figure, and his efforts in behalf of the industry were considerable. At the very least, if Essex, Terraplane, and even Hudson are gone, the network of highways Roy Chapin was so instrumental in bringing about is with us. And it was only in the seventies that the felicitous relationship between industry and government, for which Chapin can be given almost total credit, ruptured as a result of the enactment of the 1966 National Highway Traffic Safety Act and Detroit's neanderthal reaction to it.

The Big Three and the independents that survived the Depression would go on to stratospheric industrial heights—for a time at least. They were the suppliers to everyman.

The tiny portion of the industry that catered to the elite—the craftsmen, the artists, the magnificent coachbuilders of America—would all be gone by the beginning of World War II. But the brilliance of their legacy, very different in quality from the achievements of their giant brothers, was in its own way, as dazzling.

1933 Essex Terraplane
Hudson's Roy Chapin decided that in order to restore confidence in Detroit's willingness to risk capital and reputation in a depression economy, significant car companies had to continue to introduce new models and even new nameplates. Thus the Terraplane from Hudson Motor Car Company—a success despite the times, but a car with a limited lifetime.

CHAPTER 9

Chevy Ascendant

The summer of 1928 came to Sacramento hot and early; with it came a bright new 1929 Chevrolet for our Model T owner. Business had been good at the hotel he managed. His salary, like the salaries of many Americans during the boom of the 1920s, had been raised and raised again; the 1923 T was still in fine condition, but he wanted something just a little better. Cars that were just a little better were a General Motors specialty, thanks to Alfred Sloan's marketing philosophy. Ford was replacing the T with the new Model A, a very good car, but one that inherited the T's stigma; it seemed tinny, particularly compared to the contemporary Chevy.

Business was beginning to decline at the Chevy dealership, so with the introduction of the 1929 models in late 1928, it held a drawing for a free car radio. Sure enough, while the hotel manager was trying to persuade the dealer to take his T in trade, his 7-year-old son picked the winning number, so when the family drove out—they had all gone down to look at the new closed car—it was with the promise of having the radio installed at the very first opportunity.

The 1929 Chevy four-door sedan had a more-or-less contemporary three-speed transmission with the shift lever on the floor. (The manual gearbox was as easy to operate as it was going to be until 1948, when Chevy went to Powerglide, a full automatic.) It cost $595, sat five comfortably (two in the front), weighed 2,647 pounds, came standard with disc wheels, and mounted the optional front and rear bumpers. It was actually a three-tone car: the fenders were black, the body a darkish green almost from above the running boards to just below the beltline, where the color changed to a lighter, more cheerful green, which extended over the top of the hood.

Best of all, the Chevy had a six-cylinder engine—the "Cast-Iron Wonder," it was called—and although it would constantly be under development, it would be used until the 1953 model year. The engine ran extremely smoothly. It was powerful compared to the engine in the T. It was just over 183 cubic inches (3,180 cc) with a long stroke, and it made close to 30 horsepower. Despite its 3.82:1 ratio of engine to driving wheel speed, a relatively high numerical final drive, the car could reach a decent 65 or so miles an hour and still get 23 miles to the gallon (just over 200 miles per tankful).

The Chevy's smoothness gave the car owner a sense that he had stepped up in class. The car reinforced the whole notion. It may have looked square and simple, but it was a far cry from the cars that had preceded it. Because of this new, overall refinement, as well as the use of a conventional transmission, if a contemporary American were suddenly transported back to the moment of delivery of the 1929 Chevy, plunked down behind the wheel, and told to drive it away, he would have no trouble at all. The self-starter switch was not a switch at all, it was a kind of fat button on the firewall to the left of the clutch. The large, wood-rimmed, four-

1929 Chevrolet
The year marks the introduction of one of Detroit's great engines, the "Cast Iron Wonder," a six-cylinder so durable and so capable of development that it lasted until 1953. With the inclusion of a six, Chevrolet emphasized the Sloanist marketing philosophy of positioning models at the top of each market segment; this car competed with the Model A Ford, which had a four-cylinder engine, and had a distinct advantage as a result of the smoothness of its six. Chevy sold more than a million cars in the first year of production, at a price of $595.

spoke steering wheel was mounted on a column that jutted up out of the floor between the clutch and the brake pedals; the throttle was a conventional pedal in the now familiar far right slot between the brake and the transmission hump. A second foot-operated button, to the right and just beneath the brake pedal, actuated the headlight dimmer.

The instruments were oval and stretched across a larger oval in the middle of the dash. The largest, central-most instrument oval contained a rolling speedometer, a continuing odometer, and a trip odometer. Flanking the speedometer, were twin ovals, the left one containing a temperature gauge (marked "Cold" on the first quarter of its elliptical sweep face, then "Normal," and finally "Alcohol Boils"), the right one containing an ammeter at the top and an oil pressure indicator at the bottom, reading in pounds per square inch.

Except for the enormous amount of room in the back seat, everything would seem familiar to today's car owner. The car started with a key turn and then a sharp punch on the floor starter. It was virtually noiseless. Visibility was somewhat restricted by the wide A (front), B (middle), C (rear) pillars connecting roof to body. Still, you could see the front fenders and hood plainly, so parking was no problem. Nor was cranking the steering wheel around to park difficult. There was no power steering, of course, but there was not so much weight on the front wheels that this Chevy was any harder to parallel park than today's front-wheel-drive manual steering cars.

By the summer of 1928, vacationing by car was a familiar occurrence. The Sacramento hotel manager's request to his wife that *she* take their kids off to the Midwest to see the relatives might have been unusual, though. Men were almost always the ship captains on long journeys, but it was possible to see a woman at the long-distance wheel. In such a case, it was only proper that an older woman go along, not so much as a chaperone as for moral support.

Perhaps while his family was away, the hotel manager could manage to sell his T, for the Chevy dealer had not taken it in trade. Used cars were considered a great problem for auto dealers in the late twenties. "I Fired All My Salesmen" was the title of one industry magazine piece. It was the story of a dealer who became fed up with overtrades his salesmen were making and instituted a policy of no trades and no salesmen. (The 1902 Curved Dash was probably still sitting in a barn somewhere. In 1902, despite classifieds like this one: "First Check for $1,250 Takes This Factory Rebuilt Haynes-Apperson," there was almost no used-car market, which is why many collectible cars were discovered in rural outbuildings half a century later.)

In the meantime, Mother, her mother, and two young boys would set out south from Sacramento to Bakersfield, in order to turn east and penetrate what was already being called the Southern Route. They found reasonable roads on the trip. Route 66 would not be finished for almost four years, but it was being graded and parts of its bed were already macadamized. We had 694,000 miles of paved road in the United States in 1928, almost double what we had had in 1921; and we had 2.3 million miles of dirt highway. What was paved was mainly two-lane roads, but there were some three-lane as well. It would take us at least thirty years to identify the three-lane highway as a killer. Our Sacramento family was rescued from its perils—mainly of encountering on-coming traffic in the middle lane while trying to pass—only by the scarcity of cars on the highway. This need to pass, by the way, was probably another strong reason the hotel manager had given up on the Model T. A lot of hard work had to be done in lower gears—he was forever in a position of asking for more than the minimal power of the Ford's four-cylinder engine, and he was fed up with the planetary low in the T. Enough

of cramped calves and a left leg that was built up to half again the muscle strength of the right.

Anyway, there was the family driving along just as comfortable as could be in the Chevy, on a trip very much like trips today, except for the pleasure of looking at the real countryside instead of Interstates.

Mrs. Hotel Manager could make about 200 to 250 miles driving ten hours a day. The southern route was hot, so driving started at perhaps six in the morning. In the back, the kids played the same car games kids play today, perhaps a little more innocent, for they were counting the number of cars on the highway and by the end of the afternoon they were still in the twenties. Commercial traffic was mainly trucks, not the kind of long haul eighteen-wheelers we are used to, but farm trucks hauling produce to the city.

A modern driver transported to the past would be struck most by the lack of support systems along the road for the motorist. Major oil company gas stations were few and far between. There were more—but still not too many—little independent gas stations. They had gas, though, and from a pump (still about 16 cents a gallon for the regular). They also had canned oil. What they didn't have was a bathroom. So when the inevitable cry rose from the back seat, the driver pulled over at the nearest bush.

After the sun had been up for a while, the kids would begin to look for a stand selling root beer floats or orange drinks. Toward evening, the women would begin to look for an auto court. This would be a simply designed facility, an L-

of cramped calves and a left leg that was built up to half again the muscle strength of the right.

Anyway, there was the family driving along just as comfortable as could be in the Chevy, on a trip very much like trips today, except for the pleasure of looking at the real countryside instead of Interstates.

Mrs. Hotel Manager could make about 200 to 250 miles driving ten hours a day. The southern route was hot, so driving started at perhaps six in the morning. In the back, the kids played the same car games kids play today, perhaps a little more innocent, for they were counting the number of cars on the highway and by the end of the afternoon they were still in the twenties. Commercial traffic was mainly trucks, not the kind of long haul eighteen-wheelers we are used to, but farm trucks hauling produce to the city.

A modern driver transported to the past would be struck most by the lack of support systems along the road for the motorist. Major oil company gas stations were few and far between. There were more—but still not too many—little independent gas stations. They had gas, though, and from a pump (still about 16 cents a gallon for the regular). They also had canned oil. What they didn't have was a bathroom. So when the inevitable cry rose from the back seat, the driver pulled over at the nearest bush.

After the sun had been up for a while, the kids would begin to look for a stand selling root beer floats or orange drinks. Toward evening, the women would begin to look for an auto court. This would be a simply designed facility, an L-

shaped cluster of one-room bungalows alternating with open garages.

In the same issue of the *Motor* that trumpeted the worth of firing all a dealer's salesmen, there was a piece about the kinds of people who vacation in cars and stop nightly in auto courts.

"Visitors exceed 10,000 people yearly," said the article, "coming in some 3,500 automobiles from every state in the Union [to enjoy] such accommodations as running hot and cold water, electric lights, shower baths, and a dozen and one other comfortable necessities. . . .

"The average motor-tourist is away on a vacation that may last from two weeks to two years. He and his family have saved for some time. About 20% of the total [tourists] work their way from place to place. There are printers, carpenters, plumbers, electricians and even undertakers and embalmers to be found among them." Most of the cars parked in these auto courts were products of Ford or GM—Chrysler had yet to become large enough to join the triumvirate that would come to be called the Big Three.

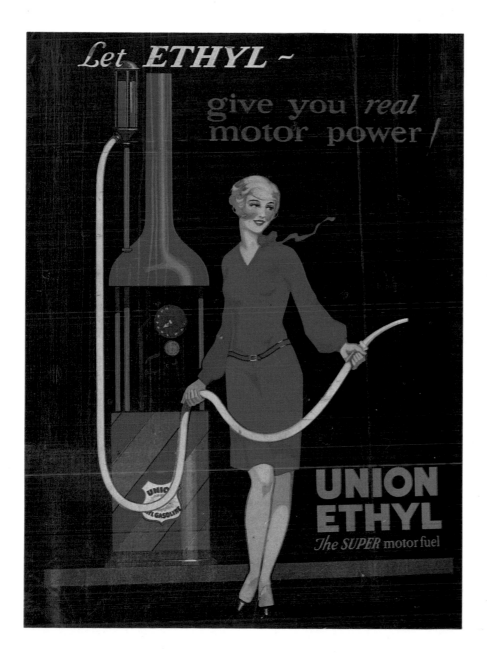

In 1929, GM ranked just under Ford in profits. Had the hotel manager's wife, driving her family across Kansas, New Mexico, and Arizona on the way back west known the figures—which was unlikely for they appeared in the trade magazines and on the financial pages of newspapers only—she would have approved of GM's rising profits. The driver was becoming more and more fond of the Chevy, and with good reason.

What had been most appealing to her on the trip so far was that the Chevy was really a two-speed car. She had to start in first, but there was no need to use second gear unless there was a steep hill to climb. After starting, she could go right into third gear, and along the car went smoothly and comfortably. (These driving habits distinguished American motorists from their European contemporaries who were forever rowing through the gears. They were habits that would lead to the extraordinary hospitality granted the automatic transmission when it arrived a decade after the 1929 Chevy's debut.)

Steering was very light, particularly given the fact that an engine considerably heavier than the Ford's sat over the front steering wheels. Although the brake pedal was spongy, the brakes were good. They were mechanically operated drums on the front wheels and contracting bands on the rears. Each brake could be individually adjusted without removing the wheels. No one was substantially bothered by lumps and ruts in the road. The Chevy did not have shock absorbers—although it could have used them—but its springing was good. The car did buck a little, but that was due as much to its being loaded for vacation as to its lack of shocks.

No, this was a good car on a long trip and everyone knew it. Passing drivers generally recognized the Chevy and possibly thought to themselves that a car from GM would surely find its way into their garage one day. For even if Ford repassed Chevy in sales in 1929, it would not hold the lead, and only twice more would Ford regain the national sales lead, neither time for very long.

There was nothing exceptional in this trip then, except that it was Mother and Grandmother in the front seat. This was just another family on vacation, journeying across the land in a motor car. This was the pattern for the next half century: the auto-mobile American family on the move. And in the Chevy's square shape moving through the dust of the two- and three-lane roads that were the immediate ancestors to Route 66, you could discern clearly the outlines of the modern car.

IV
CLASSIC CARS
1925–1948

CHAPTER 10

The Great Artists: The Golden Years

Monuments in the midst of ruin. While the nation was starving and the auto industry was undergoing an agony of reorganization—loss of four-fifths of its sales, dismissal of a huge part of its workforce—up the driveways of the great and the near-great rolled some of the most glorious cars ever produced in the United States.

America's great cars thrived best in the hothouse of Coolidge prosperity—the great boom that started in 1921 and ended on Thursday, October 24, 1929—although an occasional special-bodied carriage still whispered down Park Avenue on its way to its new owner as late as 1939. In fact, an entire company—Auburn-Cord-Duesenberg—came together only as the Great Depression started and actually had its best sales year during the Depression.

But the years of glory began in the boom for both technological and economic reasons. We were still an automobile nation discovering itself, still figuring out how to build cars the American way. Our technology was honed to meet mass demand, our capital invested to promote mass production. Our automobile industry decided early that a million cars sold at modest prices would have a far greater return on investment than a few cars sold at high prices. By the early 1920s, Detroit was becoming so efficient at building Chevrolets and Fords that it had little to offer the owner of the biggest house on the highest hill in Westchester.

"The luxury car's rise depended on acceptance of the basic motoring experience as commonplace," wrote Richard Burns Carson in *The Olympian Cars*. "And this condition had been met by 1925." Carson said that the very moment a trip in an automobile became available to everyone, it was no longer an exciting experience for the "jaded and affluent." And so, just as they took to private railroad cars once the unwashed had begun to flood the Pullmans, and just as they scorned packet boats in preference for the sway of the Blue Riband ocean liner across the North Atlantic, the carriage trade lived up to its name when it ordered its cars: big, stylish, luxurious—and expensive.

These were the last years when the master of that mansion in Westchester could still feel—and not be ashamed to let the world know he felt—part of a monied elite. Sulka and Brooks were still selling morning coats, silk hats, and detachable wing collars by the dozen. In 1929, just as the world was crashing around their countrymen, 513 Americans managed to earn $1 million or more, and a dozen of them were running their fingers through five times that much. We were about to be a nation in agony, but we were not uniformly poor.

As a result, we were not uniformly bolted into Model T's. No, some of us had cars that would become known as classics. They were finely built, silent, extravagantly trimmed motor cars, perhaps the last of their kind—with names like Marmon, Peerless, Cunningham, Duesenberg, and Lincoln, and boasting graceful (or massive) custom coachwork by Le Baron or Darrin or Brunn, reminiscent of the carriages of Versailles.

"Between 1925 and 1942 the skills and special knowledge required to make a

1936 Cord Westchester Sedan Model 810
This is the Cord of memory: 125 horsepower, advertised speed of 100 mph, body styled by Gordon Buehrig, one of the greats.

great luxury automobile were abundantly available in the five important automobile-producing nations," said Griffith Borgeson and Eugene Jaderquist in *Sports and Classic Cars*, a landmark post-World War II book that was among the first to recognize what specialist American constructors had wrought just two decades before its publication. "From the past had come craftsmanship, the ability to work with metal and wood and fabrics that made up the custom and semi-custom bodies. From the past also had come the tradition of quality as an end in itself, an intangible but essential part of the finished product.

"Both had been a major part of the luxury automobiles of earlier days...but the chassis and engines of those early cars had been primitive. Not till after World War I did the engineers catch up with the craftsmen. It was during the classic era that luxury cars first became the smooth, silent, troublefree servants they had long been advertised as being.

"A 1920 Locomobile or an earlier Crane-Simplex cost many times more than a 1932 Packard Twelve, and represented at least five times as much careful, skilled hand labor, but the Packard was a better luxury car."

So the classic was reliable and it was quiet; the same can be said for the post-World War II Cadillac. What made the classic a classic? The answer was styling, ambition, fulfillment of expectations—values of a lost generation—and craftsmen who, remembering the traditions of their trade, had been hoping that with the evolution of the horseless carriage into the automobile, there would still be customers who would cherish high style.

Until 1925, American product designers were in hot pursuit of function. Fenders were functional, meant to keep mud away from the car's occupants, and they looked like they were designed to do just that. The engine, moved forward from under the driver's seat, was contained in a little box in front of the driver, a box that stood upright and took up as little room as possible. "In the rear, the body customarily ended up directly over the axle in a sharp, vertical line, with the rear fenders extending beyond it," said Borgeson and Jaderquist. However primitive, this was attractive compared to what was done to bodies. Some were enormous, seeming to overwhelm the chassis. Furthermore, they were ungainly. Seating arrangements were haphazard, even bizarre. Seats faced forward, seats faced backward. Some cars had twin seats flanking the driver's perch but placed behind it, almost as though the driver were meant to be a navigator and his passengers bodyguards. No doubt about it, many of the cars built by Americans were downright ugly.

All this would eventually change thanks to such institutions as Alfred Sloan's Art and Color section, but the aristocrats were far more aware of aesthetic considerations than the average persons and they were ready for high automotive art well before Harley Earl, the West Coast Cadillac stylist, came to Detroit.

They would get their automotive sculptures courtesy of the carriage artisans, America's last great coachbuilders.

Bespoke Bodies

The practice survives in the trade of gentlemen's tailoring: bespoke suits. For decades Brooks Brothers—and a few of its gentlemanly competitors—have of-

LEFT AND BELOW:

1916 Crane-Simplex Touring, Model 5
This car was designed and built by the specialist firm of Holbrook to look like a yacht. It is complete with ship-style ventilators, walk-through seating, searchlights, teak gunwales, and a propeller that holds the spare tire on. The 1916 car appeared in auto shows in New York and San Francisco. Production ended in 1917.

171

fered both individually fashioned dinner suits, cutaways, three-piece pinstripes, and Chesterfields, and a slightly lower order of suiting called "special cuttings." Precut sections of, say, a jacket sit in the back shop waiting for a customer, who is fitted, and for whom the precut pieces are then artfully tailored. The practice is somewhere between mass production and one-off tailoring. Recently, mass manufacturers of suits have set up their own "special cuttings" shops.

The analogy of tailoring to the history of American custom coachbuilders is exact. In the beginning of the Golden Age of the coachbuilder, he relied for the majority of his trade on the individual customer. Carson has given us the typical sequence: The client would choose a chassis (perhaps a Duesenberg or a Packard), which included frame, engine, wheels, "everything, in fact, that went with a complete car except places to sit and bodywork to surround them." It would be shipped to a coachbuilder, who had responded to the client's queries with specific proposals, including sketches and line drawings, perhaps even swatches of interior fabric. The client would enter negotiations with the builder, and the burden was very much on the client to choose every aspect of trim and color. Then building began: "Using exact dimensionally annotated drawings as guides, woodworkers built up the body-shell frame and door frames out of cured white ash hardwood," Carson wrote.

"Metal craftsmen hammered and stretched panels over this framework [usually aluminum] which was more readily shaped into curving, molded forms." The hardware was cast in brass, and then came the finishing work, which required hundreds, sometimes thousands, of hours by craftsmen who varnished and painted, varnished and painted again, carved wood, trimmed upholstery, and assembled the whole lovely creation. Usually the process of body building took several weeks. Bespoke bodies.

As more and more builders of high-priced automobiles saw more and more trade go to custom coachbuilders, they began to commission their own series of semicustom bodies to market themselves—"special cuttings" bodies, as it were.

From the second stage, the "special cuttings" stage (the coachbuilder supplying a stock special body for a variety of chassis, each tailored to the tiny eccentricities of individual customers), the natural progression was to shift the customer emphasis from the individual car buyer to the chassis builder. A chassis maker would request design sketches and models from the body builder each year.

"From those submitted, he would select the few he wanted, and order from 50 to 200 bodies . . . for delivery to the factory. Assured of this volume of work, the bodybuilder could quote a reasonable price far below the cost of the same body built singly. The customer lost a little in individuality but he gained much in price," wrote Borgeson and Jaderquist.

The final step was inevitable. "By 1933 the growing list of former custom designers who sought refuge in mass-production work included Raymond Dietrich at Chrysler Corporation, former Cord Corporation stylist Al Leamy at General Motors, Murphy man Frank Spring at Hudson, John Tjaarda at Briggs Body and Philip Wright [also] at Briggs." said Carson. "Both Briggs and Murray [special coachbuilders] had built up a tremendous volume in low cost bodies for Fords, Chryslers, Dodges and other popular cars. They saw an opportunity to cash in on the luxury-car trade as well.

"With such mammoth corporations as these in the competition, the smaller independent body builders, most of which were still located far from Detroit, lost a major portion of their business." To them, the villains were GM, with its acquisition of Fleetwood to build special Cadillacs, and Chrysler, for acquiring Le

Baron to the same end. Why all the trouble and all the expense; what distinguished these so-called classics?

Recall that little or no attention was being paid to form, to the aesthetic relationships among sections of the car. Now, the stylists had reordered the importance of construction. Instead of engines enclosed in a tiny box at the front, the stylists decreed that cars needed long, imposing hoods—never mind the actual length of the engine. To give elegant proportions, the long car had to be narrow; running boards had to run the length of the car, emphasizing it, and the rear seat had to be placed over the rear axle. "The very impracticality of the classic designs shows that the stylists were sacrificing everything to fashion and appearance," said Borgeson and Jaderquist. The coachbuilders' customers were not in the least fazed. It was a sacrifice they were only too happy to make. Borgeson and Jaderquist had no doubts about the overall results: "Beauty and stability of design joined engineering and craftsmanship . . . to create the finest luxury automobiles the world had ever seen."

What were these monuments? Who were their coachbuilders?

A Gallery of Greats

The Importer's Salon, begun just before World War I in New York City, put American coachbuilders on the map, in Carson's opinion—and in garages of the

BELOW, OVERLEAF, AND P. 176:
1927 Lincoln Coaching Brougham
Coachbuilder John Judkins with his chief engineer by his side did a great deal of research at stagecoach specialists Abbot and Downing in Concord, New Hampshire. The Judkins Coaching Brougham engenders love or hate in viewers. One expert called it "horrendous" and said it was finally sold in Hollywood because buyers elsewhere were too sensible to own such a thing. It was used in a movie starring W. C. Fields and as a publicity device for Beverly Hillbillies sponsor McMillan Petroleum. It is painted in English coaching colors: yellow and black with red striping. The interior is a reproduction of early Concord coaches and is done in dark green Moroccan leather with red plush trim.

glitterati. "The first signs of coming luxury car consciousness," he called the show. It set out a buffet of automotive dishes irresistible to the new American strivers: Mercedes, Rolls-Royce, Isotta-Fraschini. "In their own lands [such cars] culminated a natural progression from horse-drawn to gasoline-powered transport for the titled few. Neither privation nor contest with a hostile environment had hampered their development as noble chariots," Carson said. They were not bought by many in the New World, but those who did buy cars exhibited at the show were what we'd call today an "influence group," people whose tastes were immediately accepted by others as a standard.

The only trouble for the new owners was that foreign service on a marque imported in limited quantities was as bad then as now. The cars were mechanically advanced, lovely to look at, and beautifully crafted, but you couldn't find anyone to work on them. Customers, then, were beginning to tire of having to have every replacement part individually machined or imported (and in transit for six weeks or more). Their problems were soon solved by the American coachbuilders who had gazed on the success of the Importer's Salon.

After the war, the Importer's Salon opened its doors to "fine cars of domestic manufacture," thus admitting into the most exclusive auto showroom in North America the new breed of domestic coachbuilders—and a newly interested old breed as well.

Typical of the homegrown coachbuilder was the new firm of Le Baron. The company had begun when a pair of automotive draftsmen, Raymond Dietrich and Thomas Hibbard, having decided New York needed specialists in body design, opened a studio in 1920. They were pure "automotive architects"—their own phrase. At first, the only thing they built was a reputation as the place to go for very special designs. Hibbard and Dietrich sold plans for a car in very much the same way as their more conventional architect colleagues sold the concept and details for a building—blueprints to go to the actual builder. Very soon both partners became full-on coachbuilders in their own right. By 1927, Dietrich had his own company in America, and Hibbard had gone to Paris.

Le Baron's founders came from the greatest of American coachbuilders, Brewster. Brewster was a carriage building company begun in 1810. For a time the company built its own car, using the Knight engine. Soon, it was making bodies for Rolls-Royce, and soon after that, a customer who wanted a Brewster body had to buy a Rolls. Brunn of Buffalo was particularly well known for its formal cars; its final, great product was a town car on a Buick platform. Derham of Rosemont, Pennsylvania, started as a carriage builder in 1887. It was known for its close-coupled sedans, a style that eliminated the rear quarter windows. Derham outlasted many of its competitors; it was still in business (although barely) after World War II, modifying Chryslers and Cadillacs.

Judkins of Merrimac, Massachusetts, built one of the great anachronisms of American automotive history in the 1927 Lincoln Coaching Brougham, a stage coach of a car, complete with wicker trunk. Carson called it a "horrendous" design, able to be sold only to a tasteless myopic in Hollywood, where people would buy *anything*. Perhaps. But today the car, sitting apart from its contemporaries in a museum, seems visually strong, even charming. Rollston (later known as Rollson) was America's toniest builder, or at least its most expensive. Its jewel was the Twenty Grand Duesenberg, a 1933 model based on the Duesenberg J. The Twenty Grand was originally called the Duesenberg Arlington, the name changed by concensus of the spectators at Chicago's Century of Progress when they saw its price tag. Holbrook, Willoughby, Waterhouse, and

Weymann of America each had its moment on the fashionable stage, as did Rollson, Biddle and Smart, Le Baron, Brunn and Murphy—some briefly, some for a longer time.

Some of these companies were already anticipating the later association with Detroit manufacturers. One of the first of the Detroit stylists, Joseph Eskridge, remembers being a familiar figure at Biddle and Smart as liaison between Hudson Motor Company and that New England designer of semicustom bodies. The association did not last long. Within a few years, Hudson had brought its styling inside, where it remained, except for some post-World War II efforts at jobbing out design to Italian coachbuilders—which, as we shall see in Chapter 19, was a dreadful mistake.

Perhaps the prototype for the revived coachbuilders' trade of the seventies and eighties, was Walter M. Murphy of Pasadena. It was a company that scorned decoration, placing primary emphasis on the beauty of line and minimum trim. The Duesenberg was its favorite chassis, the open car its forte. Out of Murphy came another company called Bohman and Schwartz. Neither survived.

In fact, none of these great artisans lasted. Absorbed, outdated, preempted by a world war, shoved aside by styling departments within great manufacturing companies, further weakened by the disappearance of the genus chauffeur—all these things combined to make the coachbuilder an anachronism and with him, the coachbuilder's early classic proportions. The sight of a uniformed chauffeur (and often footman) sitting in the open while owners luxuriated in a tiny cubicle way in the back of an enormous car—140-inch wheelbase, with most of that space given to engine and driving compartment—gave way to a car with a 125-inch wheelbase, with the owner/driver presiding.

But while they lasted, the coachbuilders made cars that still stand as American artistic masterpieces.

We will examine Auburn-Cord-Duesenberg in a separate section later in this chapter, for if all the cars E. L. Cord's company built were not classics, enough were that the company is thought of today as having been in the forefront of firms dedicated to their production. But even without the cars from Cord, there were still enough American classics to stun a maharajah.

Establishment Classics

1933 Cadillac All-Weather Phaeton, Series 452C

Known to its intimates as the "Al Jolson Car," this special-bodied V-16 was executed by Fleetwood for the singer in March 1933. Cadillac was a pioneer of the V-type engine; it had a V-8 in its 1914 car. By 1930, *three* V-types were being made by Cadillac, V-8, V-12, and V-16. This year's production of V-16s was restricted to 400 cars.

There were, of course, the great cars being built by the great manufacturers: Cadillac and La Salle from GM, Lincoln from Ford Motor Company, Chrysler and Chrysler Imperial from Chrysler Corporation, Packard from Packard.

We have heard Alfred Sloan talk about what Harley Earl did to the La Salle to distinguish it from its sibling Buick. Other classics followed the same approach. The classic was a lower car than any available production model, and it had an enormous hood. Sharp corners were banished in favor of gentle curves. The fenders were not left to catch the wind but brought down in compound curves to the level of the bumpers. In came the slanted windshield and the V-shaped radiator grille. The passenger compartment was considered part of the overall design of the body and was not left perching way back over the rear axle. "Classic styling was so positive in its effects on the automobile world that it eventually set the pattern for all the cheap production cars," said Borgeson and Jaderquist. Nowhere was this as true as at the Big Three.

Even before there was the notion of such a thing as a classic, Cadillac was edging toward the concept of unlimited luxury, extravagant styling, and technical daring. In 1914, Cadillac used the first V-8 in an American production car. Then, as the 1930s opened, the company introduced a V-16, only to add a V-12 in the fall. Technically, the thirties were an interesting decade for Cadillac. Just before the January 1930 introduction of the V-16, Cadillac had gotten synchromesh transmission, the first car in the world to do so. Sloan had resisted safety glass for a few years because of the cost—the 1929 car had not only the glass but chromium plating as well. Prices for the factory car ranged from $3,295 to $5,995. The V-16 *began* at $6,000 and went as high as $9,000. Power brakes were introduced in 1931. Ride-control (adjustable shocks) came the next year, and the year after that, "no draft" ventilation. Cadillac adopted independent front suspension in 1934 and "turret top" bodies in 1935.

Things languished technically for the factory car for three years, and then Cadillac's shifter went from the floor to the steering column (antedating by a year the same change on all GM cars), and both the V-12 and the V-16 were dropped in favor of a new V-16, a short-stroke, side-valve unit that was used until 1940. In that same year (1938), Cadillac introduced a model called the Sixty Special, with a light and airy four-door body, no running boards, a 5.7-liter, side-valve V-8 engine that by 1941 came in a choice of three wheelbases. It was a good car, a lovely car to some people, and an enormously important car, for despite the contrary signal of the introduction of an enormous V-16 in 1938—just as the era of Classics was ending—the Sixty Special was the shape of things to come: good, solid, wonderfully built cars from a great manufacturer, but no classic. Packard was on the same path. So was Chrysler. The decade was closing. The glory days were winding down.

Borgeson and Jaderquist pointed out that Cadillac Division was able to make all the changes it made because it didn't have to show a profit. "Other firms were not that lucky; if their models were not financial successes, bankruptcy loomed very near." Borgeson and Jaderquist suggested that Cadillac's allowed profligacy was in pursuit of prestige for the whole GM line, that any losses could be written off to the equivalent of advertising and promotion. Though it may not be gracious to argue with so rich a source as *Sports and Classic Cars*, we have Sloan's words to the contrary. Not at any time during the Depression did GM lose money. Some risks were taken, some experiments made, but all in favor of GM's purpose in life, which (as Sloan told us clearly) was to make a profit for its investors.

Some thirties Cadillacs can be instantly recognized as classics, while some of them are clearly not. They are classics (when they are) because the Classic Car Club of America says they are. However, to compare the 1930 dual cowl, dual windshield phaeton with a 1933 convertible sedan is to understand that in the classic era some of Cadillac's cars were almost equal to the greatest of them all and some were distinctly related to GM's less aristocratic car families.

Cadillac's own history is proof of the mayfly life of the classic car. Between 1931 and 1937, the division marketed three lines, with a total of sixty-two models. But by 1934, Cadillac had already begun to back away from the ultimate classic, advertising that it would build only 400 V-16s, all with custom bodies, all to special order. When the division introduced the Sixty Special, it canceled the V-12. In 1941, the V-16 disappeared forever. GM wouldn't support the building of classics within Cadillac because the competition had disappeared. Once again we hear the echoes of Sloanism—it is not necessary to lead, just to be as good as anyone else. Although Cadillac was not upset to find itself in the vanguard of prestige cars in America after World War II, that was really almost by default. The Series 75 (1946–1948) is the only postwar Cadillac considered a classic, although a late fifties Eldorado Biarritz has been placed in the category of "Special Interest," and the Milestone Car Society lists that car as well as the Cadillac Sixty Specials of 1948 and 1949 and the same years' models Sixty-one and Sixty-two in coupe and convertible form as "certified milestones." Perhaps a generation hence

1930 Graham Paige
The 1930 Graham Paige is a rare car in that it has a body designed by Ehrmann Rossi; it was unusual to send the chassis of an American car to Germany to have it bodied. The Graham Paige has no running boards, and its trunk represents European styling.

183

1937 Oldsmobile Four Door Sedan
This was a General Motors production car with an experimental transmission. The car had a semi-automatic transmission, which later developed into the hydramatic.

1934 Packard Runabout Speedster
This, the Model 1106, twelve-cylinder, Le Baron, boattail coachwork, is the only car listed in the Packard 1934 catalogue with a 135-inch wheelbase. It is a car that helped maintain Packard's high reputation.

these cars will have transformed themselves into classics, but not according to the —admittedly amorphous—definition of the day: special coachwork, particular attention to elegance, runs of a few identical models, style above function.

To emphasize its pragmatic view of the automobile market even during the classic era, GM introduced a car we have already seen, a kind of bourgeois Cadillac—the La Salle. Packard had brought out a relatively inexpensive car in 1926, which in Sloanist terms meant that Cadillac had to enter the same market segment. In 1927, it did, with what was really just a small Cadillac—the La Salle —styled by Harley Earl. Its engine was all but identical to Cadillac's; the stock Fisher bodies for Cadillac and La Salle were almost indistinguishable, as were the special bodies done for both by Fleetwood.

Then GM executed a typical flanking maneuver on its competitors, by now both Packard and Lincoln, which were producing competitive autos in the lower segment of the upper-price market. (Carson called them "pocket luxury cars.") In 1934, La Salle ceased being a Cadillac sibling and became an upmarket brother to Oldsmobile, one segment down on the sheet metal social scale. Packard, as we are about to discover, scurried to introduce the Model 120, which was racy and medium priced, to combat La Salle (powered now by an Oldsmobile engine). In addition, it was La Salle that prompted the 1936 introduction of Lincoln's Zephyr, widely loved today, but a car that diminished Lincoln's reputation, appearing from out of nowhere as a kind of poor relation. And no sooner had the Zephyr popped up to accompany the Packard 120 than La Salle reverted to its lofty status as a kind of Cadillac, dropping the Olds engine in favor of the Series Sixty V-8. The first La Salle saw daylight in 1927, the last in 1940.

Cadillac's effort to compete in the prestige market was only relatively successful compared to the king: Packard. It was a company founded on discontent with the worth of anyone else's car. It was an innovator even early in its history. Packard replaced the tiller with a steering wheel. It pioneered the H-slot shifter in American cars. It was a competition success, one of the first marques to be driven across the United States. Although Duesenberg introduced the first in-line eight-cylinder engine in 1921, Packard had the first reasonably priced straight-eight, in 1924. Henceforth—until 1955—Packards would be known for their wonderful, large, silent, reliable straight-eight engines. Packard's was even larger in piston displacement than the Duesenberg's engine, with a bore (cylinder diameter) of $3\frac{3}{8}$ inches and a stroke (cylinder depth) of 5 inches. Powerful and quiet, long-stroke (as they were called), large-displacement, relatively slow turning engines were typical of classics. Usually, the more cylinders the better, for there is an inherent vibration in all engines, and the more cylinders the more frequent the explosions and therefore an apparent disappearance of the moments between that create the feeling of roughness.

Packard's pre-Depression peak came in 1928 when its "styling was as stiff and uncompromising as that of the Rolls-Royce." The company sold 50,000 units, and 45,000 of them went to people who had owned Packards before. Said Carson: "The Packard's impressive and instantly identifiable appearance was to be so common in smart settings that the marque pre-empted the whole mass image of what luxury motoring was all about. There were always more expensive cars than the Packard, cars that were perhaps better . . . but among the huge majority to whom wealth and luxury motoring would always remain a dream the Packard was forever visible as a sign of the life's best riches and social rewards."

Nevertheless, Cadillac's V-16 in 1930 tolled a bell for Packard. The more cylinders the better, thought Americans when they sallied forth to buy a classic, and for longer than it should have, Packard stuck to its straight-eight. But two

RIGHT AND OVERLEAF:

1940 Packard Station Wagon
Perhaps the loveliest station wagon
built by Detroit, this Packard was a particular favorite of William Fisk Harrah,
owner of the world's largest car collection. He drove it daily and at such high
speeds that his museum technical director had a roll bar built into its roof
without Harrah's knowledge. Air conditioning was sufficiently novel when
the wagon was manufactured that
Packard identified the inclusion of it on
the side-mounted spare.

1934 Packard Sport Phaeton
The first twelve-cylinder Packard was
introduced in June 1915. Because of its
smoothness, it became a favorite among
clients of custom coachbuilders. A new
V-12 was added in June 1931 after
some experimentation with a new in-
line eight. This Eleventh Series twelve-
cylinder Packard Sport Phaeton with its
Le Baron body is thought of by many
Packard experts as that company's
"pièce de résistance."

years later, even given its thin resources compared to GM, Packard knew it
needed the sales impetus of a multicylinder motor, and it introduced the V-12. By
1935, the V-12 had increased to 473 cubic inches—absolutely huge—and larger
than Cadillac's engine (although second in America to Marmon's V-16). In the
V-12's first year of production, it used bodies adapted from the eight-cylinder
cars. In addition, though, Le Baron did a V-12 speedster and a phaeton. Then
Brunn built an aerodynamic coupe for the 1933 New York Auto Show as well as
cabriolets in 1938 and 1939. Given its size, the 1934 Le Baron Sport Phaeton was
a surprisingly graceful car, with attempts at either high style, aerodynamics, or
both in its downward-curved beltline and deco rear skirts.

As the Depression deepened and the V-12 fell out of favor, the eight-cylinder
engine regained its rightful position at the head of the Packard table, powering the
160 and 180 models. Le Baron, Rollston, and Darrin built bodies for these later
cars. Many consider Darrin's Victoria four-passenger convertible with its distinctive trademark cut-down doors, to be Packard's most coveted collectible.

The classicist turns away from Packards of the late 1930s. The company had
introduced the 120 and then dipped even deeper into middle-class pockets with a
six-cylinder car. Once Packard left the halls of the great, goes the argument, it lost
its cachet. The move made enormous marketing sense. It saved the company for
many years, and allowed even commercial travelers to make their rounds in a car
with the Packard logo. "Quite literally the Packard name was put on the open
market for the cash it could bring in," said Borgeson and Jaderquist. Later,
Packard had Darrin do some delicate convertibles. After the war, it pushed its
way forward with great, bulbous cars, the first of which was poignantly evocative
of its great years—particularly in convertible form. But in 1954, it was swallowed

188

by Studebaker, which produced some of the most grotesque cars on the American scene, using the Packard logo on them. In 1958, the name was mercifully dropped.

This was not the case with Cadillac's bulldog competitor, Lincoln. In fact, if there is a postclassic era classic today, it is Lincoln's Continental—brought out in 1940 for the first time and in 1956 for the last—a genuine, separate, neoclassic car. We will get to the Continental when we deal with the few elegant American cars built after World War II. In the meantime, let's see what Henry Ford's senior division was up to while the Model T was becoming the Model A was becoming the V-8.

Lincoln had a lovely start in Henry Leland's car, painted and polished and powered by a 348-cubic-inch, L-head, V-8 engine. After production, each engine was thoroughly tested, typical of the Lelands but expensive to do. "If anything there was too much emphasis on the non-visible features of the Lincoln and not enough on the visible," said Carson. Henry Leland was clearly not a man for frills. His cars were upright and sensible and unglamorous. Walter Chrysler would have approved.

In 1932 (the year of Henry Leland's death), Ford introduced a V-12 for Lincoln—the Model KB. Borgeson and Jaderquist said of the KB: "Mechanically, it was a car Leland might have manufactured." Its engine was carefully finished. It was built on a huge, sturdy frame. "It had more main-bearing area than any other American V-12, an important factor in crankshaft rigidity and thus in smoothness of operation and durability."

But the virtues of the KB were not all mechanical. It brought out the best in the great American coachbuilders. The man responsible for their interest was the

1936 Packard Coupe Roadster
By the late 1930s, Packard found it had to begin to appeal to a less select market but one that still wanted a distinctive-looking car. The Model 1404 was factory-bodied and priced at just over $3,000.

192

same one who would bring forth the Continental in 1940: Henry's son Edsel. He was a friend of the partners at Le Baron in New York, and they did a phaeton for him in 1929 that was odd but very special. That prompted Edsel to go further afield in the coachbuilding world and elicit designs from Willoughby, Judkins, and Brunn in addition to Le Baron, so that by the time the KB came along, Lincoln could offer variations on the theme in its catalogue. Edsel's education in styling influenced the design of the hood, fenders, and grille, which Lincoln would supply the specialists along with the chassis. "The result was a unity of design rarely found even during the Classic Era," said Borgeson and Jaderquist.

Only two years after the KB, the 1934 K came out. It made concessions. Although it too had a V-12 engine, it was not a V-12 of distinction. It was smaller. There were four main bearings instead of the previous seven. The compression ratio had been raised so that it could furnish as much horsepower as its rich predecessor. Although never a success, Lincoln kept the new V-12 for six years. Meanwhile, the company, at the urging of Briggs Manufacturing, which was making the stock bodies for Ford and Lincoln, took a course that would bring the introduction of the Lincoln Zephyr, a nice car but not a good one. Furthermore, it was a car that met La Salle and the cheap Packard on their own middle ground, by association depriving the great Lincolns of much of their mystique.

The third great manufacturer who also made classics, Chrysler, joins this elite company by the barest of margins. Remembering Chrysler's heritage, and Walter Chrysler's yearning to produce a very special car with his name on it, it is not surprising to find a classic just a year after the corporation saw official life. In 1926, Chrysler built the E-80, the beginning of a whole series of increasingly powerful similar cars, some of whose bodies would be built by Locke, Dietrich, and Le Baron. Then, in 1931, the corporation introduced a car that has been called "the

1932 Lincoln Convertible Sedan Model KB-241
The K and the KB are considered the great Lincolns. This one has a Dietrich body and Lincoln's L-head, V-12 engine of 448-cubic-inch displacement and is thought so splendid that it has been part of two impressive collections. The car came to Harrah's from the first of two assemblages put together by enthusiast J. B. Nethercutt, of the Merle Norman cosmetics company.

LEFT:
1926 Lincoln
Lincoln was thought of as a massive automobile; but some were commissioned in a size just large enough for two people.

1931 Lincoln Convertible Roadster
This Lincoln is a true classic, highly prized by collectors. Its body is by Le Baron, one of the first of the new style coach builders. The firm was to have an influence on Edsel Ford and the Lincoln Continental he developed.

1941 Chrysler Thunderbolt
Chrysler Corporation did two special show cars just as war was descending on the U.S. This one, called the Thunderbolt, may be the least felicitously proportioned car ever done.

greatest classic in Chrysler history," the '31 Custom Imperial. It is a sensuous car, with its semicustom Le Baron body. Not ponderous like some classics or delicate like others, the Custom Imperial was of a kind with Auburn and Cord in its lovely purposefulness. Of course, it had an extraordinary engine—the Red Head or the Silver Dome (the former had more horsepower), both were of the same specification: straight-eights with a long stroke and an L head.

In the meantime, Carl Breer, one of the trio of engineers Walter Chrysler had

*1941 Chrysler Newport
Dual Cowl Phaeton*
One of the last dual cowl phaetons
built in the United States, this car was
designed by Ralph Roberts and built
by Le Baron. It had an all-aluminum
body. Its original owner was Dan
Topping, one-time owner of the New
York Yankees. He had his name cast
into the heads and hubcaps and his in-
itials cast on the grille and then gave
the car to Lana Turner.

brought to Willys, was off doing the Chrysler Airflow (and an accompanying
DeSoto), Detroit's first attempt at mass selling of a streamlined car. It was the
Edsel of its day.

Chrysler Corporation built a few show cars thereafter, and the Milestone Car
Society recognizes Chrysler's great postwar 300 series as well as the wood-bodied
convertible built in 1948, the Town and Country. But the apogee of the company
was clearly the Custom Imperial.

OVERLEAF:

1912 Stutz Bearcat
The 1912 Stutz Bearcat is probably
America's best-known sports car. It
ran at Indianapolis and many other
races.

The Grand Independents

The one name that can be said to symbolize American classics for those who see them as lean, low, and rakish was Stutz. In fact, the histories of Stutz, which built its first racing car in 1911 (when it was still called the Ideal Motor Car Company of Indianapolis), and Duesenberg are much alike. Harry C. Stutz changed the company's name the year before he brought out the first version of the Bearcat. Based on pure race-car design, the Bearcat had a minimal body hung on the chassis that was strong and simple and that was powered by a high-performance engine (at least at the time), a four-cylinder Wisconsin, making 60 hp at 1,500 rpm. Stutz left his own company, but it continued to manufacture cars. In 1926, Frederick E. Moskovics came in and infused Stutz with money and the notion of building great luxury cars on what continued to be sporting chassis. He advertised the car's great performance made for accident avoidance and called the 1926 car "The Safety Stutz."

It was not a successful theme, so Moskovics began to offer customers a bewildering choice of bodies. Anyone doing any kind of special coachwork was called in to do a Stutz. Le Baron, Rollston, Brunn, and Fleetwood did limited-model Stutzes. Weymann did fabric-bodied cars. Some of the others might have been made of gossamer from their names: Chantilly, Monte Carlo, Riviera, Longchamps. In 1932, Stutz brought out the revived Bearcat and the Super Bearcat, again hearkening to pure racing engineering, the engines (called DV-32) were big (322-cubic-inch displacement) four-valve-per-cylinder overhead cammers. But all the original Bearcat could do—and it was Mercer's chief rival as America's sports car—the new Bearcat could not, although it was a formidable car. Stutz sales languished.

One of Stutz's problems was that the company could not afford to produce anything other than its eight-cylinder engine when everyone else was boasting new V-12s and V-16s. With the Bearcat and the Super Bearcat, Stutz had the best sports car of its day, but to no avail. Stutz, as a company, had a sad end. It turned to the building of delivery vans and finally made an urban, lightweight version called the Pak-Age car. Pak-Age-ing lasted until 1938, when the company was sold to Diamond T, a builder of large freight haulers.

We'll look at two more giants in the Depression era glitter and then come to a cruelly short paragraph on some of our great cars that passed only briefly across the horizon.

It simply would not do to dismiss Pierce-Arrow as just another great car, although Borgeson and Jaderquist seemed to: "If there is any single distinction Pierce-Arrow deserves, it is the rather dubious one of producing the most successful *un*successful classic in United States history." It's a question of perspective. Certainly from the company's point of view, its cars did not produce a lifeblood of revenue. But from the view of the car lover, particularly the lover of classics, Pierce-Arrow was a shining jewel in the American tiara.

George N. Pierce, having learned the trade in bicycles and bird cages, had been building cars in Buffalo, remember, since 1901. His early cars were typical of the day until 1903, when he came out with a 15 hp two-cylinder auto—the Arrow. The next year the engine was upped to 28 hp, and the car renamed, appropriately, Great Arrow. The last of the Great Arrows was made in 1908, powered by a motor that made 60 hp at 1,000 rpm.

In 1909, Pierce combined the company name with the car's. From the beginning, Pierce-Arrow was a maker of fine motor cars, including a limousine (in 1911) with a bulging top and a rear entrance so ladies with huge bonnets could

1912 Stutz wheel

enter and sit up straight with never a worry for ostrich feathers or furbelows. Pierce-Arrow's distinguishing feature, the headlight mounted on top of the front fenders, first appeared on the 1914 model; by 1915, the company's reputation as a builder of an elite motor car was firmly established. Three models were available with a complete line of bodies. Prices started at $5,850 and went to $7,300. This was serious money. In 1920, Pierce-Arrow finally dropped right-hand drive, perhaps in response to dropping sales. Things got so bad in 1923 that the company brought out the Model 80, a smaller car with four-wheel brakes and an L-head six-cylinder engine, selling for $3,000 to $4,000.

Nothing really helped. By 1928, Pierce-Arrow was sold to Studebaker, which got rid of the by-now antiquated and outglamored six-cylinder engine, replacing it with a Big Eight. Obviously, if Pierce-Arrow were to compete with Lincoln, Packard, and Cadillac, it would need a multicylindered engine in a V configuration. The parent company, Studebaker, was not doing well; in fact, it resold Pierce-Arrow in 1933 to a group of Buffalo businessmen. Yet the engineers at Pierce-Arrow went ahead with a V-12. It was an undramatic engine. Customers familiar with other V-12 engines could see little that was different in the Pierce-Arrow V-12. In desperation, the company tried to give the engine panache by hiring famous race driver Ab Jenkins to set records at the Bonneville Salt Flats. Jenkins drove a Pierce 12 around the standard ten-mile salt circle, averaging 112.9 mph for twenty-four hours. For that sales year (1933), the company managed a tiny profit, but its sales and engineering conservatism finally put an end to Pierce-Arrow in 1938 — not before Le Baron and Brunn did some remarkable bodies, though, and not before Phil Wright executed a stunning car called the Silver Arrow, which sold for $10,000 in 1933.

It is accurate to say that the Silver Arrow was aerodynamic, enclosing running boards and spare wheels, but this description does not convey the sense of

1913 Pierce-Arrow Seven-Passenger Touring Model 66A
This was the first year for the distinctive headlamp-atop-the-front-fender treatment that would come to characterize all Pierce-Arrows. The Model 66A is one of the largest antiques ever built. It has a 147-inch wheelbase and is powered by one of the largest passenger-car engines ever manufactured in the United States, a monster of 824-cubic-inch displacement. All that for $6,000.

1933 Pierce-Arrow Silver Arrow
This Silver Arrow was the official car of the 1933 Chicago World's Fair. It was a high performance car, making up to 115 mph. The Silver Arrow came with power brakes, a speedometer in the back seat, and recessed door handles. Only five of these cars were built, and this one was dredged up from the bottom of a river in Ohio.

photo by Joseph Kugielsky

1926 Pierce-Arrow Runabout Series 80
The Pierce-Arrow copywriters were at it again with the Runabout in 1926, calling it "fleet" and "silky." By now, colors were important to car buyers. The Runabout came in "six options of gay colorings: Brilliant Black with a striping of Grosbeak Vermillion; Cruiser Gray; Desert Sand; Ambato Green; Sport Blue Light; and Marne Blue." At $2,895, it was the lowest-priced Pierce-Arrow ever offered.

massiveness yet gracefulness in so early a car. It can't be said that Pierce-Arrow built commonplace cars. But it was a commonplace company, and one always slightly behind its time (even the Silver Arrow was a follower, taking a path already blazed by Cadillac, Briggs, and Packard with their aerodynamic sedans).

The last car Pierce-Arrow produced (in 1938) and the final auctioning of assets in the same year were yet two more doleful episodes in the death agonies of the classics. Most were already gone, one in particular that had been as brilliant as any during its day: Marmon.

Howard Marmon had built his first car in 1902. By 1904, he was already using aluminum, in his constant search for lightweight, high-performance materials. He introduced the Model 34 in 1916, with an engine made almost entirely of aluminum. It was so successful that the model was not replaced until the first eight-cylinder appeared in 1927.

In the meantime, Marmon had been to France and had brushed up against that stunning automotive creator, innovator, autocrat, and pioneer, Ettore Bugatti, who was building a sixteen-cylinder aircraft engine for the French military. Marmon wanted the United States to use the engine, but as we saw, Washington opted for mass production of the Liberty. At the same time, though, it allowed the French V-16 to be built at the Duesenberg plant in New Jersey. The brothers Duesenberg would introduce a straight-eight with echoes of the Bugatti engine after the war.

When Howard Marmon's turn came to build a multicylinder, he also found inspiration in Bugatti's creation. Still, the result was a V-16 all his own. It was aluminum, but it had steel sleeves. It was the largest engine made in America, but it was very light weight and enormously smooth. The New York branch of the Society of Automotive Engineers gave Marmon a gold medal for technical

1933 Marmon Five-Passenger Sedan Marmon was a great name in American car manufacture but one that did not survive the Depression. There are Marmon devotees who insist that no finer car was ever built in this country. This one has a Waterhouse special body, one of a very few special coachwork bodies mounted on the Sixteen. This car came from the collection of Governor Winthrop Rockefeller.

1924 Wills Ste. Claire
The Wills Ste. Claire was named for
its inventor, Childe Harold Wills, who
had also helped to develop the Ford
Model T. This luxury car was produced from 1921 until 1927.

1925 Doble Coupe Series E-24
An imposing car, often considered the
pinnacle of steam-car achievement,
this Murphy-bodied coupe was Abner
Doble's own car and his test bed. Its
four-cylinder, 213-cubic-inch engine
produced a rated 75 hp and a top
speed of 90 mph. This large, finely
made car is very much a classic.

BELOW:
*1930 DuPont Royal Town Car
Model G*
The DuPont was a glorious
automobile, little known today but
revered by enthusiasts. Only 125
DuPonts were built in 1930; because
the market for quality cars was limited
during the Depression, one by one great
marques like the DuPont disappeared.
The Model G was an eight-cylinder,
40-horsepower car with a body by Merrimac. Price when new: $5,750.

achievement for the engine. Nor was the V-16's body without merit. An industrial designer who later became a postwar legend in packaging, Walter Dorwin Teague, did simple, unadorned coachwork for the Marmon that conveyed a feeling of elegance and simplicity. Nonetheless, Marmon offered only a few alternatives to the factory body. However splendid, the car needed to compete in the luxury market with marques whose catalogues showed a great variety of styles from a galaxy of coachbuilders. As a result, Marmon suffered. So the eight *and* sixteen were dead in the water. Very well, Howard Marmon would build a V-12. But it was 1931; there had been few customers, and there was no money to finish the radical body on the V-12, much less to put the car into production. Another great name passed from history.

Gone with it was Cunningham (not the manufacturer of the same name that would appear after World War II), which Borgeson and Jaderquist said was the producer of a car "that probably came closest to being an 'American Rolls-Royce.'" Cunningham offered no stock bodies. Everything was made to order and everything was expensive. The simplest sort of roadster started at $6,500. Cunningham's cars were known for their silence, massiveness, and exclusivity; their forte was certainly not clever engineering. There was nothing about Cunningham to recommend it over any other car during the Depression other than its understatement. In 1931, only seventy-five customers took enough note of that to buy one.

Gone too were Peerless, Franklin, Wills Ste. Claire, Doble, DuPont, and, yes, even the American Rolls-Royce, an abortive effort to build in Springfield, Massachusetts, a car every bit as good as the English Rolls-Royce. The American company even imported English supervisory workmen to insure that standards were met. But Americans of the Depression era (and one suspects of today as well) wanted the real thing, not a pale colonial version. American Rolls-Royce buyers

1931 Springfield Rolls-Royce
To deprive the United States of the finest car in the world simply because import duties were high was not the Rolls-Royce way. In 1921, the company put the Silver Ghost Rolls into production in Springfield, Massachusetts. Nearly 3,000 American Rolls-Royces were built before the company realized that U.S. buyers during the Depression were willing to pay large sums for a Rolls-Royce, but they didn't feel an *American* Rolls carried the proper imprimateur. U.S. production came to an end in 1931.

would import them; they would never pay good money for a car made in their own backyard.

The Cars of E. L. Cord

Of all the great cars of the Depression era, none are so exciting to the modern car fancier as the ones that came from Auburn-Cord-Duesenberg. The company was brought into existence in 1926 by Erret Lobban Cord. Cord was born in 1898 in Missouri with what the Indianapolis *Star* would call almost a century later a kind of inherent "Whiz Bang Supersalesman, Superpromoter" talent. He was brought up in Los Angeles by a family that "had just enough money to spoil me." He was promoter enough to have made and lost three $50,000 fortunes by the time he was twenty-one. He was also fascinated by cars, enough that some of the money that came from his building of trucking bodies for bauxite haulers from Death Valley, California, was spent making and selling Model T racing bodies.

At the end of World War I, he had exactly $20. He managed to parlay it into a successful auto agency in Chicago within four years. At that moment, destiny called.

The Auburn Automobile Company wanted E. L. Cord to run it out of debt. He was sponsored in his efforts by a group of investors including William Wrigley, Jr. Auburn had been building a variety of highly interesting cars since its

photo by Joseph Kugielsky

founding in Auburn, Indiana, at the turn of the century. The latest, prior to Cord's arrival, was the 6-51. Instead of the streamlined bodies and beveled edges on the sides of the fenders of its predecessor Beauty Six, the 6-51 had cycle fenders and step plates in place of running boards.

Cord brought some of the most energetic and imaginative engineers and stylists in America to his new company, including the Duesenberg brothers, Gordon Buehrig, and Phil Wright. He introduced a Duesenberg, he incarnated a Cord. He pumped health into an Auburn subsidiary called Lycoming Engine, which was in both aircraft and automotive power plants. He owned his own coachbuilding firm, first called Central, later Le Grand.

Borgeson and Jaderquist praised Auburn: "From the beginning of the Classic Era until the demise of the Auburn Supercharged Eight in the mid-Thirties, the buyer could get more for his money in an Auburn than in any other automobile." It was a fact that did not escape buyers. In 1931, Auburn sold 28,130 cars, more than DeSoto, Hudson, and Packard. That year, with Auburn in thirteenth place in the industry, Cord signed up 1,000 new dealers. The car that did it was the 8-98, which had a 286.6-cubic-inch Lycoming engine, making it, at $1,395, the performance car for the masses. At this moment, Cord decided that what Auburn needed was a V-12. The engine would power an Auburn Speedster to records that remained in the books until after World War II. But the V-12 was not a success, and using it raised the car's price so much that Auburn dropped into a lowly sales position in the industry. By 1934, Cord had given up on the V-12 and was bring-

1933 Auburn Custom Speedster Model 12-161A
E. L. Cord took over the Auburn Automobile Company in 1924 and spent the next two years recreating it in his own image to become Auburn-Cord-Duesenberg. By 1933, he was producing a group of stunning cars including this one, which has been called "the high point in the history of the company" and a "classic among classics." It is powered by an enormous Lycoming 6.4-liter, V-12 engine, making it a true 100 mph automobile.

photo by Joseph Kugielsky

1936 Cord Westchester Sedan
Known as the Coffin-Nosed Cord,
this was the top of the line of the
Cords and was probably the most
cohesive body style produced in an
American car.

ing back a six-cylinder that had the same bore/stroke dimensions of an eight-cylinder offered for the same car. The cars shown in 1935 were disasters, so Cord called in that remarkable stylist Gordon Buehrig and engineer August Duesenberg. Together, they managed to do a car that is the best known of the company's production, the 851 speedster. "It had everything," said Borgeson and Jaderquist: "long, low hood; tiny cockpit; rakish boattail deck, and a plate on the instrument panel which stated that the car had been driven at a speed greater than 100 mph." The price was $2,245. (Today a good one can cost $150,000.) Not even that was allure enough. Nineteen thirty-six was the last year for Auburn.

It was also the first year for the car made in E.L. Cord's name, almost the only Cord most people can recall today. The 810, or Coffin-Nosed, Cord was a wonder—too much of one, perhaps, with its front-wheel drive and preselector gearbox. Cord's L-29 had been born in 1929, powered by a 5-liter (302-inch), L-head Lycoming engine. It offered a variety of coachwork by a number of builders including Murphy and Hayes. Overseas, the English firm of Freestone and Webb also built special bodies for the Cord. But the L-29's price was high, and production was halted in 1932. Then, with the financial climate threatening to turn good for a change, Cord reintroduced the car in 1935 as "the weirdly beautiful" Coffin-Nosed Cord. Some people took it as a classic, some as a sports car, some as a freakish stock car. Each had claim to some accuracy. Today the 810 is a classic. It was handsomely fitted and furnished, and carefully put together. It had a Lycoming V-8 engine that could turn as high as 4,500 rpm and was rated at 125 hp. It had a Bendix preselector gearchange in which the driver operated a miniature gearbox, but the gears did not actually shift until the clutch was engaged. It was an anticipatory automatic transmission, if you will.

However, the credit for the most memorable aspects of the car goes, quite

1929 Duesenberg Model J
While to build the Model J in town-car form was the equivalent of dressing a prize fighter in a dinner suit and sending him out on the town to mix with society's elite, some of the special coachwork cars tried to suggest Duesenberg's split personality visually, using the equivalent of Safari luggage details—fabric or leather coverings for the top and side mounts.

rightly, to the stylist, Gordon Buehrig: It was—this is the widely held contemporary view—as startling and lovely a car as had ever been designed. It was dramatic, with its long, and yet cohesive and compact bonnet, with a passenger compartment that continued the lines of the hood and came back into a sleek, low pod. It was a sensation when it was shown—but the company could not produce models for reliable on-time delivery.

The component of E. L. Cord's company that is remembered as a builder of the ultimate American classics was Duesenberg. Fred Duesenberg, originally a bicycle maker, produced his first car in Indianapolis in 1904: the Mason. With his brother, August, he made race-car engines for the Mason until 1912. Then, in 1913, the brothers went into the car business for themselves. A Duesenberg won the French Grand Prix in 1921, using a straight-eight engine that had a little of Ettore Bugatti's thinking in it. The year before, the first of the Duesenberg passenger cars had appeared. Called the Model A, it was advanced, expensive, and luxurious. It used the straight-eight engine, much influenced by racing practice, but with only two valves per cylinder. It was America's first production car with hydraulic four-wheel brakes (so much mistrusted by one of its overseas drivers that he detached the front brake mechanism for racing). By 1926, the Model A had been transformed into the Model X, but by then Cord had insinuated himself into the company, and he was as anxious as the Duesenbergs for an entirely new, spectacular car to be designed and built.

The result was the Model J. It was more than anyone had anticipated. The J was powered by a four-valve engine with twin overhead cams that put out 265 hp and propelled the car at 116 mph on the Indianapolis Speedway. In an era when most radiators were flat, the V shape of the 1929 car was a sensation. It was so large, and with such important goals of performance, that much of the J was made of aluminum to keep the weight down.

1931 Duesenberg "Torpedo"
Although most Duesenbergs used special coachwork done in the U.S., some were done by overseas designers. This semi-fastback was bodied by the Swiss firm of Graber.

Murphy of Pasadena built 125 special bodies for the Model J, a great many of them roadsters. In 1932, Duesenberg added a supercharger and claimed 320 hp for the Model SJ. The bearings, reciprocating parts, and valve springs were strengthened to cope with the added power, particularly since the smallest J body possible was frequently used with the supercharged engine, offering the temptation to stress the engine to its limits by driving the car impossibly fast. There is no question that the Duesenberg had a split personality. It had a pure, if detuned, racing engine. Yet its appointments and coachwork were often far more suitable to docile town use than to high-speed road work. It roared and it vibrated, surely offending both the ears and the sensitive seats of its aristocratic owners. Somehow, nobody could quite get used to a high-performance classic (although Bugatti did not have the same trouble in France). It has been called an anachronism—even a paradox—a car with brutal strength sold to a market that preferred the delicate and refined. Still, modernists have been kinder than the Duesenberg's contemporary critics. A particularly rare car of the marque cost as much as $500,000 in 1982, and properly so.

It was all over for Auburn-Cord-Duesenberg by 1936, the same year that GM recognized the United Auto Workers and Henry Ford declared militantly that he would never give the UAW or any other union recognition. The next year, E.L. Cord, who had moved to England in the face of threats to kidnap his children, returned and sold his interests in the company. He died in Reno, Nevada, in January 1974 at the age of 76, a man who had brought the United States some of its genuinely remarkable cars.

Echoes of Greatness

We saw a revival of the coachbuilder's art in Italy after World War II, and, of course, in England the specialist builder survives to create the carriages of royalty. But they are parts of larger entities, Rolls-Royce swallowed up the makers of its special bodies long ago. Recently, we have been witnessing a new phenomenon: constructors converting production cars such as the Cadillac Seville into cars with some of the cosmetic features of the classics—outside-mounted spare wheels, trunks that look like trunks, wire wheels, opera windows. Some of these Cadillacs and Lincolns are handsome enough, although most have so many detail changes that the inherent shape of the car is lost.

Successful firms modifying existing bodies are profitable primarily because of the limousines they build on stretched platforms; their quasi-classics are a sideline. But this is not true of a group of specialist constructors called Replicar builders.

These builders attempt to duplicate the great cars of the 1920s and 1930s, using contemporary parts. The oldest and best funded of this group is Excalibur of Milwaukee, founded by Brooks Stevens, an industrial designer. From its beginnings as a sports/racing car company in 1951, Excalibur has tried to faithfully impart a sense of elegance rather than to copy the details of its exemplar, the 1936 Mercedes-Benz roadster. It has been successful because its workmanship is exact, its materials good, and Stevens' sons have continued to be committed to building a cohesive car rather than an image superimposed on somebody else's design. Others, particularly Panther Westwinds of England (now undergoing financial agonies) and Sbarro of Switzerland, as well as Cumberford of the United States, build cars every bit the equal of Excalibur. Sadly, the shortage of real classics has prompted many buyers to seek badly done reiterations of Auburns and Stutzes and Duesenbergs made by companies that are usually underfinanced and exist only very briefly.

Still, for the lucky few, there remain some great classics, restored to their original condition to be seen and even to be driven.

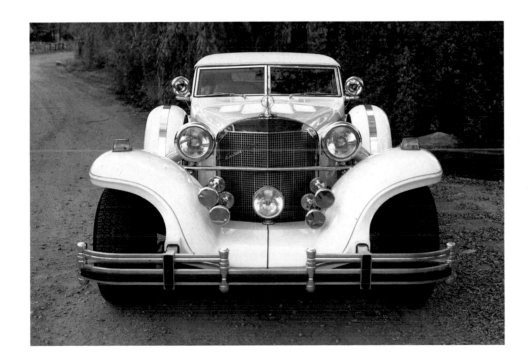

1980 Excalibur
Milwaukee industrial designer Brooks Stevens took inspiration for the first of the important American "replicars" in the early 1950's from the great Mercedes sports cars of the late 1930's. Excalibur began as a race car and evolved into a highly civilized street sports tourer based on Chevrolet components. The company, now joined by platoons of replicar builders, is one of the few reputable firms making cars whose styling hearkens to the classics.

217

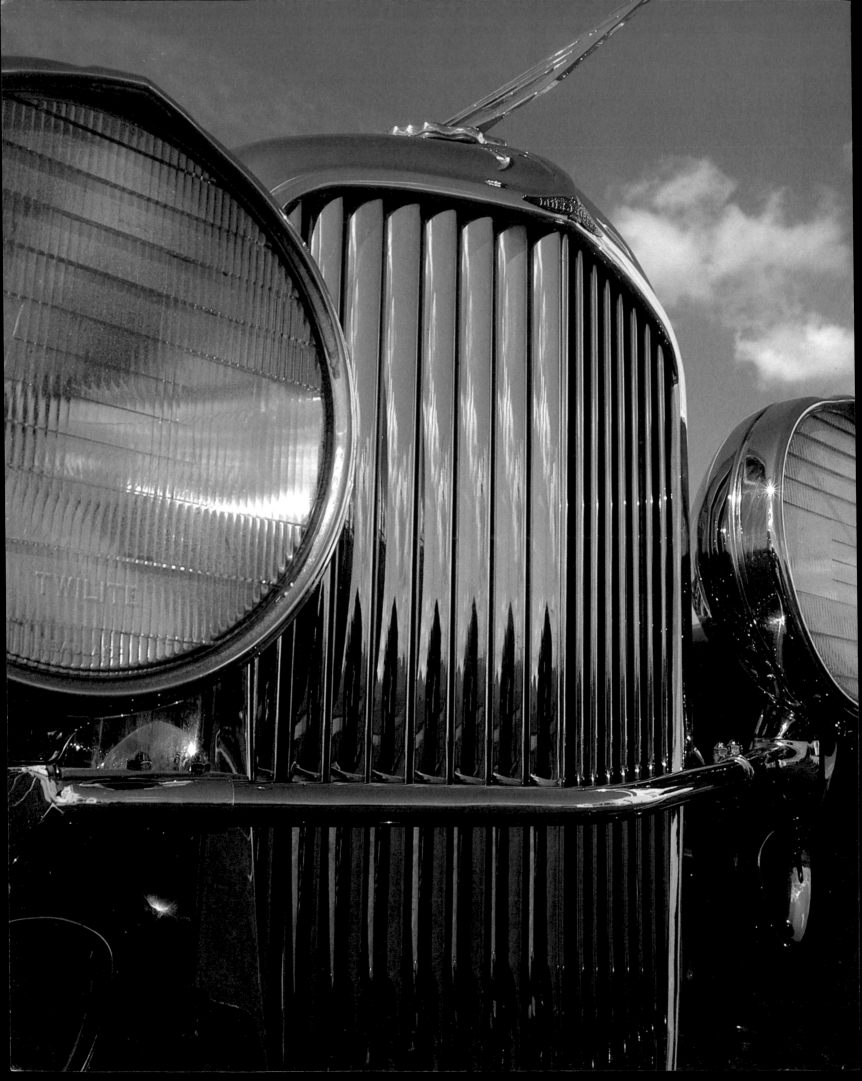

CHAPTER 11

She's a Duesy

"It was a rich cream color, bright with nickel, swollen here and there in its monstrous length with triumphant hat-boxes and supper boxes and tool-boxes, and terraced with a labyrinth of windshields that mirrored a dozen suns." It was Gatsby's car. And F. Scott Fitzgerald's description of a Murphy-bodied Dual Cowl Duesenberg SJ Phaeton is the best ever written.

Gatsby was a prototypical Duesenberg owner—perhaps a bit better bred than many, but since the book was published in 1925 and the SJ did not appear for six years, it's likely that the description is of generic automotive glitter—a description that turned out to be an accurate prediction of the future. First there was the J, which appeared in December 1928 at the New York Salon, "a natural place for such a revelation," said a contemporary commentator. "[The car is] for people of long-established culture and wealth, possessing the inevitable good taste which accompanies these . . . characteristics and the inclination to cater to them."

New York Mayor Jimmy Walker would own one. So would William Randolph Hearst, Howard Hughes, Tommy Manville, Mae West, Joe E. Brown, and King Alphonso XIII of Spain and King Victor Emmanuel of Italy. But it is misleading to cite Debrett's or Louella Parsons to convey a sense of the community of Duesenberg owners. No, it was far more likely that of the 530 cars of the J and the SJ series that Duesenberg built, the typical owner would be a member of heartland aristocracy.

There, then, on a balmy spring afternoon in 1929 in Chicago, would sit a Dual Cowl Phaeton J, a monster of a car. It was an uneasy time on the South Side, for most people were sliding toward the trough of our Great Depression or were already in it. The owner of the car could be aware of surrounding misery, but it would have barely touched him. In fact, the Dual Cowl might have been parked in front of the Chicago Yacht Club members' lounge, its owner inside watching the fancy launch summoned to pick him up and take him to his 165-foot yacht out by the breakwater.

He was, obviously, a man of wealth—a manufacturing heir or a department store magnate, for example. During the summer he lived aboard ship (crew of fifteen), taking an occasional cruise into Lake Michigan to avoid the city's heat. In the winter, he lived along Lake Shore Drive. He was deeply involved in living the life of what was then called a "wealthy sportsman" (Tommy Manville, of the Johns-Manville asbestos family, was constantly referred to in tabloids as "the oft-married sportsman"), which meant he kept a string of ponies at the Oak Brook Polo Club or he shot skeet from the stern of his yacht.

And he drove a Duesenberg. Nothing else would do. Anything else built in America was a lesser car; anything he could buy from an overseas manufacturer—with the exception perhaps of Bugatti—was effete. Duesenberg was

1929 Duesenberg Dual Cowl Phaeton Model J/SJ
The Duesenberg was a very special American aristocrat: a car valued both for its high performance and its luxuriousness. In this sense, it has been called a paradox. This particular model sits at the head of the Duesenberg table. It began as a J and then went back to the factory for an update to SJ specifications three years later. This example has been the centerpiece of two great American collections and was used in the film *Annie*.

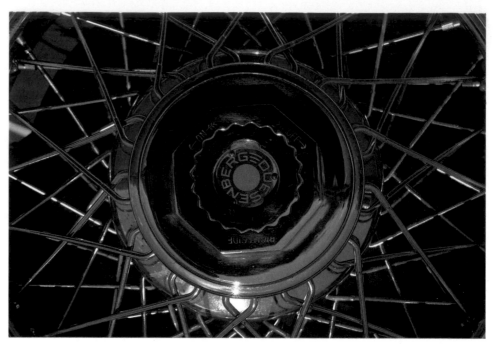

everything that proclaimed such a man's persona. It was big. It was expensive. It was flamboyant. It was tough and fast and brutal—refined in the tradition of racing cars rather than cars created for comfort, silence, and ease of driving on the street. There were Duesenbergs with fixed tops, but not many. Murphy of Pasadena made almost half the bodies for both the J and SJ series, and 150 of them were roadsters or phaetons. Moreover, a sedan, or town car, would have been bought against the advice of the owner's chauffeur, for it was almost a roughneck in the delicate company of the soft and silent Rolls-Royces, DuPonts, Packards, and Minervas that whispered through the midwestern summer darkness to the opera or the theater.

It was that difference—the elegant roughneck quality—that made Duesenberg so desirable to the yacht owner. From enormous, chromed, V-shaped grille to the four outside exhausts coiling downward on the right side of the hood and gleaming in the same chrome, to mahogany running boards, with three chrome strips, to raked chrome-bordered windshield in front of the driver and a second windshield for the rear passengers, the car was an expensively tailored athlete.

No Duesenberg came straight off the rack; there simply was no such thing as a complete car to buy. The customer went to his agent, who showed him a book of specially designed coachwork from the finest craftsmen of the age. These original designs came first from Duesenberg, whose people had gone to the coachbuilders specifying body styles and suggesting lines and shapes. The customer might choose a Murphy roadster (the least expensive of the cars in 1929), to which he would add a few personal touches. Or he might want a car done by Bohman & Schwartz, Judkins, Rollston, Holbrook, or Brunn.

These were years during which the art of coachbuilding flourished, a last brilliant display of craftsmanship from a dying trade. The Willoughbys and Dietrichs, Le Barons and Weymanns were glad to get a Duesenberg commission, not only because of the business but because it was a lovely chassis on which to create a body. It was long, low, and rigid, the ideal combination. The order might come in from Chicago, but it would go straight to the body design department of

Duesenberg, which was not at all anxious to have just any pile of metal haphazardly placed upon its car. "These styles, as shown in the first J catalogue," said a profile of the car written in England by T. R. Nicholson, "comprised a Phaeton, an All-Weather Cabriolet, a Five-Passenger Sedan, Seven-Passenger Sedan, Enclosed Drive Sedan, Convertible Sedan and Convertible Roadster. The first one and the last two were the most popular. . . . the 1932 catalogue listed no fewer than 18 models by Derham, La Grande, Le Baron, Rollston, Murphy, Willoughby and Judkins."

In 1932, prices in the Duesenberg catalogue ranged from $13,500 to $17,500. A very special car cost one customer $25,000, but that was the top price (legend has the cars priced far higher). This was inexpensive compared to European special coachwork cars, but it was a very high price in the United States. The bodies represented about a third of the cost. In the 1932 catalogue, the Murphy roadster body was $4,000.

The Murphy Dual Cowl was usually built on the longer of the two available chassis, the almost 13-footer (a foot longer than the smaller one). It dazzled with its size, the brilliance of its paint scheme, often in vivid two-tones of blue or of green, the massiveness of its engine.

Its engine came straight from the race track. In fact, every Duesenberg was tested at Indianapolis in chassis form before delivery for top-end performance (116 mph in the J). This was a Lycoming-built straight eight of 420 cubic inches (6,882 cc) with twin overhead camshafts operating four overhead valves per cylinder, two intake and two exhaust. The hemispherical combustion chambers were machined. The enormous heat-treated chrome-nickel crankshaft, which weighed about 150 pounds, was carried in five bearings and was balanced. It was pure race car: huge, powerful, magnificently designed, brilliantly executed, exhaustively refined. So refined, in fact, that given the brute nature of the engine, the crankshaft was damped by a pair of copper-lined cartridges filled with mercury, one on each side between the first two cylinders, in order to minimize torsional vibration.

The engine would turn up 4,250 rpm. This was a good thing too, for overhead cam engines are at their most efficient at high rpm. That high speed performance was the characteristic of the Duesenberg, again despite legend, which had the car a powerhouse all through its performance range. Today, we think of a car with such a huge engine as being able to rocket away from a stop, spinning its rear wheels with a great surge of power. That was not the Ducsenberg's style. It was a top end car. You drove sedately away in first—the three-speed shifter was on the floor—pushed the long, knobbed lever up, over, and up again into second (it almost touched the dash in that position), and then brought it straight down into third.

In 1932, our yacht owner would have taken his Murphy Dual Cowl back to the factory for conversion from J to SJ, which meant adding a supercharger, an even larger crankshaft, tubular steel connecting rods (the originals were aluminum), and stronger valve springs. Now the car would make 320 hp (the engine in the J had made history with its 265 hp), and if its driver wished, he could tromp the throttle in high at 60 mph and spin the rear wheels. That is where the power really came on. Up there in the 70 to 100 mph ranges, the supercharger gave off a constant whirr, turning 20,000 rpm at top speed—110 mph? 120 mph?—and the car was happiest. The driver too. For the SJ Phaeton weighed about 5,250 pounds and it tracked magnificently. What's more, the final drive

ratio (3.78:1) was designed for high speed instead of quick acceleration. Higher numerical ratios, which were available, were meant to overcome the reluctant acceleration habits of the car, but they lowered the fuel efficiency from 10 to perhaps 8 mpg.

These were the moments when the car was at its best—flat out on the road to Woodstock or Springfield, bullying a two-lane macadam, high-crowned pathway. Inside, the driver was being fed a torrent of information, much of it completely useless on an average trip. An altimeter told him his height above sea level. Other devices told him the water temperature, number of engine revolutions per minute, fuel level, time (to the second—the car came with an eight-day clock complete with full sweep second hand), speed (the speedometer, reading up to 150 mph, was in a rolling number design, a bubble of glass just large enough to accommodate three digits), barometric pressure, and brake pressure. He also had lights, but not the "idiot" lights that would be used in sixties cars, to tell the driver the engine had just run out of oil or was boiling over. No, in the Duesenberg, a light went on at 75 miles to indicate that a chassis lubrication pump was at work replenishing all the lube points on the car. (Curiously, this light flashed red when the lubrication pump was working and green when the pump system itself needed refilling.) Another light winked every 700 miles to tell the driver to change the oil in the engine. At 1,400 miles, on would come yet another light to indicate that the battery water level needed to be checked.

When the driver wanted to come to a stop, the Duesenberg would show off again; it was the beneficiary of the first production hydraulic brake system used on an American automobile. Hydraulic brakes were first fitted to the Duesenberg that won the French Grand Prix in 1921 —the first American Grand Prix winner.

There were brakes on all four wheels and they were servo assisted; today we would call them power brakes.

Contemporary magazine driving tests called the J and the SJ "light and easy to handle." While the car did have synchromesh transmission on second and third gears, and surely by comparison with any other cars of its day it was easy to drive—particularly at high speeds—it was not light and easy to handle. In fact, today's driver would be likely to call it a truck. The cockpit was hard to maneuver in; it was small on the Phaeton, barely two-people wide. The wheel was large, but with a surprisingly narrow rim, the shifter intrusive, and the car generally a handful. It steered hard, no arguing with that. It shifted easily on the way up, but despite the synchro, the Duesenberg driver had to double-clutch on the way back down.

"With the exception of the Type 41 Bugatti Royale [the largest car ever built] . . . it [the Duesenberg] combined the technical characteristics and the performance of a racing car with the smoothness, if not the silence of the most sophisticated luxury car. For this very reason it attracted the enthusiastic owner driver." The driver would not have wanted a mere slip of a thing anyway and didn't at all mind the hard mouth of the Duesenberg. In fact, he probably loved it, for it was a skill to take a Duesy to its limits.

Entire production of the two models of our most glorious car lasted less than a decade. They were last shown in 1936, after which E. L. Cord, who owned the company, shut down production. Since then, there have been efforts to revive Duesenberg, the last of them producing a plastic replica SJ based on a contemporary Ford sedan, complete with power steering, cruise control, and air conditioning. One such device was sold for $101,000 at an auction in a gaudy Nevada hotel in 1981.

The magic of the Duesenberg name is with us still.

V
POSTWAR CARS
1948–the Present

CHAPTER 12

Postwar Prosperity

In 1917, the Lelands and their Detroit confreres had had to beg Washington to recognize the automobile industry as a war resource. In 1941, Detroit was the first place the federal government turned. The building of passenger cars was halted entirely. Every manufacturer converted completely to the production of war materiel. By the war's end, Chrysler Corporation alone had made these parts, pieces, bits, and wholes: 25,000 tanks, 18,000 Wright B-29 engines, 60,000 Bofors guns, 5,000 B-29 fuselage assemblies, 29,000 marine engines, 10,000 Corsair landing gears, 30,000 fire pumpers, 300,000 rockets, 360,000 bomb shackles, 12 million Duraluminum forgings, 435,000 Army trucks (the famous Dodge 6 x 6s), 12,000 tank engines, 5,500 Curtiss Helldiver center wing sections, 2,000 radar antenna mounts, 5,500 Sperry Gyro compasses, 3 billion rounds of small-arms ammunition, 100 miles of antisubmarine netting, and 1,586 searchlight reflectors.

Tracing the increase in the federal budget from the onset of the Depression to the middle of World War II is a good way to understand how much money was being poured into Detroit and the automobile industry so it could produce war materiel. There is no understanding postwar overproduction of passenger cars and the resultant abuse of Sloanist sales methods and the notion of annual model change without an appreciation of just how large Detroit became during its period of war-induced nourishment.

During the early Roosevelt years, annual federal budgets were $8 to $9 billion. In fiscal 1942, the federal budget rose to $34 billion (five times the peak during World War I); in 1943, it was $79 billion; and the year after, it rose to $95 billion.

A great deal of this government spending made Detroit fat. But the auto industry was more than just enlarged. "The miseries of the Great Depression had obscured a striking fact," said historian Frederick Lewis Allen. "Under the spur of necessity American industry had gained sharply in efficiency during the nineteen thirties."

Just how sharply? The first two decades of the twentieth century had seen productivity increases of 12 percent and 7.5 percent, respectively. From 1920 to 1930, productivity rose 21 percent, and in the Depression decade, it went up 41 percent, "But always the brakes had been on," Allen points out. "Now with the coming of war, the brakes were removed." By the end of the war, the GNP (even taking inflation into account) had risen a real two-thirds over the 1939 figure, from $91 billion to $215 billion.

These numbers represented dramatic drops in unemployment, unprecedented prosperity for social segments previously excluded from sharing the consumerist dream, and (as in the first war) a huge leap forward in all kinds of technology, much of it readily convertible to peacetime use. These and other side effects of World War II would mean much to the postwar auto industry.

1943 Jeep Model MT-TUG
At the very least, the most famous vehicle in the world and the basis for a number of similar types including Britain's Land Rover, the jeep was built by both Willys-Overland and Ford during World War II to a design based on a 4 × 4 Bantam.

The first was rationing. In 1942 (the year in which the last new car had been built), the government rationed tires and gasoline. Sugar made the list in the spring. Shoes were added next, then meat, followed by cheese, flour, fish, and canned goods. A good deal of this was more appearance than substance. Many rations were more than ample, and Americans were by far the best-fed people on earth. Gas was a problem; the 35 mph wartime speed limit was an unpleasant reminder of it. And as long as rationing was official and noticeable (rationing stamps were issued), people felt deprived; at the very least they felt they were making sacrifices and looked forward to having the freedom *to buy* when the war was over.

Second, the conversion of consumer industry to the making of war materiel reduced unemployment (down two-thirds from the 1939 figure) and put money in more pockets than ever before, creating further pent-up demand for postwar consumables. At war's end, "the farmer bought a new tractor, a corn picker, an electric milking machine. . . . the farmer's wife got the shining electric white refrigerator she had always longed for . . . an up-to-date washing machine, and a deep-freeze unit. The suburban family installed a dishwashing machine and invested in a power lawnmower. The city family became customers of a laundromat and acquired a television set for the living room. The husband's office was air-conditioned. And so on endlessly," said Allen. The *real* focus on this acquisitiveness, as we shall see, was the automobile. But first let's mention some further influences of the war that affected the industry in its efforts to produce those automobiles.

The enormous increase in the number of employed, their extraordinary wages, and their feeling of importance (now that wartime restrictions on the degree to which they were allowed to combat management were lifted) resulted in a postwar labor force that felt its oats and would embark on a long series of strikes—several of the earliest and nastiest against the auto industry.

Overseas service by hordes of men and women, who previously had never been beyond the boundaries of their home towns, introduced an interest in other cultures, other values, other peoples. Some of this interest led to understanding, but even if some of it was *not* understanding but contempt or anger, those feelings too would be influential. Beginning in 1947, the first sports cars from England landed in New York and San Francisco and were snapped up by the vanguard of an enormous number of foreign car buyers, eventually depriving Detroit of almost a third of its home market. This broadening of horizons—particularly of hardware horizons—would turn the American market almost upside down by the 1980s.

All Those Toys

Great upheavals reshaped American social topography after World War II. We had discovered suburbia almost at the same moment that we discovered the car. Said Ernest Kohlmetz in *The Study of American History* about our lemminglike rush to the suburbs: After World War II, "construction boomed because the car and the road redistributed the population to the suburbs and countryside, where housing developments, shopping plazas, consolidated schools, hospitals, churches, factories and high-rise office buildings sprang up on former farm and woodland."

In 1947, we got the housing development when Levittown, Pennsylvania, brainchild of Abraham Levitt and his sons (who had learned the mass-housing

business from building navy quarters during the war), set the pattern for the housing tract. Eventually, the Levitts built 17,000 more houses in Pennsylvania and 12,000 in New York, all of them using precut materials that were plopped down on concrete slabs.

The next year saw the birth of McDonald's, a hamburger manufacturer that would spread its "golden arches" from sea to shining sea as a result of the marketing genius of Ray Kroc; and Baskin-Robbins, the Praline/Huckleberry Finn/Chocolate Divinity ice cream franchise—both of them, naturally, in California.

In 1952, Howard Johnson opened his 351st restaurant. The first Holiday Inn sprouted up, and was franchised by Kemmons Wilson two years later. While Wilson was at work with his Holiday Inns, Victor Gruen Associates began the "Malling of America," with Northland Shopping Center in Detroit. Northland comprised more than a hundred stores, including J. L. Hudson, named after the man who had invested in one of the devices that made suburbia possible. In 1955, we got Kentucky Fried Chicken, and the year after that, Midas Muffler opened its first shop in Macon, Georgia. Truly, the sleazing of the nation was gathering irresistible momentum.

Levittown, McDonald's, Baskin-Robbins, shopping centers, muffler shops, Kentucky Fried Chicken—indeed, the whole franchise phenomenon—not only depended on the automobile and the highway, but they also saw their work force become a labor statistic labeled "auto-related." Henry Ford put us on wheels just before and immediately after World War I; Abraham Levitt, Colonel Harlan

ABOVE LEFT:
1942 Packard "180"
Although Packard had sold its name and reputation in 1935 by introducing the low-priced 120, it continued to build some extraordinary cars. This is one of the last, a sporty roadster with cut-down doors styled by Howard Darrin.

ABOVE RIGHT:
1947 Packard Clipper
Packard's postwar Clipper was a clean, handsome car, but it was indicative of the company's determination to penetrate the middle price range. Ultimately, the marketing plan was disastrous, and one of the great names in American auto manufacturing disappeared.

Sanders, Ray Kroc, Howard Johnson, Kemmons Wilson, and others lashed us to those wheels in the wake of World War II.

So we moved to the suburbs, those of us who could afford it (and the government was doing all it could to make suburban housing affordable to veterans, with guaranteed low-interest housing loans). And when we got there, we multiplied. We created a baby boom, which produced a huge new age cohort, car dependent, and—as its members grew into adolescence—car sophisticated and car addicted. The birth rate had been about 18 per 1,000 in the thirties. It was 23.3 in 1946 and 25.8 in 1947. All those future consumers! And couples could afford such family expansion because of the new prosperity. Remember the dreadful income figures of the Depression. Now after-tax wages (as of 1949) averaged $3,000 for a steelworker, $8,000 for a car salesman, and $10,000 for a dentist—at a time when gas was 25 cents a gallon, Coke cost a nickel, a loaf of bread was 15 cents, and a shiny new Cadillac $5,000.

Soon the baby boom would produce an unprecedented demand for education, but before the young would have to face the first grade, their fathers were going to college. Many of them had never dreamed of being able to go, but now they had the G.I. Bill, enacted by Congress in 1944, to pay their way. From 1950 to 1960 college attendance rose from 3 million to 10 million.

Prosperity, education, and migration brought a coalescing of classes in America, and not only in the suburbs. "Millions of families in our industrial cities and towns, and on the farms, [were] lifted from poverty or near-poverty to . . . middle-class [status]," said Allen. There were "decent clothes for all, an opportunity to buy a better automobile, . . . go to the dentist, pay insurance premiums." There was also something else promoting this coalescing, thought Allen. He saw a process of "Americanization" occurring in the children and grandchildren of earlier immigrants. "The sons and daughters of the immigrants had resolutely acquired American customs and manners; the third generation who possessed [English-speaking parents] were as American as Mayflower descendants." As delightful evidence of this Americanization, Allen cited the 1950 Yankee World Series first-game lineup: Woodling, Rizzuto, Berra, DiMaggio, Mize, Brown, Bauer, Coleman, and Raschi.

That was only the beginning. We were about to see two more dynamics that would blur class lines even further. The first was the rise of the expense-account class. Tens of thousands of middle-management employees who ordinarily could not have afforded once-a-week theater and twice-a-week dinner out suddenly found themselves living an almost Rockefellerian life. We can blame it on Ralph Schneider in part. In 1950, he started the Diner's Club, which permitted average Americans to rent cars, buy clothes, eat out, book hotel rooms—all on credit.

More important still in the homogenization of the country was the beginning of the communications revolution. In 1945, 5,000 homes in the United States had television sets. Two years later, Bell Telephone Labs developed the transistor, which would allow miniaturization of not only television but everything else electronic (leading to a stunning change in auto technology thirty years later). By 1948, a million homes had TVs, and Earl "Madman" Muntz was selling 4,500 sets a weekend in Los Angeles. Not long after, he brought his blitzkrieg sales techniques to the merchandising of Kaiser and Frazer cars. Then he built an automobile in his own image called the Muntz Jet.

In 1947, America got its first phototypesetter, allowing entrepreneurs with minimal capital to go into the magazine and newspaper businesses. At the same time, AT&T's stranglehold on telephonic communication was shaken when the Department of Justice accused it of monopolizing manufacture. It was a long, hard fight, but it ended with competitive telephone companies charging lower rates and building their own equipment. In 1950, Haloid Company produced the first Xerox copier, and the first Japanese tape recorder came out of Sony's shops in the image of an American model its maker had seen three years earlier.

This was bright-side America after World War II. There were also shadows.

Strife And Insularity

Two groups in America had to fight their way into the new prosperity—labor and blacks. Labor had the easier struggle. For blacks to become a part of the great middle class was a longer struggle, tougher by far and still not over.

Said Robert Kelley in *The Shaping of the American Past* about the causes of labor's fight: "In the Spring of 1946, wartime price control legislation was allowed to lapse, and the cost of food and other necessities rose with breathtaking suddenness. All the raises that labor had won were cancelled out in a brief few weeks, while corporate profits boomed upward to their highest point in history—and more strikes began."

During that year, 4.6 million Americans walked picket lines. More than a quarter million went out at General Electric, Westinghouse, and General Motors in January 1946. About the same number in the same month struck the meat-packing industry, and three-quarters of a million walked away from the steel industry. In the spring, President Harry Truman ordered troops to take over the railroads; a brief strike followed, and then Truman thought better of his hard-line response and recommended and got wage boosts for railroad workers. More troops were sent into the soft-coal mines not five days after others were riding the rails, ending a strike called by John L. Lewis on April Fool's Day. Despite his apparent opposition to labor and its strikes, Truman vetoed the Taft-Hartley Act—which passed despite his veto—in 1947. The act was a defeat for labor. It outlawed the closed shop, led to the passage of right-to-work laws in a number of states, prohibited the use of union funds for campaigning, set up an eighty-day cooling-off period before a strike could begin, and, worst of all for the unionists,

1951 Muntz Two-Door Hardtop
When TV supersalesman "Mad Man" Muntz started building cars just after World War II, he had Kurtis-Kraft (of Indianapolis race-car fame) build the body, and at first used Cadillac engines in a car he called the Jet. After production of the twenty-eighth vehicle, the company moved to Illinois and switched to Lincoln engines.

gave government the right to enjoin labor in cases of strikes that might "imperil the national health or safety." By the late 1940s, "the public was angry at the unions. The national economy staggered along from day to day through a seemingly endless series of crises," said Kelley.

One key consequence of the labor movement for the auto industry was a 1948 settlement between Walter Reuther of the United Auto Workers and GM's president, "Engine Charlie" Wilson, establishing the principle of automatic cost-of-living pay raises tied to the consumer price index. The next year, GM workers accepted a small wage cut when the cost of living went down.

Then the government took over control of the railroads again, not to relinquish it until twenty-one months later, at just about the same time (spring 1952) that Truman ordered federal seizure of the steel mills. That set off a firestorm. The steel companies went to court, and the seizure was ruled illegal. Immediately, 600,000 CIO steelworkers left their jobs and didn't return for fifty-three days. Truman's steel order was the high-water mark of federal intervention; his bloody defeat marks the beginnings of its retreat.

In 1953 came a second auto-labor landmark. "The UAW began another campaign with crucial implications," said Kelley. "A demand for a guaranteed annual wage. The first national response was the traditional one: the notion was rejected as absurd. . . . Finally, Ford agreed to such a contract, which quickly became standard in similar industries." That about did it for the great period of labor turmoil. Although the phrase *guaranteed annual wage* was not descriptive of the fact, the contracts were good enough—six months' pay for the qualified unemployed at about two-thirds of their regular wage. According to Kelley, "These measures eased the buildup of annual pressures within the economy for wage increases. . . . the vast turbulence of the late 1940s, when millions of workers struck for long periods, died away."

Labor had not achieved all of its goals, but its progress had been enormous, enough so that union members felt a part of the American mainstream.

This was not the case with blacks. A series of battles and court decisions from the abolition of unfair employment practices (1941) to the right to vote (1944) to the beginning of an end to restrictive covenants in real property sale (1948) to the 1954 Supreme Court case of *Brown* v. *Board of Education,* putting a stop to the sham of "separate but equal" schooling, was placing the federal government's strength behind what was becoming known as the Civil Rights Movement. There were agonies to come, worse even than the Detroit race riots of 1943, but at least federal troops would not be sent in on the side of the repressive forces as they had been in Detroit.

The battle for equality affected the Detroit auto industry profoundly. A black migration north that had begun before the war revealed northern cities to be less tolerant than the South had been, and working conditions—in the auto industry specifically—not much better. Successful battles by blacks against northern discrimination fueled white migration to the suburbs, polarized attitudes in midwestern states, and exacerbated racial frictions. Many industry managers pointed to the influx of blacks into auto manufacturing as one factor encouraging the militancy of the UAW locals. Others, even more willing to shift the blame from themselves for the decreasing quality of domestic cars, accused black assembly-line workers of being undependable and uncaring about their work.

There were riots in the sixties, particularly in Detroit, where the inner city was all but burned out. White executives, hidden away in Bloomfield Hills or Grosse Pointe, saw only the shells of buildings on their drives to work on Jefferson Avenue (just down from the Solidarity House headquarters of the UAW) or

Highland Park. This insulation from the real world was part of the pervasive provincialism of the white executives. Detroit the Industry had become paralyzingly insular, and this showed in their products. Said automotive journalist Maurice Garapedian: "These people simply have no idea of what it means to own one of their own company's cars. They get free cars every six months and then their executive garages fix them for nothing if something goes wrong and even wash them every day. They talk only to each other; their wives speak only to wives of other Detroit executives. They meet in the locker room of the Lochmoor Country Club or over cocktails at the Detroit Yacht Club. Provincial? What else could you expect?" By the mid-seventies, only one Detroit senior manager lived in the city of Detroit; every one of the others drove in and out of town on the freeway.

Roads, Roads, And More Roads

The *freeway*. By the beginning of the last quarter of the twentieth century, this had become the generic term for an immense system of interstate highways blessed and funded by a nation totally committed to the automobile.

"The Interstate Highway Act of 1956," said historian James J. Flink, "was the most ambitious public works program undertaken in our history. It committed the federal government to pay from a Highway Trust Fund 90% of the construction costs for 41,000 miles of toll-free express highways to be completed by June 30, 1976.

"Between 1947 and 1970 the combined highway expenditures by local, state and federal governments in the U.S. totaled $249 billion. . . . [In 1973] the timetable for completion was extended to 1979."

State and federal governments have a long history of financing road building. The Federal Aid Road Act of 1916 had appropriated $75 million. Further congressional action in 1921 required the states to contribute to the cost of roads. But only in 1944 did an enormous appropriation come: $500 million a year for three years under the Interstate and Defense Highway Act, extended for two years in 1948 (the amount was cut by $50 million during this extension). What had we received for all that money?

In 1968, a Special House Subcommittee of the Committee on Public Works, assigned to look into highway safety, design, and operations, peered into what Congress and the American people had wrought and came to some unpleasant conclusions.

"Who could believe it," the subcommittee asked, "that millions of dollars' worth of guardrail has been incorrectly installed along the nation's highways, some of it actually endangering rather than protecting life?

"Or the clearance distances marked on overpasses are so unreliable that some trucking firms make their own measurements and publish their own guide for drivers?

"That a maintenance crew assigned to remove a hazardous roadside tree would cut it off so high as to leave an equally hazardous stump?

"That a commonly used minimum standard for lettering on road signs is so small that 20 percent of the driving population can't read the message?"

There were further indictments, but they obscure two facts. The first is that the acts of 1944 through 1948 and 1956 that put a topper on our road-building appropriations achieved what they set out to do. We have a system of highways that is a marvel. They enhanced auto-mobility by orders of magnitude. They encouraged Detroit to build land cruisers. They afforded the average American

family a way of vacationing with the car, at a cost well below that of any other means of transportation. They prompted B. Bruce-Briggs, the last great auto advocate, to call our privately owned automobile and publicly built highway the most effective mass transit system in the world. They caused the more sentimental Garapedian to say: "The builders of those roads succeeded too well. Traversing their endless spans, the traveler loses the sense of the richness of the country . . . blanked away by the Stuckey signs, the Howard Johnson's, the rest stops, the Holiday Inns, the Shell Islands that occur and reoccur with numbing regularity as the miles spin out. The Interstates have homogenized the landscape. There is no Ohio as distinct from Indiana as distinct from Pennsylvania. The fine, rich mixture of America is turned into a pale broth."

That may be valid criticism, but it was not the storm center when the Interstate Highway Act of 1956 was passed, nor when the auto critics of later years really began to kick up dust. No, the storm center was the Act's establishment of the Highway Trust Fund. Money was appropriated for *roads,* their building and their maintenance. But while we were constructing highways and manufacturing cars to cruise along them, we were also creating a class of people denied the use of both. These were the so-called transit-dependent, the old and poor, the young and deprived. But the Trust Fund was sacrosanct. It could not be invaded for conventional mass transit funds until it was amended in the mid-1970s.

Nor did environmentalists approve. Said *The Nation* in 1965, junkyards, secondhand car lots, service stations, "hideous 'automobile rows,'" drive-in movies, neon-lit hamburger joints all contributed to a war waged by "a good

photo by Joseph Kugielsky

many communities" against the highways. "The spirit of revolution is growing and it is evident that uncontrolled highway construction will not much longer be feasible." Three years later, the *Saturday Evening Post* added complaints: "We are taxed brutally to build the highways that disperse us from one dull suburb to another equally dull suburb, but we suffer shamefully from over-burdened schools, inadequate police, overcrowded recreation areas, poorly staffed hospitals and ill-supported libraries." The critic was Lewis Mumford, planner, visionary, philosopher, and long-time adversary of the automobile.

He might better have spent his energies fuming at another target, for by the time he wrote "Speaking of Autos," the managers of the industry were already undermining the long-time love affair between Americans and the automobiles Detroit was building.

CHAPTER 13

Detroit Closes Its Borders

While General Douglas MacArthur was standing at attention on the fantail of the U.S.S. *Missouri* in Tokyo Bay receiving the surrender of the Japanese in 1945, Americans were forming lines in front of automobile dealerships across the nation. All that deprivation, all those pent-up desires, all that postwar prosperity were somehow encapsulated in the need to own a new car.

In fact, there was nothing new about the cars that were sold after the war, but as the industry cranked up once again and cars trickled into dealerships, the retail establishment chose to behave in a way that would make its customers suspicious of its ethics forever. With far more buyers than cars, the dealer who put names on a list and delivered cars in order was the exception. Most sellers plunged into an orgy of greed. To get delivery of anything, buyers were told—not even asked —that they would have to bribe the seller. So-called under-the-table (there was nothing covert about it) payments were commonplace. Did a buyer who was fiftieth on the list for a Ford or a Cadillac or a Chrysler want the car within the month? All he had to do was pay the dealer from $100 to $500 in cash above the price of the car at the moment of order, and his name would suddenly go to the head of the list.

Lines had already formed in front of the nation's dealerships when Henry Ford II ("Deuce") drove the first postwar car produced by Ford Motor Company off the line on July 3, 1945. Ford began full production on July 6. A new company begun by Henry J. Kaiser, who had made his fortune in construction of dams and highways before the war and in shipbuilding during it, was announced July 26. By fall, production of civilian cars had begun at Chevrolet, Buick, Cadillac, Pontiac, Oldsmobile, Studebaker, Nash, Hudson, and Packard. On November 21, the UAW struck GM.

That was not only frustrating to General Motors and GM buyers, but it must have seemed particularly unfair to GM management. After all, the company had led the entire industry in what had truly been a staggering wartime output.

As we've discovered, the strike at GM was just the first of many walkouts and sitdowns that plagued the industry and confounded the waiting consumer. For GM, a strike became a familiar problem. Ford faced far more trouble than a mere strike.

Recall that Henry Ford the Original had allowed his company to fall into the hands of Charles Sorensen and Harry Bennett's gang of thugs and that any worthwhile executive had quit in disgust. Ford suffered a stroke in 1938, which affected him profoundly. Already slipping into senility, now he became virtually deranged. He allowed his son Edsel to become president of Ford Motor, but Edsel died of stomach cancer in May 1943. In the meantime, Franklin Roosevelt had named GM president William S. "Big Bill" Knudsen Commissioner for Industrial Production of the National Defense Commission. Ford, who, according to historian James J. Flink, was convinced that Roosevelt was "a warmonger con-

1953 Allstate and *1951 Henry J Two-Door Sedan Model 513*
The Henry J was an early attempt at an "ethical car," small enough to be used in urban traffic and to keep its owner from being accused of consuming conspicuously. The wheelbase was 100 inches, and the price was low at $1,363. Henry J. Kaiser tried to break the mold in another fashion, when he attempted direct-mail marketing with Sears Roebuck of a special version of the Henry J called the Allstate. Differing from the original only in trim, the Allstate was a sales disaster.

trolled by General Motors and the du Ponts and that United States involvement in World War II was part of a conspiracy to get control of his company," refused to allow war work to be done in any of his manufacturing facilities. It had taken great effort by Sorensen and Edsel to convince Ford that unless he changed his mind, a takeover of Ford Motor could become reality. In November 1940, the firm began production of Pratt and Whitney airplane engines. The next year Washington approved subsidies for the building of the Willow Run plant to make B-24 bombers, and naturally there was a considerable contingent of military overseers among the Willow Run staff. "Henry Ford feared that the military personnel at Willow Run were spies sent by Roosevelt to assassinate him and took to carrying an automatic pistol under the cowl of his car," said Flink.

It is no wonder, then, that Ford's reassumption of the company's presidency upon his son's death so appalled his family that his own wife and Edsel's widow threatened to sell their stock unless he turned the job over to his grandson, Henry II.

Deuce took over in September 1945. Flink described the legacy left by Ford: "The Ford Motor Company was losing about $10 million a month. The Ford Service Department [euphemism for Bennett's gestapo] had made fear and demoralization a way of life. . . . Few executives worth their salt were left. The company lacked both a program of research and development and college-trained engineers. Accounting was so primitive that at least one department estimated its costs by weighing the invoices. There was no coordination between purchasing, production and marketing."

Nevins and Hill, in the third volume, *Ford: Decline and Rebirth,* of their monumental work, went even further: "The company was not only dying, it was already dead and rigor mortis was setting in." But a benevolent eye was gazing down on Dearborn. Not sixty days after Henry II took over, a telegram arrived on his desk. "We have a matter of management importance to discuss with you," it read, and it was signed by Charles B. (Tex) Thornton, an Army Air Force officer who had been sent to Ford by the military to be sure things ran right with wartime production. He represented not only himself but a team of nine young men (mainly Harvard MBAs) who were looking for work. "Of the 10," *Car and Driver* said in a mid-seventies piece on the rescue of Ford, "Thornton, George Moore, Wilbur (Gene) Anderson, Charles E. Bosworth, J. E. Lundy, Robert S. McNamara, Arjay R. Miller, Ben Davis Mills, Francis C. Reith and James Wright (Moore the youngest at 26 and Wright the oldest at 34), six would become vice-presidents of Ford and two would be presidents of the company."

Not only did Henry Ford II agree to meet with them, he hired them all, and off they went sniffing and snooping to find out just how enormous a disaster area they had descended upon. In the meantime, Henry II knew perfectly well that he needed more than a group of bright young men (known later as the Whiz Kids). However energetic and diligent they might have been, they were not car folk. Somewhere, somehow he had to find a competent executive with an automotive background to be their leader and his chief deputy. He found his man at General Motors: Ernest R. Breech, former accountant for the Yellow Cab Manufacturing Company and after its merger with GM, that company's general assistant treasurer, president of its aeronautical division, and ultimately a GM vice president. Breech thus represented finance *and* product, the perfect combination. "I [had been] the cleanup man for GM," Breech said later about what he discovered when he arrived at Ford, "but this one was *really* a mess."

In his turn, Breech went hunting for a chief engineer, whom he discovered in an ex-Oldsmobile, then Borg-Warner, man named Harold T. Youngren.

It was 1946. Henry Ford's company had $685,034,892 in the bank; Henry's grandson was in the chief executive's office; Henry's grandson's uncle, Ernest C. Kanzler, who knew all about cars *and* the family, was there for Deuce to go to for advice; Breech was at the helm; Youngren was in the engine room; and the Whiz Kids were swarming everywhere. But there wasn't even a *current* car, just a rewarmed version of the 1942 model. It would all be made right, but only because of a crash program we will watch in the next chapter when we drive the model B-A. In the interim, how was the remainder of the industry faring?

Invaders Repelled

Studebaker, which had hired Raymond Loewy to style its cars, introduced its famous "coming or going" car in 1946. The car was much influenced by curious notions of streamlining (as aerodynamics was called) that had come from the great trains of the immediate prewar era. Shrink the Super Chief or the Twentieth Century Limited or the Hiawatha to one car-sized module and the result would look much like Loewy's slab-sided, wrap-around-rear-window, turret-topped, double-ender. The car offered a choice of 2.8-liter or 3.7-liter six-cylinder engine, both proven power units, and despite or because of its startling appearance—maybe simply as a consequence of the drought in automobiles—it was a sales success.

Almost everybody else was still selling reheated 1941s and 1942s, but there were exceptions. Crosley was one. Tucker and Kaiser-Frazer were two others.

Kaiser was an interesting case. Born in 1882, the son of a German immigrant shoemaker in western New York State, Henry J. Kaiser left school before

OVERLEAF:
1953 Studebaker
Studebaker Corporation could never have been faulted for failure of styling daring after World War II; its first effort had been the "coming or going car" which was eventually succeeded by this remarkably cohesive coupe. Later, the company added flash, glitter, and a supercharger—a mixed signal to people who found the '53 a pleasant and handsome tourer.

1947 Studebaker Champion Deluxe Coupe
The 1947 Champion shocked the civilized world with its styling. It was the first American postwar car to try a startlingly different approach from what had been done before 1942. Studebaker hired industrial designer Raymond Loewy to style the car, which was facetiously referred to as the "coming or going" Studebaker.

The great shipbuilding/steel-making/dam-constructing firm of Kaiser entered the car business after World War II. Its products (this one styled by Darrin) were far ahead of their time, and for a few years the company prospered. But when the Big Three came out with all new models in 1949, lines in front of the new Kaiser dealerships began to shorten. The name *Pinconning* comes from the home town of the Kaiser plant superintendent.

finishing the eighth grade to take a job at a salary of $1.50 a week. Kaiser made his way to the Pacific Northwest, evidently to prove to his prospective father-in-law that he was the stuff of pioneers. In short order, he was both a gravel and cement dealer and married. In 1914, he opened his own construction business in Vancouver, British Columbia, and began building highways in both the northwest and California. His break came in 1927 when he received a $20 million subcontract to build 200 miles of highway and 500 bridges in Cuba. Returning to the West in 1931, Kaiser became a partner in Six Companies, Inc.—a consortium of contractors—and launched a career as a dam builder. Six Companies built Hoover (or Boulder) Dam on the Colorado River. Associates at Six Companies joined Kaiser in a successful bid (as Columbia Construction Company) to construct Bonneville Dam on the Columbia River. As a member of yet another consortium, Kaiser built Grand Coulee Dam, also on the Columbia. Almost at the same time, he was busy building piers and levees around the country. With the other hand, he was making improvements at naval bases on Guam, Wake, and Hawaii. His final dam-building project was Shasta in northern California in 1939.

With the war in Europe came the German Atlantic submarine campaign, so successful it got within days of starving out the British, principally because the German U-boats were sinking Allied ships faster than new ones could be built. A ready supply of merchant bottoms became necessary for survival. Kaiser, who had never built ships, stepped up in 1941 with the claim that he could not only build hulls faster than anyone else, he could build them before their keels were laid. (At the same time, he became involved in steel, magnesium, and aircraft production.) His shipbuilding techniques were so successful that by April 1943, Kaiser's three Liberty shipbuilding yards were averaging 39.2 days from keel to delivery compared to the national average of 52.6 days.

The belief that he could enter the closed club of automobile manufacturers after the war came quite naturally to him. (One associate had said of Kaiser that he made his achievements only because nobody had told him beforehand that they were impossible.) But Kaiser had not anticipated the problems of coming into auto manufacture so late in the day. He bought the assets of Graham-Paige Motor Corporation at the urging of its head, Joseph W. Frazer, and in 1947, Kaiser-Frazer brought out its first car.

Frazer had rented, and the company had later bought, the huge Willow Run plant that had been subsidized by the government during the war for Ford's B-24 production. There, K-F planned to build the Kaiser and a more expensive car named after Frazer. The Kaiser prototype had been styled by Howard Darrin, but it had been much revamped by K-F styling under Robert Cadwallader. It featured unit construction, torsion-bar suspension, and front-wheel drive. Its sister car, the Frazer, followed the Kaiser's lead with full envelope styling, anticipating the industry by at least two years.

The proposed mechanical advantages represented by the prototype proved far too expensive to be put into a production car. Front wheel drive was dropped, and unit construction was reluctantly scrapped, as was the notion of torsion bars. What emerged was a handsome but conventional car with a box-section frame, and independent rear suspension. The engine was an updated Continental six-cylinder design of 3.7 liters developing 100 horsepower. (In later years, this would be increased to 140 hp in the supercharged Kaiser Manhattan.)

During its eight-year life span in the United States, Kaiser-Frazer was an innovative company. It built the Kaiser Traveler, a combination sedan/station wagon; the Virginian, one of the first of the so-called hardtops (no visible middle, or "B," pillar between the windshield and the back of the top); and the Kaiser Darrin, a sports car with sliding doors. For a time, the company was the most suc-

OVERLEAF:
1953 Kaiser Hatchback
The Kaiser is remembered for different and innovative designs; among these was the Traveler. It was an early hatchback that opened up at the rear like a station wagon and had large drop-down seats that created a flat-bed effect.

1951 Frazer Manhattan Convertible Sedan
The Frazer was never as innovative or as attractive as its sibling, the Kaiser. Usually built in the old Ford Willow Run plant, this Frazer was assembled at Jackson, Michigan. It had a six-cylinder, 226.2-cubic-inch engine carrying around a large car weighing almost 4,000 pounds, so performance was not startling. This was the last year of production for Frazer.

cessful of the postwar independents, selling almost 150,000 cars during both 1947 and 1948, which put it ahead of Hudson, Nash, and Studebaker.

In 1953, the company changed its name to Kaiser and bought Willys-Overland. From 1950 until 1954, the company built an interesting car and marketed it in an extraordinary fashion. It was named after the company's founder, Henry J., and was an early attempt by an American manufacturer to build a small, agile automobile. It was not distinguished from an engineering standpoint, but both Kaiser-Frazer and giant Sears, Roebuck attempted to break the conventional franchise-dealer sales network by marketing a version called Allstate through Sears. Its production by K-F resulted in an association between Willys-Overland, which had started a civilian version of the Jeep after the war and then added a pair of undistinguished sedans, and Kaiser. Willys supplied four- and six-cylinder engines for both the Henry J. and the Allstate and became a part of K-F in 1953. By 1954 K-F gave up on everything but Jeep, moving manufacture of the Kaiser Manhattan to Argentina, where it was known as the Kaiser Carabela and lasted until 1962.

A fascinating company, Kaiser-Frazer. Decently funded, producer of what still seems almost a contemporary design in the immediate postwar Kaiser (the Frazer was far less distinguished), it was one of the first to use the envelope body, to build a hardtop, to introduce an early version of a hatchback, to try to build and market an "ethical car" in the Henry J. and the Allstate, to bring back the sports car to postwar Americans. At the same time it was a victim of slaked thirst for product once the wartime drought in cars was over, and it was unable to compete with established manufacturers represented by dealer networks. Nonetheless, K-F did try to break a mold by marketing through dry goods/mail order channels. Among other things, Kaiser gets credit for a real effort to bring choice to the marketplace.

Powell Crosley was another pioneer who actually began manufacture of a tiny car in 1939. When postwar production resumed in 1945, Crosley took advantage of a Navy-developed, 722-cc, overhead camshaft, four-cylinder engine originally made of brazed copper and sheet steel and featuring a fixed cylinder head. This proved both troublesome and expensive, so Crosley went to a cast-

1941 Crosley Convertible Coupe
Powell Crosley was a midwestern radio manufacturer with a better idea; he would build a sub-compact. This is a rare prewar version; 1,800 were sold through Crosley radio and appliance dealers. Postwar cars used an engine developed by the U.S. Navy with Crosley. Price of this car: $299.

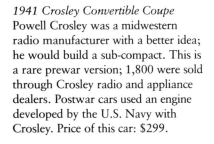

iron block but continued to innovate with aluminum pistons, intake manifold, and bell housing. The company built a whole line of what today would be called microcompacts, including a sports car, the Hotshot, which actually won an American endurance race at Sebring, Florida, in 1950. Crosley, who had made his money in the radio business, was too far ahead of his time. His company went out of business in 1952.

The final postwar effort of significance was Tucker, certainly the most notorious and most spectacular of the attempts to break into auto manufacture, and probably the one with the least chance of success. The car was the product of a combined design of Preston T. Tucker and Alex Tremulix, a former stylist for Auburn-Cord-Duesenberg. It was as spectacularly different from its contemporaries as it was ugly. The car was originally designed to have a central steering wheel and front fenders that turned when the wheels did, as well as a horizontally opposed 9.6-liter engine. This was far too radical. The car, named the Tucker Torpedo, appeared in 1948 in semiprototype form as a fastback weighing 3,600 pounds, powered by a flat six-cylinder engine developed from a Franklin design originally meant for helicopters but remade as a liquid-cooled unit. The car had disc brakes (well before anyone but Crosley had used them) and independent suspension. It sported three headlights, one a cyclops middle eye. Only forty-nine cars were made in the two-year life of the company (1946-1948), every one different from every other in one or another detail. Most used a preselector or electric transmission, some using the prewar Cord gearbox, others a device called the Tuckermatic, an automatic transmission with fewer than thirty parts. Legend has

1948 Tucker Four-Door Sedan Model 48

Designed by engineer Preston T. Tucker, this began as a sports car to be called the Torpedo, with projected front-wheel drive and front fenders that turned with the wheels. The innovations were the work of Tucker and former Auburn-Cord-Duesenberg stylist Alex Tremulis. After a costly court battle with the Securities and Exchange Commission on charges of fraud, Tucker was acquitted, but his car never went into production.

it that the cars were capable of going 120 mph. Legend also has it that the car was so revolutionary and so good that the Big Three conspired against Preston Tucker and forced him out of business.

The truth is that Tucker was enough of a wheeler-dealer to attract the attention of the Securities and Exchange Commission, which charged him with fraud. That put paid to his company, and the fact that he was cleared of the charges in 1950 would not revive the car. Tucker died in 1956, a disillusioned man.

Although new products of some merit were introduced, with the exception of Hudson, the balance of the industry was simply trying to build cars to satisfy demand. Hudson came forth with a long, low "stepdown design" Hornet in 1948, a stunning car with high performance. It achieved enormous success on the new late-model stock-car racing circuit, enhancing the reputation of a company already known for engineering excellence. Hudson's last effort at innovation was a car about the size of the Henry J. and called the Jet; it turned out to be too little, too conventional, too uninspired, and too late.

1957 Hudson Hornet Four-Door Sedan
The Hornet had a very low center of gravity and handled beautifully as a result. Even with its six-cylinder engine producing only 145 horsepower, it was very successful on the early stock-car racing circuits.

1953 Hudson Super Jet Four-Door Sedan
Anticipating Nash's preoccupation with small cars, Hudson introduced the Jet as a competitor to what was already on the market from Kaiser and soon to come from Nash, a small, inexpensive car. The cost was $2,230, and for it Hudson product planners insisted that every comfort found in their larger car be included in the Jet.

1948 Chrysler Town & Country Convertible
If Chrysler had a postwar classic—at very least a collectible—in addition to its great 300 series, it would be this 1948 Town & Country wood-paneled convertible.

1951 Chrysler Newport
During the early 1950s, American enthusiasts complained bitterly about the lack of excitement in the cars built by Detroit. Today, cars like the '51 Newport are almost collector's items, prized for their simplicity.

To give some notion of the failure of boldness by the Big Three, the principal efforts on the part of all of them (with one engineering exception by GM, which was to offer the high-performance Kettering engine) were in the direction of new styling that would distinguish postwar from prewar products and in the pursuit of power accessories. Olds had pioneered the automatic transmission for the masses. in 1939; now automatics and semiautomatics were popping up everywhere. Buick introduced a variant it called Dynaflow. Pontiac and the rest of GM's divisions offered Hydramatic, a far better design. All of GM was going to the high-compression Kettering engine. For example, Oldsmobile's version of the motor was put in its medium-sized car, the Rocket 88, in 1949. At the same time, Dodge introduced the Wayfarer, a short-lived "business coupe" (with storage room where the rear seat would ordinarily have been) with a convertible top. The top GM divisions copied Kaiser with hardtop models. The all-steel station wagon appeared when Plymouth brought out the Suburban. Next, Chrysler stunned the world with the key-start. By 1950, Ford had *its* automatic transmission, the Fordomatic (on Mercury it was called the Merc-o-Matic), and Chrysler introduced what is now considered a postwar classic, the woody convertible called the Town and Country.

The Korea police action was cutting availability of strategic materials again, but in 1951, Ford and Chrysler came out with hardtops; Nash introduced a sports car in the American idiom, developed with England's Donald Healey. Willys added a smaller all-steel wagon to the seven-passenger wagon it had produced right after World War II. The year 1951 also saw another great leap forward in the American builder's efforts to make it easier for drivers to conduct their cars down the suburban byway: power steering. To give some indication of how undistinguished the changes of this period were, the Automobile Manufacturers Association listed the following breakthroughs for 1952: "Innovations included Oldsmobile's automatic headlamp dimmer, a suspended brake pedal under the dashboard and ball joint front wheel suspension on the Lincoln; suspended clutch and brake pedals on the Ford; dual range Hydramatic on the Pontiac; 12-volt electrical system on the Chrysler Crown Imperial; four-way seat adjustment on the Packard; automatic overdrive on the Plymouth and DeSoto offered a V-8 engine."

Still, cars built by Detroit were simple. The age of excess and stagnation was only just beginning to show itself on the horizon. Today we look back on the cars of the late 1940s and early 1950s with admiration. They were highly utilitarian, reasonably priced, uncluttered, almost handsome devices. And some were enormously significant.

For example, the current chief stylist of Daimler-Benz AG, an aware auto historian, considers the 1949 Ford one of the "most important cars of post-war American production." On this, he would get no disagreement from Dearborn. The car probably saved the Ford Motor Company.

CHAPTER 14

The Car that Saved FoMoCo

Ford Motor Company was rich and talent laden in 1946. It was also bereft of a competitive product. The postwar car sitting in dealerships was a thinly disguised 1942 model, itself an update of a design that had evolved gently through the Depression years from the time of the introduction of the V-8 (1932) and representing only the third major model in the history of the modern company. It had only recently gotten hydraulic brakes (1939), and the flathead engine was making 100 horsepower, up only 10 from the pre–Pearl Harbor car. It had transverse leaf suspension all around, and the shifter had moved from the floor to the steering column in 1940. It was a truly uninspired automobile.

The problems that lay before the new management team of Henry II, Ernest Breech, chief engineer Harold T. Youngren, and the Whiz Kids was formidable. Soon enough, they all were aware, a public that was willing to snap up anything new would become more exacting as competitors changed to genuine postwar models and as demand was sated. The warmed-over prewar car would be embarassingly antiquated compared especially to what might come from General Motors—not to mention Chrysler Corporation.

Design cycles had long been part of planning at Chevrolet, Pontiac, Olds, Buick, and Cadillac, following the principle of the annual model change instituted by Alfred P. Sloan, Jr. At Ford there was no such legacy. A rhinoplasty here, a chin tuck there, were the extent of the changes that the company stylists and engineers were used to. Now Breech and Deuce were faced with the need to crank out an entirely fresh model. If a completely new car were to be introduced for the 1949 model year, it would have to have its debut in the summer of 1948.

Never mind that the company was still a shambles, nor even that Youngren had just come aboard in 1947. A new car there had to be and a new car Ford would produce. To update the old was out of the question. Said Breech, "Such a course seemed a capitulation to disaster, for the Ford was the company's chief product and there should be no question of its novelty or distinction." In late summer of 1947, Breech announced to the company's Policy Committee, "We [will] spend no time or money phonying up the old Ford, because this organization will be judged by the market on the next car it produces, and it had better be a new one."

In effect, this gave FoMoCo (as the company was being called) less than twelve months in which to produce the new automobile, and that was unheard of in terms of lead time, even at GM. The only concession Breech and Deuce were willing to make was the inevitable one: The V-8 engine would stay, for tackling the problems of designing and producing a new engine at the same time as they were creating a new car was unthinkable.

The greatest part of the burden fell on chief engineer Harold Youngren for creation of the overall package; Henry Ford would make the styling decisions

1949 Ford Custom Tudor Sedan Model B-A
Called by *Car and Driver* magazine "The Car That Saved Ford," the 1949 was a complete reskin done by the new management team brought in by Henry Ford's grandson, Henry II. Daimler-Benz chief stylist Bruno Sacco considers the car's envelope body "trendsetting—a very important step that had worldwide implications."

based on the designs of two men. The first was the company's own stylist, Eugene Gregorie. The second was an outside consultant named George Walker.

Cars are shaped in a variety of materials before they get to sheet metal. First, of course, come the sketches and drawings, which are committed to clays and then wood bucks. Often by the time the clays appear, the variety of concepts have come close enough so that one clay model can represent two versions of the eventual car—a schizophrenic full-sized replica with the left side exhibiting one visual entity, the right side another of the same size but different in something more than detail, something less than concept. In the case of what would become known as the Model B-A, yet inchoate 1949, there seem to have been two separate clays, one representing Gregorie's view of Ford's future, and the other representing Walker's.

When Ford, Breech, Ford's brother and company director Benson, and the top management of the company met to view the results, neither clay was identified as to its creator. The Product Committee decided on Walker's styling and rejected that of its own in-house designer. This was not the first time such a thing had happened in the auto industry, nor would it be the last. (When VW was desperate for a replacement for the Beetle, its styling department's design was put aside for one done by Italian stylist Georgetto Giugiaro. The result was the VW Rabbit—like Ford's Model B-A, a car that saved its parent company).

Gregorie pouted in his office for four days and then quit Ford flat. Walker, who had been a stylist at Nash and was called in by Breech himself on the B-A project—perhaps *this* was the reason for Gregorie's desertion—took complete responsibility for its shape.

By now it was October, with the introduction date no more than ten months away. The schedule called for the completion of a preproduction prototype in February. Although this early version of a regular model could be assembled by hand quickly enough, it would take time to make all the necessary tooling and to reorder the lines as needed. If the kids Henry II had hired were indeed whizzes, this was the first time for them to prove it.

To confuse matters even more, FoMoCo had already done a new Lincoln (the bulbous Cosmopolitan), and Mercury had been reshaped in Lincoln's image. Further, an earlier decision had dictated that 139 new truck models would precede the introduction of the company's flagship. Showing of the 1949 Ford was locked in for June at the Waldorf Astoria in New York.

And of that showing, *Car and Driver* said: "Imagine the scene that June 8, 1948 evening. Everyone in the industry and everyone in the *Social Register* had been invited. Circling among them, surely uncomfortable but commuting with regularity to the six bars in the room, was the press. Black-tied waiters circulated with trays of champagne, and there was an orchestra to soothe the doubts of nervous executives and admen alike.

"Each guest received [a model of] the Ford, while certainly through the minds of the sales executives, seeing these constant reminders of their new product and watching the faces for reaction as the guests looked upon the...cars displayed, there must have passed like a litany the words of the 1949 Ford sales data book: 'You are presenting the most sensational—the most talked about—automobile that has been built in the past two generations.'" Reactions to products at lavish receptions, competing with endless supplies of free champagne, are predictably, invariably favorable. Press and FoMoCo executives alike would have to await the market's verdict—not long in coming.

You were very likely a World War II veteran of about thirty if you ordered a B-A in 1949. You were working, rather than going to college under the G. I. Bill,

because you couldn't have afforded school *and* a new car. You'd put up a down payment consisting of most of your separation-from-service bonus. That left $1,103 of the selling price ($1,471) of the Ford due Ford Credit over a year at $50 a month—at an interest rate of 4 percent.

You were what was then called a "junior executive" in an advertising firm or in retailing; you were a new suburbanite; your house was bought in Levittown using a G. I. loan. For a year you had waited for the new car; by now you and your wife were fed up with the walk/bus ride/train trip into New York City, and the new Ford represented freedom.

You had ordered a Ford because you were still part of a "Brand Loyalty" generation. More than that, the choice of Chevy or Plymouth or Ford carried clear social implications. Plymouth buyers were staid. Chevy people were unimaginative. Ford owners still sought the magic of performance the car stood for as a result of its prewar prowess on the dry lakes or as a street racer. From your brief prewar experience with Ford and perhaps because you had had an opportunity to drive a Ford staff car during your time in the military, you remembered a hard-riding, balky shifting, noisy piece that somehow always managed to smell as if the exhaust were venting into the passenger compartment.

The car came as a surprise, for it was unlikely the dealer had been able to spare a demonstrator for you to drive beforehand; he was selling every car he could get his hands on. Your new car was a mouse gray tudor—you certainly had no choice of color and almost none in model. It was a color and style that came to characterize the B-A.

It was a simple car, very unlike the bedecked and trimmed monsters that evolved from it. It had a three-speed shifter mounted on the column, and shifting was smooth. You found you could upshift to second or third without using the clutch, and first was easy even without synchromesh to find and use. Compared to its later sisters, the 1949 had a high numerical final drive, which means that speeds in each gear were restricted. (Thus the gearing is called "short.") If first gear (using the same V-8 engine of the 1946 to 1948 models for power, remember) felt almost automotively British in its limited capacity for use—at 15 miles an hour and left in first gear, the car felt like it was in enormous pain—the short gearing also meant that the car would *almost* start in third gear, and third was useful in almost every situation except for climbing Annapurna. The short gearing was clearly deliberate, since American drivers were lazy and automatics were coming into vogue. If a manual transmission car couldn't be put into top gear and left there, its driver felt cheated, forced to be a slave to primitive technology.

When you climbed into the B-A, you had a feeling of being perched quite high above the ground, but this is in comparison to cars of much later vintage. That is the problem with the B-A: It was so close to the cars that followed it and so far from the cars that immediately preceded it that one tends to compare it with designs of the late sixties.

The view out the windshield from the driver's side of the plain-jane bench seat was restricted, but only in relation to the view from the passenger compartments ("greenhouses") of cars of the eighties. The windshield was split, and the front pillars ("A" pillars in the stylists' jargon) seemed very wide, even in 1949.

If our junior executive—by the 1980s a very senior executive—could have left his 1980 car to sit again in his 1949, probably the B-A would have evoked strong feelings of contemporary or near-contemporary Detroit designs. Its broadcloth upholstery and handsome headliner material though, would seem almost plush. The comparison, of course, is with the plastic that eventually replaced them—the

better for wear, manufacture, and expense, but at considerable cost in the feeling of interior hospitality.

Ford bragged in its sales brochure that the B-A had "Hydra-Coil" front springs and "Para-Flex" rears. Translated, that meant that Youngren had redesigned the front suspension to be independent by coil springs while he retained the leaf elliptics for the rear solid axle. The difference in feel between the cars of 1946 to 1948 and the 1949 is principally a result of that change. It was this change that put the company in contemporary engineering competition with Chevrolet and Plymouth. But its use by all three led the American car down the road to handling complacency. Part of that complacency is noticeable in the degree of softness of ride ("compliance"). The B-A's ride was far harsher than that of today's cars with their wider wheel rims, fatter tires, and much advanced shock absorbers; but the ride was still the clear beginning of the marshmallow feel that would characterize Detroit products for the next three decades.

The B-A could not compare in speed with its contemporary Oldsmobile, whose Kettering high-compression engine made it a very fast car for its time. Nor did the B-A's handling come close to that of the low-center-of-gravity, step-down Hudson, introduced the year before the Ford.

Still, the 1949 Ford was a marvel, particularly for FoMoCo. In 1948, Ford sold less than half a million cars. In the first year of the B-A, sales almost doubled, as did profits—a clear answer to the question in everyone's mind at the moment of the B-A's debut.

"It was visible evidence of the successful revitalization of the Ford Motor Company," says the sign identifyng a B-A in Ford's own museum in Greenfield Village, Michigan.

Said Nevins and Hill: "That Henry Ford II, Breech and their chief associates had rebuilt the company had by 1949 become generally recognized. By mid-1949 there was a quiet confidence throughout the organization that it had the resources for dealing with the unfolding postwar era."

For that, credit the Model B-A.

VI
MUSCLE CARS

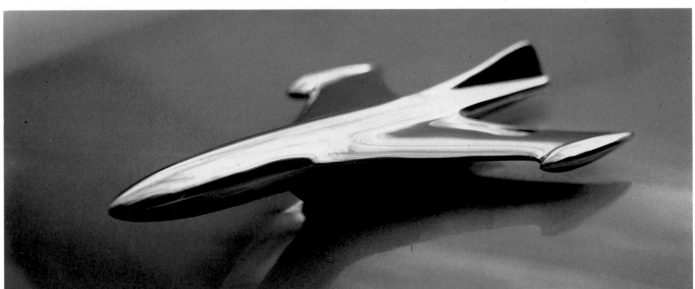

CHAPTER 15

Hovering Sloanism

By 1955, the American consumer was auto-sated. Detroit was not. What followed is a disgraceful chapter in the history of the industry. In an age of engineering complacency, product men at the top found themselves replaced by managers brought up on balance sheets. The whole point was to concentrate on what the industry called "Moving the Metal."

Manufacturing efficiency had indeed increased during the Depression; then along came the war to fund huge factories, train an enormous workforce, and stoke Detroit's rage to produce, until it no longer had the vaguest notion of adjusting output to demand. It knew better, and its teacher had been Alfred Sloan. It would create a burning need for cars in a country that had taken its fill in the decade since V-J Day. How would it create demand where demand did not exist? First, by forcing cars on independent dealers, and then, by pressuring those dealers to increase their sales by threatening to pull their franchises or to plop a factory-owned dealer right next door to them.

In order to satisfy the auto manufacturer's chief executive accountants, the retail establishment had to sell enormous quantities of cars. Truckload after truckload of cars were forced on dealers whose markets were already dwindling. The dealers (the wholesale customers of uncaring manufacturers) turned to methods and practices of sale that would make a black marketeer shudder.

The age of the Great Sales Blitz was upon us. What little reputation the dealers had managed to salvage after their routine ripoff of war-deprived buyers was about to disappear forever. "Would You Buy a Used Car from This Man?" became the scornful epithet applied to the hawker of cars.

We will examine the devices of deceitful selling forthwith, but let's pause a moment to make two observations. First, blame could not then nor can it now be put entirely at the dealer's door. He was the visible villain, no question. But those managers at Chrysler or GM or Ford, pretending that the abuses of the marketplace were entirely the responsibility of the nation's retail auto dealers, were equally responsible—perhaps, as initiators of the problem, even more so. Dealers became thieves because the holders of their franchises forced them to steal or go out of business. Second, it has been a generation since the Great Blitz, yet suspicion remains the tone in an auto transaction. If we take the time to figure out why, we can see that it is all coming back. Although more skillfully packaged now, many of the abuses of the Blitz are echoed in the early eighties. The reason is clear enough. Detroit is agonizing in the early years of this decade as it has not done in thirty years. "When the nation catches cold, Detroit has pneumonia," it has been said—echoes of a self-pitying city. "When Detroit's sales go cold, it makes its pneumonia a contagion," is equally true.

If, as automotive economic writer Emma Rothschild said in 1973, Detroit

OVERLEAF:

Nash Metropolitan
Nash's early attempt at a subcompact, this car was built with English components, was based on the Austin/Morris, and had specifications identical to the MG Midget series.

set sales patterns for all hard goods, we were a nation in trouble in 1955. Sales had almost quadrupled between production revival in 1946 and 1950—a year in which Detroit sold more than 6 million cars. Then the nation's consumers paused for a breath, and industry sales fell a million in 1951, and another million in 1952. There was a two-year stabilization period, and then, in 1955, production figures leapt upward from the 4 million plateau to almost 8 million. "The auto industry broke all records," trumpeted the Automobile Manufacturer's Association. "Output totalled 9,204,049 units including 7,950,477 passenger cars." It was force-feeding—and even that was getting hard to do. Sales fell to 5.8 million in 1956 and did not approach 8 million again for almost a decade.

Clearly this trend was unacceptable to the accountants. The passenger car population was a mere 50 million or so (it reached 122.5 million in 1980), which to Detroit meant there was half a nation out there as potential car buyers—*new* car buyers; the problem was that most of them didn't know it. Detroit would fix that. It invented a whole new buying population by making "owners" of people whose own common sense rightly told them they couldn't afford a new car, but who became persuaded to the contrary by a savage campaign of deception and double-dealing.

The idea was this: If a consumer who had never considered buying a new car because he hadn't the money or the credit (much less the need) could be convinced that suddenly a dream he had not allowed himself could be realized, he would become so entranced with the notion of owning something heretofore unobtainable that he would override good sense and agree to take possession of a new car. Notice that this is not the equivalent of buying a new car—the customer just allowed himself to become its registered owner. At that point, the manufacturer was out of the transaction (he had sold the car to the dealer, after all, and could now sell him another one *and* increase the dealer's quota). The dealer was almost totally out of the deal. It was now a matter for the possessor and one or another kind of financial institution to whom he owed the money for the car. Metal had been moved. But how?

"We appeal to the larceny in everybody's soul," said one veteran car salesman during the Great Blitz. Detroit dealers could sell cars to people who had never dreamed of owning because it was able to convince the heretofore scorned and unqualified buyer that a new car could be bought for little or no money down and miniscule payments for an indeterminate period of time. To achieve that tiny miracle, the dealer body lied. It advertised cars that did not exist for prices so low that if they *had* existed, they could not have been sold so cheaply.

This was only the first step in what was becoming known as "The System." The name came from an unvarying sales ritual devised by a number of sales management consultants, the best known of which was a southern company called Hull-Dobbs. The System said that if the dealer was able to convince a living body to appear at its door, by one means or another that body could be detained long enough to buy—through the use of devices ranging from cajolery to intimidation to threat.

The body was brought in by "mooch" advertising, a term from the Depression originally meaning "beggar" and transmuted to stand for "indigent." If a pitchman repeated it enough times on late-night television or on radio, or if the message were appropriately emblazoned in full-page newspaper advertising, a person with no money at all could be convinced that the dream of mobility could be his. A new car cost nothing down, went the pitch. A trade-in, no matter how old or infirm, would be appraised at almost the full price of the new car. No lie was too big, no absurdity too blatant, to faze the dealer catering to his new

271

1955 Ford 40A Thunderbird Convertible Coupe
A revived Ford Motor Company under the stewardship of the founder's grandson, Henry Ford II, replied to Chevrolet's 1953 introduction of the Corvette with the T-bird, which appealed to the American buying public even more than GM's sports car. It was produced in this form for only three years and then became obese and almost unrecognizable.

be in production. Ford's FX-Atmos was as removed from reality as its name. We got new sealed-beam headlights in 1955, still not as good as the European quartz halogens; the same year saw the introduction of the two-passenger Thunderbird, a lovely little car although totally conventional, which would last three years in production until it blew up into an obese caricature of itself.

We had already seen the introduction (in 1953) of a six-cylinder Corvette, the Blue Flame: rebirth of the American sports car and the only one that would continue in manufacture. Safety door latches appeared on the T-bird, which prompted Ford to try to market safety in a collapsible steering column and seat belts during the following year, only to find either that it couldn't discover a way to sell protection or that people weren't willing to buy it.

1952 Plymouth Hardtop
Chrysler was experimenting with engineering, but not with styling. Its management was deathly afraid of changing the shape of its cars—particularly its most popular car, the Plymouth. Even the 1952 Ford was visually more interesting than the Plymouth, although Chevrolet was not exactly setting the styling world on fire either in 1952.

clientele. The whole point was to get a breathing person into the dealership. The System would take it from there.

In its immediate operation The System was without mercy. A prospect would have his trade taken from him for "appraisal." Often, it would be parked around the corner, its keys literally thrown on the dealership roof or the car actually wholesaled. The point was to "unhorse" the buyer—to leave him without transportation unless he drove out in a new car. Then a novice posing as an experienced salesman (he was called the "liner") wrote on an order form a deal that was as outrageously impossible of fulfillment as were the deals promised in the advertising: a new car for $1,000 or a trade-in worth $100 valued at $900 against the $1,000 car. To the dealers, this was fantasy land, but the buyer was at the door because he believed he could buy a new car for nothing. The liner's job was to get the buyer's signature on a piece of paper agreeing to a deal—any deal.

Then the brutality started. The customer was turned over to the closer, called the "T. O." man (for "turn over"). It was the T. O. man who had to be tough, mean, and experienced enough to "bust" the buyer off the written deal. His devices were many, including: a "bug" in the office so he could eavesdrop on the customer's conversation with his companion; the sad admission that the customer's car had disappeared; the blank contract—on which anything the customer would agree to was accepted so that his signature would appear at its bottom, after which it would suddenly be filled with real figures, impossible for the buyer (who couldn't afford the car in the first place) to meet. There were also: the "stick man," a finance expert who would take the buyer's furniture as security for a down payment; the "price pack," which was a fictional sum built into the

price of the new car to be given away as a "discount" or an "overtrade;" the "Okie Charmer," sales Blitz terminology for the commonly used Friden calculator on which the T. O. man would work the deal backwards to confuse the customer, knowing that of the three elements of any sale—trade-in, new car price, and monthly payment—he could manage to make at least one incomprehensible to the buyer—which meant he could inflate it to match the actual price of the car.

The limits of the new buyer's credulity were endless. There are stories of customers with sufficient cash in their pockets to pay the full price going out in a new car for which they had agreed to pay half again the original cost in install-ment interest payments over three years; of buyers taking delivery of a car on a weekend and writing a check on a nonexistent bank account for the down pay-ment at the encouragement of the seller, only to be called the following Monday and threatened with prosecution for fraud by that same seller; of people being promised after-delivery additions of everything from air conditioning to power steering, which the dealers then blandly denied promising, but for which the buyers were obligated to pay or had already paid. There were also stories of the switching of cars, from the $5,000 beauty the buyer thought he was getting to a $2,500 stripped version; of the substitution of demonstrator models for new cars—wound-back odometers and all; and ultimately of threats to tell the buyer's family or friends or employer that he had obligated himself to a bank or finance company and that consequences would be terrible for him if he didn't take delivery. The pretense was over; it was war between car seller and car buyer.

It is still war. These days most sellers complain that they are not treated as reputable members of the local business community. Some are right to object; there are far fewer System dealers today than there were in 1955. But there are still many, and the 1950s reputation of the retail car establishment still clings to the rest like a stockyard stink.

Symphonies in Pink

What were these people selling, that it put so much pressure on the buyer and required the abandonment of all decency to "Move the Metal"? To the car critics of that day, American automobiles of the late 1950s and early 1960s were abominations. It was an age of three-color paint; (Chrysler Corporation offered a particularly startling white/pink/purple combination), huge slabs of pot metal on quarter panels; spears, darts, fins, and breast-shaped bumper overriders; and double, triple and quadruple lights, lamps, and flashers.

Mainly, it was the age of accessories. The semiautomatic transmission was offered to the American public in an Oldsmobile show chassis in 1938 and made standard in full automatic form in 1939, with other divisions of GM following suit. After the war, in came power brakes, power steering, power windows, power headlamp dimmer, power seats. As early as 1953, automatic transmission was standard on expensive cars; air conditioning was coming into common use; the 12-volt electrical system was replacing the 6-volt to take care of all the accessories; and lights were replacing gauges so drivers couldn't actually see how profoundly their cars were being strained to support all these gewgaws.

The cars were routine, but to give them glamour, manufacturers were touring the country with "show cars"—slyly suggesting reality just around the corner for the car lover. The trouble was, not many of these show cars ever went into mass production. Packard had a 1954 fiberglass sports car called the Panther that never materialized. GM's turbine-powered Firebird XP-21 was never intended to

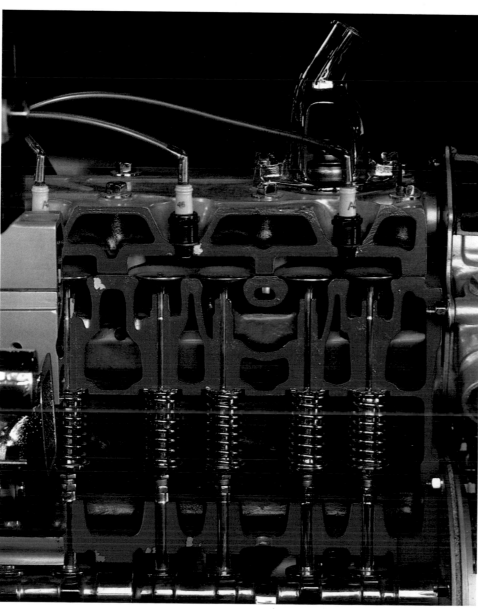

1938 Oldsmobile Display Chassis
Detroit manufacturers had begun to float trial balloons, this one to take around the country to show its new semiautomatic transmission, advertised as a "safety transmission." The gearbox would evolve into GM's hydramatic.

1955 Ford 40A Thunderbird Convertible Coupe
A revived Ford Motor Company under the stewardship of the founder's grandson, Henry Ford II, replied to Chevrolet's 1953 introduction of the Corvette with the T-bird, which appealed to the American buying public even more than GM's sports car. It was produced in this form for only three years and then became obese and almost unrecognizable.

be in production. Ford's FX-Atmos was as removed from reality as its name. We got new sealed-beam headlights in 1955, still not as good as the European quartz halogens; the same year saw the introduction of the two-passenger Thunderbird, a lovely little car although totally conventional, which would last three years in production until it blew up into an obese caricature of itself.

We had already seen the introduction (in 1953) of a six-cylinder Corvette, the Blue Flame: rebirth of the American sports car and the only one that would continue in manufacture. Safety door latches appeared on the T-bird, which prompted Ford to try to market safety in a collapsible steering column and seat belts during the following year, only to find either that it couldn't discover a way to sell protection or that people weren't willing to buy it.

And still came the show cars. GM's V-6 powered La Salle II was one—no V-6 was contemplated for mass production, none appeared for twenty years, and the model name was never revived. Chrysler showed something called the FlightSweep II. Ford did introduce a final, real Continental, the 1955, considered the last of the series of these classics begun by Edsel Ford in 1940. Begun as a one-off for Edsel himself, it was a clean, graceful, distinctive car with the proportions of the classic Classic: long hood, short coupled passenger compartment. Only a few were made before the war, and production was temporarily discontinued in 1948. But from the beginning, it captivated the car-buying public. It had the aura of a very special car about it; its limited production contributed to the allure. The Continental was coveted by most but owned by a very few during its production

OVERLEAF:
1940 Lincoln-Zephyr Continental Cabriolet Model 06H
Continental production started on December 13, 1940, and would contribute some of the handsomest cars ever production-built in this country. The first actual customer car, #3, bore a plate with the name Jackie Cooper on it. This car was shown in Los Angeles and later given or sold to Mickey Rooney.

279

1956 Lincoln Continental
This is the car considered by purists to
be the last of the "real" Continentals
built by the Ford Motor Company.

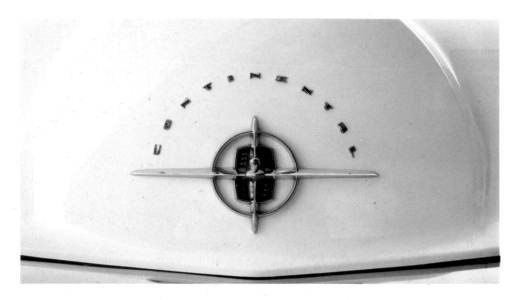

lifetime. The 1955 model was criticized as being "no longer a Lincoln." It was said
to have taken very little from Edsel's original design.

We got V-8 engines in everything in the decade after 1945. We got pickup
trucks that were primitive by today's standards, and we got dual headlight
systems. We got torsion bars, push-button shifters, fuel injection (not very good),
14-inch wheels instead of 15s or 16s, and rear-facing seats in station wagons. On
those wagons, we were spared the burden of having to care for wood; wood-
grained plastic was substituted—no care required, never mind the peel.

Ford brought us the convertible hardtop in 1957. And then American
Motors, whose president, George Romney, was ranting and raving about the
"Dinosaurs in the Driveway," capitalized on Detroit's automotive elephantiasis
with a line of small cars that sold very well for a short time. To aid the consumer,
Congress passed the Automobile Information Disclosure Act of 1958, which required a manufacturer to affix a label to every new car revealing: make, model,
serial number, final assembly point, name of receiving dealer, factory-installed

Ford Pickup Truck
After the war, pickup trucks began to be used outside rural areas as passenger vehicles. Their use became so ubiquitous that Ford and Chevy pickups were at one time the two top selling vehicles in the U.S.

optional equipment, delivery and transportation charges, and suggested retail price. It didn't change a thing. "Suggested" was taken by the dealer to mean only that. Additional stickers put on side windows by the dealers themselves added charges, many of them fictitious. If the act had been meant to undercut the abuses of The System, it had failed.

Many manufacturers decided unit construction (no frame) had manufacturing advantages; American Motors, Lincoln, and Continental used it. GM, with Cadillac, and Ford's middle-line car, the Mercury, went to an air suspension system that was a horrible failure. Chrysler Corporation broke the technology barrier in 1958 with an electronically controlled rearview mirror that switched into "dim" whenever it was hit from behind by the glare of bright lights. Ford unveiled the automatic trunk-latch switch under the dashboard or in the glove box. Rambler introduced reclining seats.

In 1959, while the rotary engine was being prepared overseas, Dodge gave birth to the immortal Dart; Plymouth introduced its sibling, the Valiant; Ford

1955 Chrysler Sports Coupe Model 300
Ah, the Chrysler 300—tough, massive, brutally fast. At first the company didn't realize it had built a car that would appeal to performance buyers. Those who bought the 300 in its first production year for $4,110 got a car now worth five times that. Subsequent 300s carried initials to indicate the year of production (e.g., 300B in 1956).

gave us the Falcon; and Chevrolet made history of a sort with the Corvair.

Intermediates, large cars but not so large as the so-called Standards, appeared in the early sixties. Chrysler continued its brilliant high-performance 300 Series, perhaps the recognized beginnings of a Muscle car tide that would sweep down the main streets of nighttime America in the next few years. Edsel and DeSoto went away. Imperial became part of the Chrysler line. The Packard name was dropped. Chrysler continued to work on a gas turbine for passenger cars in a project that it had begun right after the war and that is still in the research and development stage.

It was not a shining engineering epoch in the annals of Detroit.

A couple of people, John Keats and John Jerome, let the industry know all about its failures. Said Jerome in his book *The Death of the Automobile*:

"The stodgy car died in 1955. All our clinging Calvinist sensibilities of practicality, economy, simplicity, all the cramped guidelines of American Gothic were junked. We wanted more. We got it: bigger engines, more 'zestful' performance, more options, chrome, jazz, sex." This age of accessories was symbolic of industry solutions that were something less than elegant. "When technological intelligence fails, pile more power on top, in hopes the oversupply will trickle down to absorb the jangling harshnesses of inadequate engineering. In hopes that the customers' wide-eyed wonder at ever another machine to insert between man and function will preclude examination of either machine *or* function. Putting toys on toys to help you play with your toy.

"To try to pick the single symbol of the decline of the automobile is to stagger in bewilderment among the dazzling array of appropriate choices. But perhaps it is not a gadget at all that finally betrayed the car. Perhaps it is the vision behind the machine, the philosophy that generates such waste. That philosophy...created both a product and an industrial structure doomed by their inability to respond or be modified to suit the changing demands of a fragmented society. It is a philosophy that larded every single element of its own universe with excess."

As for Keats, he was every bit as critical. He spoke in *The Insolent Chariots* of our original love for cars, a love affair that blossomed into marriage. He found, after fifty-eight years of bliss, that the increasing obesity of the automobile was taking the bloom off the romance and, choosing a particularly insensitive metaphor, decided to malign both cars and women: "As the frightful marriage wore on, the automobile's original appeal shrank in inverse proportion to the growth of her demands. She grew sow-fat while demanding bigger, wider, smoother roads. The bigger and better the road, the fatter she became, and the fatter she grew, the greater her demands for even bigger roads. Then, with all the subtlety of the madam affecting a lorgnette, she put tail fins on her overblown bustle and sprouted wavering antennae from each fin. And, of course, her every whim was more costly than the last."

Keats excoriated the American industry for copying European technical development, starting with Duryea's copy of Daimler, Benz, and Panhard-Levassor. Stutz's Bearcat, said he, was nothing more than a "plagiarized" Fiat racer. Fluid (semiautomatic) transmissions had appeared in boats at the turn of the century. English buses had them as well by 1926. Europe was first to use the direct driveshaft, split axle, torsion bar, and disc brake. "During the 1930s, electric starters, hydraulic brakes, demountable wheels, all-steel bodies, safety glass and automatic windshield wipers were with us, and the only wonder is why they were so long in arriving," said Keats. Keats' Bill of Particulars (only slightly flawed) constituted a reasonable indictment. What were we up to?

1957 Chrysler Model 300

Chevy's Shining Hour

In 1954, Chevrolet announced a new car for model year 1955. Its 1946–1948 cars had been warmed over prewar items; its next six years were spent in putting out a six-cylinder automobile that was anything but exciting. "For more than 20 years," said Jerome, "the company had struggled along with its hoary 'Hot-Water Six,' a dead-reliable, easy to repair, parsimoniously economical design...that performance enthusiasts insisted was far better suited for use as a boat anchor than as the engine of a modern passenger car. Even the Southern California hot-rodders, who seemed to be capable of drawing horsepower out of anything vaguely metallic, had given up on it."

The 1955 had a new V-8 and it was a wonder. It was light, small, but with room for development (265 cubic inches in piston displacement), and it was reliable. It could be turned to high revolutions (eventually as high as 9,000 rpm). In terms of power output, it made enormously efficient use of its fuel/air mixture apparatus—carburetors and manifolding (the jargon is that it "breathed" well). It increased in size—in its second year it was bored out to 283 cubic inches—and so in power. In fact, the second-year engine could turn out 1 horsepower for every cubic inch of displacement, heretofore considered, by *European* standards of performance, the kind of power to be expected only from a competition engine.

The car could be bought in three versions and dozens of models, the most expensive of which was the BelAir. The three-speed shifter on the column was standard with an optional overdrive (the first year) coupled with a 4:11 rear end, a high numerical ratio. But automatic transmission was an increasingly ordered option. The windshield—on previous models shaded by an outside visor—could be ordered with a slight tint. The windshield glass curved dramatically at both

1955 Chevrolet Bel Air Sport Coupe

"It's got glamour—and plenty to go with it!" proclaimed the sales brochure for the 1955 Chevy Bel Air Sport Coupe and then went on to talk about vinyl interiors and a new instrument panel. Had they only known, the brochure people would have proclaimed this a landmark car, which it turned out to be. It stunned its competition upon introduction, a simple, elegant car that anyone could own, with a marvelous new V-8 engine. Chevy enthusiasts still think of the 1955 Sport Coupe as *the* Chevrolet.

sides, shifting the "A" pillar out of the driver's immediate vision but significantly distorting the view through the curved glass.

Instruments were in pods, and there were not many of them; so-called idiot lights had replaced the ammeter and the water temperature and oil pressure gauges, except on the BelAir, where they could still be ordered as extras.

The headliner material was still cloth, but the seats were "color-keyed" plastic, this being the year of the two-tone exterior paint. The back seat was cavernous, as was the trunk. For the first time (to the rage of gas station attendants then and for generations to come), the gas cap was hidden inside a door. Radial tires were not available on new American cars. The Chevy came with bias-ply tires on its 14-inch wheels. On a good day with a tail wind, the car could make 100 mph in stock form. On a balmy day with a lightfooted driver, an average of 18 miles per gallon was entirely possible.

This was all good stuff, but the thing was massive. Although not the 17 feet 6 inches it would grow to in eight years, it was only a little more than a foot shorter. It weighed nearly 4,000 pounds, depending on the number and the weight of accessories ordered. It took a fair amount of time to walk around. One of the size problems with the new car—as with all that would follow it for a long time—was something called "overhang." The wheelbase of the car was significantly shorter than the overall length. Wheels and axles were set in quite a bit from the front and rear bumpers, which skewed the weight bias of the car unnaturally forward and so needed far too much pressure by the front brakes in stopping.

Compared to some contemporary European cars, the 1955 was primitive. Its suspension was very compliant. The shocks and springs were designed to coddle the passengers, not tauten the car in curves and corners. The steering ratio—the number of turns of the steering wheel to go from lock to lock of the front wheels—was absurdly high, on the order of 4.5 to 1. And the Chevy shifted its weight as it rumbled down the highway. Because of the soft springing, the car would drop to its haunches under acceleration and dip its beak in the pavement under hard braking. As its driver pointed it around a curve, the Chevy would take several "sets"—angles of roll—depending on the length and radius and camber of the curve. (European cars of the same vintage—with their stiffer springs, lighter weight, and smaller size—were far more predictable.) If the Chevy had been ordered with sintered metallic brake linings, it would stop in a reasonable distance. But they were an expensive option, used mainly for the Corvette under competition conditions. Few Chevy salesmen, much less buyers, knew such an option existed. Few Chevies stopped very well in 1955 as a result.

In this year, the division introduced a version of the Chevy called the Nomad, a station wagon with rounded lines in back, swept-around rear windows, and indentations in the roof following the pattern of the luggage rack as it swept backward. It was and is a handsome car, relatively clean of chrome, cohesively styled. Inside a high-line Nomad (a redundancy really since all Nomads were BelAirs and all had the full trim treatment) there could be switches for every accessory imaginable.

Given the time, the car, and now almost three decades of hindsight, how do Keats' criticisms stand up?

Let us take a sidestep for a moment to look at the terrain. We were about to pass the great Interstate Highway Act, but that didn't mean we were without roads. Americans crossing the country, in 1949, say, could travel endlessly across a two-and three-lane highway as straight as a hoe handle through Montana or Texas. They had Route 66 at their disposal, Chicago to Los Angeles. they had parkways in Connecticut and turnpikes in Pennsylvania. If they were anxious or

desperate enough, they could make New York to Dallas in under two days.

Now this introduces an enormously interesting thesis proposed by B. Bruce-Briggs. Writing a few years later than Keats and Jerome, in *The War Against the Automobile* (1977), he insisted that America had then and has now the best mass-transportation system in the world, consisting of publicly funded highways, individually owned and operated automobiles, and the operators themselves. According to Bruce-Briggs, "There are about 3.8 million miles of... thoroughfares and they give access to almost all the land in the U. S." The automobiles have great "flexibility," which means they require only one operator, can carry up to eight persons, are bought and maintained by individuals who can "decide where . . . to go, [and have] control of the speed, route, destination, time of departure and time of arrival."

The individual, the third element in Bruce-Briggs's mass-transportation system, is easily trained and charges no one for his labor. The system is financed in a variety of ways. "The thoroughfares, being state owned, are almost entirely paid for by direct levies on their users," although there are some toll roads and bridges.

"The vehicles themselves are individually purchased through small businessmen who have franchises from the manufacturers of the vehicles."

Bruce-Briggs cited the following statistics to prove the workability of the mass transportation system. It represents perhaps 10 percent of the GNP, but it's a buy at that because it "accommodates 94% of all intracity trips, 85% of all intercity trips, and 80% of all trips to work." He calls it the auto-highway-driver complex.

Now, let's get back to the 1955 Chevy and see whether the criticisms stand up. The car was easy and comfortable to drive, although it offered only a bench seat, which was covered in plastic, so driver and passengers slid around some in curves. But the Chevy was easy to point, easy to turn, and relatively willing to stop. Shifting was no problem; steering and braking were power-assisted. It could carry six people with ease, heating them thoroughly and quickly in the winter,

1955 Chevrolet Bel Air Nomad Station Wagon
Chevrolet thought of its Nomad as "the luxury leader of the new Chevrolet line." Indeed, it was, but the times dictated use of absurd descriptions, and so it was hard to tell real advances from sales garble ("Motoramic Styling"). Certainly, the Nomad had better visibility front and rear than any previous wagon, with its wrap-around windshield and curved rear-quarter windows. It was also the first Chevy wagon with a two-piece tailgate/liftgate.

cooling them equally efficiently in the summer with a device derived from the primitive icebox made by that little company Billy Durant had bought, Frigidaire. It had a push-button radio for entertainment. It was easy to clean inside and out. It was large, but not too large to park. Vision was good except where the windshield curved and distorted the view. It would go for miles and miles without need for nourishment. The tires were reliable and rarely needed changing. Mainenance consisted of an oil change every 3,000 miles if its owner was conscientious, 6,000 if he wasn't. It could stand new spark plugs, points, and perhaps condenser at 25,000 miles at a cost of less than $50.

A 1955 Chevy driver could take his car on winding roads in Vermont, confident that he would be safe as long as he was reasonably prudent. Certainly he could point it across the country and have a fast, safe, pleasant trip—knowing that if by any chance his car broke something along the way, there would be a knowledgeable repairman nearby, equipped to deal with any mechanical emergency.

Nomad owners could stuff a family of eight in the car with room left over for a Maltese terrier, luggage on top, games and toys in the back seat, a cooler attached to the drivers' window if they were going through the desert, and a water bag hanging below the front grille as well. With gasoline available at every crossroad for less than 30 cents a gallon, they had prospects for as cheap a trip—particularly calculated on a passenger/mile basis—as could be taken.

So if we accept the Bruce-Briggs thesis, the 1955 Chevy was just fine for the conditions under which it lived. It would not bend around alpine corners like a Mercedes, but we had precious few alpine corners in the United States. It would not negotiate a race track like a Jaguar, but very few Chevy owners had any reason to whirl around the Watkins Glen road circuit. It would not stop on a microdot as its contemporary MG was supposed to do, but neither did the MG.

All it did was transport its driver and passengers comfortably, cheaply, and relatively safely down the highway. What's more, it did this in what was con sidered high style.

"The 1950s were [a] golden age of the automobile. This was the period when family automobile ownership went from 55% to 80% of the population.

"This was the period when the announcement of new car models was a major news event, when the sales race between Ford, Chevrolet and Plymouth was watched with the interest of a World Series game, when ferocious competition drove Kaiser, Willys, Hudson and Packard to the wall, when the horsepower race and the tail fin race were cause for excitement."

So Bruce-Briggs thought. To the Chevy driver, who had waited two weeks for his dealer to take the soap off his showroom windows so he could see—at last—the wonderful new '55 and had then signed an order blank on Introduction Night with searchlights playing and balloons floating, the logic of Bruce-Briggs's arguments would have been taken for granted.

To the citizens of a world that is coming to recognize limitations to resources, the 1955 Chevy represents innocence—a lavish car, still handsome, if excessive, boasting a motor that was exciting and that would go on to become one of the great power plants in Detroit history.

Keats and less so Jerome had a problem. Keats wanted a VW Rabbit twenty years before it came off the drawing board because he did not see romance in an appliance. He wanted something small and something simple. Jerome, who was—and is—an enormously sophisticated car man, looked across the Atlantic from his office in New York and yearned for high-speed, agile, trim, elegant, grand touring cars for everyone.

The only trouble with either argument was that the American buying public disagreed.

1955 Packard Caribbean Convertible
By 1955, Packard had lost all sense of taste and proportion, as this car indicates.

293

CHAPTER 16

Muscle Flexing in Motor City

If accountants replaced engineers in the offices of the mighty during the late fifties and early sixties, and Detroit indeed built cars so obese and absurd that John Keats could name his book *The Insolent Chariots* after them, what technical developments of any interest whatsoever could have been going on to engage our attention?

Lovely ones.

It was all very simple, really. Accountants wanted black ink, so they turned to marketers. Marketers swirled around in their offices and, trying to follow their Great Sales Blitz Act, concluded that if one model in one line was good, twenty models in the same line would be twenty times better. Was America auto-sated? Only if demand were identified as the need for transportation. But our whole history with the car said that transportation came somewhere down on the list of auto-mobile advantages. There were also: pure acquisitiveness, pride of owner-ship, keeping up with the Jones-Rockefellers, dissatisfaction with last year's car. Detroit knew all about these things because Detroit invented them. If such all too human (if irrational) processes were propelling us into new-car showrooms, there must be a thousand more reasons Detroit had never considered. Now the accoun-tants were insisting more metal be moved, and the marketers were getting desperate for new kinds of customers. A slew of automoton market researchers, a combat brigade of clipboarded motivational researchers, a plague of attitude ex-aminers went forth in the land and came back with a delightful surprise for Detroit. Indeed, there were whole new markets out there. In fact, they had been there all the time.

There was a market for the single man or woman (a two-seater) and a market for newly marrieds (a cute little hardtop without much of a backseat.) There was a market for large families (station wagons) and for smaller ones (a hatchback). Older people wanted something very different (staid four-doors) from the young (a steering wheel attached to an engine). Better still, within those markets were submarkets. Large families in housing developments would want station wagons with stick shifts and blackwall tires. Large families in tract houses would want a plusher version of the same wagon, whitewalls and automatic transmission and air conditioning, perhaps. Large families in exurbs in the sunbelt had yet different deisres, perhaps a station wagon with lots of trim, chrome luggage rack, wraparound rear window, and a special name like, say, *Nomad*. It was called "market proliferation." It was segmenting the market by demographics and psychographics and then building a variant of every car in every line to suit each segment and then, as Detroit became entranced with the notion, segments within segments: minisegments.

It was all very well for American Motors to produce a fastback Rambler and call it a Marlin, a two-seater with vestigial back seat for the "California market."

1955 Chevrolet Bel Air Nomad Station Wagon
This was the introductory year for one of Chevrolet's most successful cars, the Nomad. Based on the Bel Air station wagon, it began life as a show car and was then put into production. It is a so-called special-interest car, and as such, is rare and much in demand.

1949 Mercury Club Coupe
The so-called Jimmy Dean car named after its owner, this Mercury encapsulates everything that can be said about its possessor, the era, and the pastures in which it roamed: Southern California. It is a Kalifornia Kustom (albeit an understated one), with its leaded-in seams, "frenched" headlamps, and lack of chrome.

was all very well for Dodge to do the same thing and call its result the Charger. But these were fakes, new cars that weren't new cars, sleight of sheet metal.

It was when Detroit fastened on the "youth market" that things began to happen, things that mark the period as one of the ages in which Detroit produced memorable cars—not great ones—but cars of a kind we will likely not see again. These were cars that in their day startled the nation if not the world, uniquely American cars, in their ways wonderful cars.

The first was the Muscle car. The second, the Pony car. As they matured, the lines of demarcation blurred; often one make and model was certifiably both. In an age of sameness and bigness, they were exceptions. It was a tribute to Detroit that out of the same stuff as they made their go-to-supermarket cars and their family vacation cars and their drive-to-visit Grandma cars, they managed to devise both the Muscle and the Pony.

What made Muscle, Pony, Sunbelt, High-Line Wagon, and Stripper versions—minisegmentation—possible was the computer. Even futurist Alvin Toffler took notice of the multiple-choice cars the new technology was making possible: "Thus the beautiful and spectacularly successful Mustang [first of the Pony cars] is promoted by Ford as 'The one you design yourself,' because [here he cites the calculations of a colleague] 'there isn't a dang regular Mustang any more, just a stockpile of options to meld in combinations of three bodies × four engines × three transmissions × four basic sets of high-performance engine modifications minus one rock bottom six-cylinder car to which these modifications don't apply × two Shelby grand-touring and racing set-ups applying to only one body shell and not all engine/transmission combinations.' This does not even take into account the possible variations in color, upholstery and optional equipment. . . .

"Anyone who has attempted to buy a car lately soon finds that the task of learning about the various brands, lines, models and options . . . requires days of shopping and reading. In short, the auto industry may soon reach the point at which its technology can economically produce more diversity than the customer needs or wants."

We can cheerfully dismiss the besequined hardtops and the bedraggled tudors. What counts is that the computer sorting through the infinite number of choices of engines, transmissions, bodies, and suspensions, managed to come up with The Terror of Street Racing Heaven, Woodward Avenue: the Muscle car.

According to John Jerome, formerly executive editor of *Car and Driver* magazine, Chrysler really started the performance race, with its "Fire Dome V-8" in the early fifties. Chevrolet followed, of course, with its 265 V-8 in the 1955 model year. Immediately thereafter, Ford produced a new V-8 of its own,

originally a 260-inch motor, but stretched thereafter and still in use. But the powerful engine was only a component of the Muscle car. The creature itself had to be conceived, and that was left to a flamboyant man in an unlikely place for such a Frankensteinian achievement: John DeLorean of Pontiac Division of General Motors.

Its creation in 1963 is another classic case study for the Harvard Business School—from one outré suggestion made in somber committee came a Tyrannosaurus, a pavement ripper, a machine that would grant industry recognition to the illegal practice of street racing, a hype car that turned out to be all too real, and all too savage.

In 1956, William "Big Bill" Knudsen's son, Semon "Bunkie" Knudsen took over Pontiac Division. Knudsen was a car man through and through. He hired a pair of soulmates in chief engineer Pete Estes and, as Estes' assistant, John DeLorean. Estes proved himself a classic GM type—although perhaps too interested in hardware to suit the new arm garter and eyeshade set that had taken over at the top. DeLorean was another matter entirely. He was an engineer who was not at all sure that GM would allow him the freedom he wanted and needed. He was neither shy nor conventional. In a sea of sack suits, he wore tailored Italian clothes; in a field of shorn skulls, his hair curled around his ears. John Zachary DeLorean was his own man.

But Pontiac's 1956 problems were DeLorean's as well as his boss's as well as his boss's boss's. Out there in the world, Pontiac was seen as a constipated car. In a word association test "Pontiac" might prompt responses like "old," "stodgy," and "unimaginative." Given the marketers' new understanding of a market pie sliced into an infinite number of segments labeled from Young Punk Kid to Rich Palm Springs Matron, Pontiac seemed to be appealing to a tiny slice called "Middle-Aged Appliance Buyers on the Verge of Retiring to an Airsteam Trailer Park." Not much excitement there. Not much opportunity to spread the market and increase division sales either. Yet DeLorean saw this as opportunity. "We could find a niche in the market and exploit it. We could choose where we wanted to be in the market by being daring, innovative and by taking chances," DeLorean was quoted in *On A Clear Day You Can See General Motors,* an autobiography he co-wrote with J. Patrick Wright and then disavowed.

"We could ignore over half of the whole auto market . . . and still grow," said DeLorean. And how? By grabbing the youth market and shaking all that discretionary money out of its pockets. "Knudsen was the first in the industry to recognize the emerging importance of the youth market, not just in automobiles, but in everything from fashion to food. Capricious, energetic, and impressionable, America's young people have always been excited by cars. But their influence in car buying increased as the post–World War II economy grew, producing two-, three-, and even four-car families."

Since its name change from Oakland, Pontiac had had the Indian chief, after which it was christened, sitting arrogantly (in plastic after the war) as its hood ornament. Off came the chief. Pontiac had been suitably garbed in strips and stripes of chrome. Knudsen banished chrome. This was the first step in pursuing his policy of turning a stodgy car division into "a freewheeling, forward-thinking operation."

Then Knudsen looked over the option list—with a little help from his friends Estes and DeLorean—and decided that in addition to air conditioners and idiot lights and fuzzy dice for over the rear-view mirror, he would make available big engines, stiff suspension parts, varying axle ratios, and close-ratio transmissions. He would do more than that; he would call attention to their availability in the most vulgar way possible. Pontiac would go racing.

The southeastern United States had no mainstream professional sport in the 1950s; the National League Braves were still in Milwaukee. The Falcons and Dolphins of the NFL did not exist. The Southeast *did* have a sport grown at home, however, and it was almost more a religion than a sport in places like Level Cross, North Carolina; Hueytown, Alabama; Charlotte; Atlanta; and Daytona Beach. The Good Ol' Boys of the Carolina piney backcountry and Georgia red clay one-laners had been playing with stock cars since they were old enough to watch their daddies and their uncles run moonshine. In all of the United States there were probably only two places outside of Detroit engineering labs and test centers where mechanics were getting incredible performance out of regular production engines and cars: in Southern California, where hot rodding was king, and in the Southeast, where a quick car had taken the place of a good horse as the sign of a dirt road sport. This had quite naturally evolved into a money-making enterprise—late-model stock-car racing first on short dirt tracks and the sands of Daytona Beach, then as it became big business, on huge concrete ovals all over the South.

One of the people who helped it become such big business was Semon Knudsen. He saw southeastern racing as a perfect showcase for the new, high-performance Pontiac. And he as right. "Win on Sunday, Sell on Monday," went the slogan in the Carolinas and Florida and Virginia, which is just what Pontiac did.

But cars sold in sections of the nation other than the South, so Knudsen sent a legendary Southern California hot rodder named Mickey Thompson off to the endless salt flats of Bonneville, Utah, to set a few records. Thompson, like his Los Angelino colleagues, was no believer in understatement. He stuffed four Pontiac engines into one fragile chassis and blasted down the salt at 400 miles an hour. Stodgy car indeed.

Nor was this all. Across the land, DeLorean's postwar generation was deeply involved with a uniquely American motor sport called drag racing. Using a plumb-straight half-mile strip of concrete with a runout area at the end, pairs of cars would line up at the top waiting for a Christmas tree of lights to flash green, and off they would go to see who could cross the line in the least elapsed time. Although each drag race took no more than fifteen seconds to complete (and some took as little as six), an organized event would draw as many as 1,500 cars and would sometimes go on for several days. Drag racing had become an enormously popular sport in the United States—particularly since there were a number of classes in which owners of stock cars could compete. This was a very different definition of *stock* from that used by the southeastern racers, whose cars *looked* more or less like their showroom counterparts but underneath were really racing cars. Drag-racing stock cars really *were* stock—classes existed for the young, the innocent, the less-than-rich who "run what they brung."

All this was perfect for Pontiac. A youngish advertising executive named Jim Wangers worked for Pontiac's agency during the early Knudsen-Estes-DeLorean days. That is to say, he worked in advertising during the week. On Saturdays and Sundays, he climbed into his Pontiac and went drag racing. What's more, he was good at it.

From stock classes, he progressed to more and more sophisticated cars, until he was at the top rung of the sport, racing cars that—like their southeastern counterparts—looked like the cars anyone could buy but that were in fact much modified. With Wangers leading the way, Pontiac won every drag race in sight while Mickey Thompson's banzai run down the Bonneville flats was fresh in

OVERLEAF LEFT:
Supercharged Rail Dragster
This dragster is typical of the cars used by the top-level drivers in the uniquely American sport of drag racing. Fierce devices like this one could get to the end of a quarter mile in less than seven seconds from a standing start.

OVERLEAF RIGHT:
1974 Garlits' "Wynn's Charger" Rear-Engine AA Fuel Dragster
Designed by the best-known drag racer in America, Don Garlits, this revolutionary rear-engined racer was built to go from a stop down a quarter-mile strip, reaching the end in five seconds, at a speed of over 200 miles an hour. It is powered by a supercharged and injected Keith Black Hemi engine of 501 cubic inches that produces 2,000 horsepower.

OVERLEAF BELOW:
1962 Herda Land Speed Record Streamliner
This car set a land speed record in class at Bonneville at 346.462 mph for the flying kilometer and 345.755 mph for the flying mile. It used either a 471.7-cubic-inch Ford engine or a 299.3-cubic-inch supercharged Chrysler engine to conform to engine regulations in class. It was designed by Lockheed aerodynamist Robert Herda, also an excellent road racer for Porsche.

299

everyone's memory at the same time that the division was winning forty-three of fifty-two top stock-car races in the Southeast. By the time the Pontiac triumvirate was finished, there wasn't a stodgy car in any Pontiac dealership in the nation.

In combination with an ad campaign built around a necessary engineering change that moved the wheels outward so Pontiac was broader than its competitors—the campaign made a virtue of necessity by bragging about the car's "Wide Track Look"—all this foofaraw jumped Pontiac up to third place in industry sales behind Chevy and Ford. The credit for this went to Knudsen, and he moved on to Chevrolet, for that is the way at GM—successful general managers of the smaller divisions are always headed for the largest of them all, Chevy. Estes

succeeded Knudsen as division chief, and DeLorean took Estes' place as chief engineer.

During DeLorean's years at Pontiac he honored the division with three-quarters of GM's engineering innovations. "A goodly number of the 200 patents and pending patent applications I have amassed over my lifetime came out of my work at Pontiac," to which he might have added one invention that he didn't patent but that was as much his as anyone else's.

For some time, DeLorean had been looking at "car-crazy Southern California" for styling inspiration. Now, encouraged by his new position as chief engineer of the division and the successes of Pontiac at the drag strip and on the race track, entranced by the whole notion of a youth market, DeLorean, along with Estes, drew glory from a car that was becoming a corporate disaster. GM had introduced a line of "erstwhile compact" cars that were going the way of all small cars born in Detroit in the sixties. They were getting bigger and fancier by the year. Part of the reason for this was that the cars were not selling, and one way to make money from a slow seller is to stuff a bigger gross profit into it for which there had to be an ostensible reason. In the case of Pontiac's Tempest and Oldsmobile's F-85 and Buick's Special, the reason was increased girth.

DeLorean had a different idea. The compacts had been powered by an anemic six-cylinder engine. It was entirely consistent that he order his minions to stuff an enormous V-8 engine into one of these relatively small, light cars just to see how fast he could go with it. He could go very fast. So he had a *bigger* engine put in it and went even faster. Eureka! A Southern California car-crazy 'shine-

LEFT, ABOVE, AND OVERLEAF LEFT:

Pontiac Gran Turismo Omologato (GTO) a.k.a. "The Goat"
When progressive management took over at Pontiac Division of General Motors the first conclusion reached was that the car lacked identity and interest. As a result, chief engineer Pete Estes and his assistant John DeLorean latched onto a midsized car already in production called the Tempest, installed the largest engine available, and by 1964 created the first of the so-called Muscle cars. The ploy was so successful that Pontiac soon became the third largest selling car in America.

running backroads-blasting drag-strip-gobbling darling for the youth market. DeLorean had his engineers strip a Tempest to the bone, add heavy duty brakes, stiffer suspension, and three, two-barrel carburetors for performance and make both the big- and bigger-engine choices as power plants. The Muscle car was born at last. The pieces had all been there; the cars were cheap to build, they were light, they were fast; just a new synthesis had been needed, and eccentric John DeLorean was the synthesizer.

He named the new car after a Ferrari designation—GTO—and launched it in 1963 despite dire predictions of a sales disaster. How wrong they were, the Cassandras; how right, John Z. DeLorean. With a little help from Jim Wangers, who devised a promotional campaign around a rock group named Ronnie and the Daytonas (created for the occasion) who recorded a hit song called "Little GTO," and a flood of GTO T-shirts, emblems, and shoes, the "Goat," as it was coming to be called, took off. It was the start of a series of Muscle cars including Ford's Torino Cobra, Mercury's Cougar Eliminator, and Plymouth's Road Runner. Europeans could have their real Ferrari GTOs. The American young, for $3,200, could get a car that would go almost as fast in a straight line, and survive to take its driver to work at the car wash the next morning. In a land where straight lines stretched from one coast to the other, who needed an alpine racer?

Getting a Different Kind of Horse

Some Americans thought they needed an alpine racer. At the very least, they needed a car that *looked* like one. Fortunately for them, there was a man in Dearborn who was just a little ahead of them and who had looked at market proliferation himself, smacking his lips all the while. Lido Anthony Iacocca was an engineer and a salesman, brought up in the Ford organization. He had just celebrated his thirty-sixth birthday when he was made head of Ford Division in 1960. Iacocca is not in the DeLorean mold, although the two men share some attributes. Both have a clear sense of self, both are large thinkers. Both, when they have started down a track and gathered momentum, are extremely hard to stop. What's more, both had similar ideas about what sold cars during the Ocean Liner era in Detroit: Somewhere, somehow, a company had to be seen as exciting.

DeLorean, Estes, and Knudsen had understood that very well when they arrived at Pontiac. Iacocca saw it just as clearly over at Ford, particularly from the point of view of the young: "When they heard the name Ford they just associated it with their parents and things that were fuddy-duddy; they hadn't lived through the prewar era." Almost immediately, the new division general manager began a series of meetings to determine how Ford executives wanted their car seen out there in the world. They felt they had all the advantages that the Knudsen team had at Pontiac: Because Ford carried no emotional luggage in the minds of consumers, they were at a considerable advantage in starting from scratch. Iacocca

and his people looked at the same devices Pontiac had employed, selected some—racing, in particular—and then hit on another one.

The advertising scheme—the tone of Ford's new campaign—the Iacocca group decided, was to be "Total Performance." The target audience was the youth market. Iacocca had already opened every door by saying, "When you don't have anything, the quickest way to generate something is excitement. Earlier it had really built up inside of me that we were going to go racing on all fronts. . . . I wasn't as interested in stock cars per se as I was [in] a more sophisticated approach."

One problem he had in plunging FoMoCo into the ambitious racing program it eventually undertook was budgetary. And one of the budget constraints came from a large amount of money being devoted in-house to the development of an entirely new kind of car, code named Cardinal. Nothing about the Cardinal promised Iacocca a solution to the lack-of-excitement problem. It was to be a small, simple car, very much a competitor of the VW Beetle—but far more conventional in design. Iacocca hated it, and he campaigned brilliantly to have it extirpated—with success. "The greatest thing I ever did for [Ford]," he later said, "was killing the Cardinal at the beginning of the youth boom; we would have gone back to basic transportation and bombed!"

The timely passing of the Cardinal offered an opportunity for Iacocca's more sophisticated approach, and he plunged right in. A Ford Division product planning manager named Donald Frey had brought up a little item in 1961 that was

LEFT AND OVERLEAF:

1965 Ford Mustang Notchback Coupe Lee Iacocca pushed for excitement in product when he was at the Ford Motor Company; the result was the first of the Pony cars, the Mustang. The car put Iacocca on the cover of *Time* magazine, set an all-time first-year sales record, and ended up increasing Ford sales overall far less than it might have, since its sales came at the expense of other Ford products. But it *did* show Detroit that the American buyer wanted something other than plain vanilla cars and it paved the way for a number of exciting products from other companies. Today, a good '65 Mustang notchback is worth its original price, a fastback twice as much, and a convertible about five times what it cost new.

based on one of those endless show cars. In its test-the-waters form, it was a small, mid-engined sports car. Iacocca and Frey picked it up, shook it some, re-arranged its insides, retailored its outside, and produced the first Pony car—the Mustang. "It was the first of the long-term plans to put something together for the kids. The components were in the system; all we had to do was put a youth wrap-per around it—and this was done for less than $50 million," said Iacocca.

The Falcon, which Iacocca meant when he said "the components were in the system" was an early Cardinal. It was one of Detroit's attempts to attack the in-creasing market for imports, an appallingly incompetent car too large to be con-sidered small, too small to be considered true-blue American, too stark-looking to appeal to anyone but VW buyers, but too badly assembled and insufficiently engineered ever to be seriously considered by them.

But it had several great virtues as far as Iacocca and the Mustang were con-cerned. Its platform was a perfect size upon which to style a 2-plus-2-seater coupe. It had underpinnings and steering and transmission options that would be perfect for the kind of car he wanted to market.

Fifty million dollars is a drop in the bucket for a vast revision of an automobile, even less for a whole new kind of car. And that's precisely what the American public took the Mustang to be when it was introduced in April 1964. Although Mustangs and GTOs would come to share the same audience, the same drive-ins, the same late-night drag races, when the two cars appeared, they were not understood to have even concept in common. The Goat was a pure street bully. The Mustang, first brought forth as a long-bonnet, notchback coupe, was a "personal car." It was available as a six-cylinder, automatic-transmissioned wallflower. But it could also be bought with the 260-cubic-inch (soon to be 289-cubic-inch) V-8, a real horse of an engine, which could come with a four-speed floor shifter. The price for the tough Mustang was $2,480 plus options. It was the most sensational introduction of modern times. Ford sold half a million Mustangs in less than eighteen months; Lee Iacocca made the cover of *Time* magazine, a legend at barely forty. Very quickly, Ford fleshed out the line with a

lovely fastback and a convertible. (Today, a 1964 notchback in good condition brings more than its price as new; a convertible, about four times its original sticker price.)

Ford's dazzling success with the Mustang was only partially the result of the youth market's response to it. Shortly after it established a reputation as a kind of cheap Thunderbird, Mustang became the darling of the high-speed set. These were thrill seekers, in their late twenties and thirties, who worked by day as middle managers and accountants, but by night put on the cloak of the superdriver. The Mustang was perfect for them. It was a stylish, smallish car that set its owner apart from the Valiant/Dart/Coronet/Fairlane/Impala drivers, whose modules all looked so much alike.

Only later did the Mustang come to wrap itself in Iacocca's "excitement" in terms of pure performance. It was a remarkable race driver turned promoter turned car constructor named Carroll Shelby who transformed the Mustang into a real racing car. Actually he began to tinker with the car—with Iacocca's blessing—in its very early stages of development. In 1965, Shelby's company, based in Los Angeles, marketed a version called the GT350 which was as mean, as nasty, as savage a street machine as was being built anywhere in the world. In *fourth gear* it put so much power down to the rear wheels that they could lose traction, cocking the car sideways, and spinning evilly against the pavement, sending up great clouds of blue rubber smoke as they ground their tires smooth.

Predictably, it had been a Los Angelino, Carroll Shelby, who transformed the docile pony of Dearborn into a fierce stallion; equally predictably, it had been the influence of the car-crazy Southern Californians who gave DeLorean inspiration for the Pontiac GTO. Southern California had discovered the youth market even before World War II. Southern Californians were drag racing when drag racers were considered social felons. In Southern California, the "excitement" of the automobile had been a kind of illicit drug that people had been high on for a decade before Detroit had even discovered its existence.

Low Slung and Laid Back: The "Kalifornia Kar Kulture"

It was probably inevitable that both the drive-in and the hot rod were born in California. In the conception of the latter at least two influences were at work. First, nobody had walked any appreciable distance in California since Father Junipero Serra's Band of missionaries and bearers marched the royal route—El Camino Real—up the coast. California was the land of the highway. It was populated by Americans who had migrated there by car. Once they became Californians, they saw no reason to change their mode of transportation. There had, moreover, long been a tradition of car mania in California. California had board-track oval racing in the northern part of the state, at Cotati, in the 1920s. That strange and wonderful evocation of Italy, Venice-by-the-Pacific, held a pre-World War I Grand Prix race through the city streets "with drivers of the likes of Dario Resta, Ralph DePalma, and Barney Oldfield and a wonderful variety of cars: Peugeot, Mercer, Stutz, Delage, Simplex, Maxwell and Chevrolet" according to automotive historian Noel Frobe.

The second great influence on the development of the mutant car in California was the state's distance from tradition, geographically and intellectually. California was new, distances enormous, the Establishment guarding The Way Things Are Done not yet established, so if a Californian awoke wanting to be a

1924 Ford Speedster Model T
This year marked the first appearance at Indianapolis of the Frontenac sixteen-valve, dual overhead camshaft head for the Model T Ford block. Fronty Fords finished fourteenth, sixteenth, and seventeenth. Fronty heads were also used by sports drivers, who wanted to increase the performance of their T's. This Speedster has a body built by Mercury Body Corp. in Kentucky, Winfield carburetors, and Bosch ignition.

racer, by noon he had a car, and just before sunset he was screaming down a dry lake bed. Who was to say him nay?

Before World War I, the Model T Ford was king in California; after the war it remained so but was joined by the A and then the flathead V-8. The first step Californians took was to improve their car's performance. With the T, that meant overhead valves, which in turn meant buying one or another of the cylinder heads made for the car. As early as 1915 or 1916, said Leo Levine, author of the Ford racing history, Craig-Hunt in Indianapolis was making a single overhead cam, sixteen-valve (four for each cylinder) conversion. Robert M. Roof marketed his first sixteen-valve head just before 1917, but it was after the Armistice that the *real* performance enhancers became available. One of the heads was called the

1929 Miller Race Car
Ralph Hepburn qualified this lovely
Packard Cable Special third fastest for
the 1929 race at Indianapolis but lost
his transmission after fourteen laps in
the actual race. Owner/driver Leon
Duray then took the car to Europe
and broke a number of records before
running the car in a Grand Prix race
at Monza, Italy. After the race, the car
was sold to Ettore Bugatti. It was
discovered in the Bugatti factory in
France in 1959. The Miller was the
first to use De Dion suspension in a
race car. Front-wheel–drive Millers
won the Indy 500 in 1930, 1932, and
1934. This particular car used to
belong to Griffith Borgeson, co-author
of *Sports and Racing Cars,* as well as
an important collector.

Rajo, the other the Frontenac. The latter had been designed and built by the
Chevrolet brothers in Indianapolis. It was so successful that it actually gave its
name to the cars that used it—they were Frontenac Fords, which everyone
shortened to Frontys.

"The postwar boom is what [really got Model Ts] racing," said Levine. "It
began, of course, with the kids, those who were mechanics and perhaps had $10
left over at the end of the month and an old Model T on which to spend it. One
month you couldn't buy anything and the next month, when you had $20, you
could get the 'underslinging' parts from Craig-Hunt for $20 and lower the car a
few inches. Later . . . an eight-valve Roof head (complete with intake and ex-

haust manifolds, plugs and wires) cost $65. Wheel discs, to hide the spokes and help them support the rim, cost $10 a set, and if you could come up with $150 you could buy a Morton and Brett single-seater racing body, the *ne plus ultra* of the day. In the 20 years the Model T was being built, accessory manufacturers managed to produce more than 5,000 different items for the car, and a good many of them were in the speed equipment category." The likes of Wilbur Shaw, Frank Lockhart, and Mauri Rose began with a T-based race car, but that story waits until we get into American auto racing.

The full-bore oval-track racers were far from the only people interested in—and using—all this equipment. The lovely coincidence of car-crazed kids living in California and the dry lake beds nearby saw to that. "There was something *about* southern California, and in time those [racers] who didn't live there managed to migrate to the area. . . . [In] recent years, the beginning of May sees what amounts to almost to a mass exodus from Southern California to Indianapolis for the 500; Indiana may be where the cars are run, but California is the place where they are made," said Levine.

Yes, and starting right after World War I, they were made to take their builders out to the dry lakes of the Mojave Desert—especially to a dry lake bed called Muroc—where the current land speed record was set in 1979—which sits on what is now Edwards Air Force Base in the Space Shuttle runoff area.

Ed Winfield, who provided a great part of the intellectual stimulus, is considered by Levine to be the father of hot-rodding and its first prodigy. After Winfield came just a few other mechanical wizards of automotive performance who trained in the Mojave sunshine, including John Holman (who supplied Ford Motor Company with winning race cars after World War II), Bill Stroppe (who did the same and then went into building desert racing trucks), Phil Remington (key to Ford's finally winning at LeMans in his capacity as engineer for Shelby Racing), Fran Hernandez (a principal player in the establishment of a performance reputation for the Cougar and the Mustang). There were also race drivers: Dan Gurney, Phil Hill, Parnelli Jones, Rex Mays, Sam Hanks, and many others.

Winfield's growing up was first and typical; we must remember that he was the rule not the exception and that the same demons that drove him also drove the likes of Robert E. Petersen, who started *Hot Rod* and *Motor Trend* magazines, and also produced Dean Batchelor, who was almost as influential in another auto magazine company, which published *Road & Track*.

Anyway, there was Winfield, born in 1901, in love with cars almost before he was old enough to walk around his neighborhood in La Canada, near Los Angeles. Levine talked about an 11-year-old Winfield, his room stuffed with car literature, stripping down a Model T and reworking its engine. He went to the YMCA technical school. By the time he was fourteen, he was building Model T racers for others. Winfield became one of the great performance-parts manufacturers of what is called the "aftermarket," that part of the industry supplying parts and service for a car after it has been sold, but with the special meaning in Southern California of being the designers, builders, and suppliers of high-performance equipment.

In 1924, race driver Tommy Milton went 151.3 mph at Muroc in a Miller racer; three years later, another famous driver, Frank Lockhart, took his 1.5-liter supercharged Miller up to 164 mph there. From then on, Muroc was a legend and thither went the Ts and then As and the V-8s from Los Angeles, eventually in special-bodied form including land speed-record cars. "Had anyone in Dearborn taken note, they would have realized this was the youth market," said Levine.

So it was, although the youth were not confining their activities to Muroc.

They were also street racing on Sepulveda, Manchester, Crenshaw, and Avalon Boulevards in Los Angeles—the birthplace of street racing.

Still, Muroc was the place to go, if you could. "It was a wild scene," said Levine. Those late 1920s, early 1930s nights at Muroc: groups of kids, many with their girl friends, huddled together on the flat floor of the lake, while almost everywhere you could hear the raucous noises of engines being revved up as their owners sought an extra few horses. . . . And in the background, out on the vast expanse of the lake bed, some of the wilder ones, with a couple of beers under their belt, were already racing around in the night.

"The meets themselves were run in the early morning, before the sun got too hot and boiled the water out of the cars, and at the beginning they were staged en masse.

"By noon it was all over, and the dog-tired kids headed home, preserving what water they had to pour into their radiators. Many were practically snowblind from the experience, and the kids and the cars were both covered by a fine, talcum-powder-like dust that was sprayed over everything, but that was OK too—when they got home, they wouldn't wash their cars for days; the dust was the way everyone in Los Angeles could tell they had been to the lakes."

Out of all this came: belly-panned roadsters and, after World War II, aircraft-belly-tank record cars, Model T Frontys and Rajos, Model A engines with Cragar heads and Winfield carburetors and manifolds, flathead V-8s with Offenhauser heads and Stromberg carburetors, other flatheads with overhead-valve Ardun heads, the word a combination of two names of the man considered responsible for the Corvette, Zora Arkus Duntov.

Really, there were a few points to all this activity. Americans were developing an automotive sport of their own; California was the home ground for that sport, and something called the "youth market," which, as we have seen would not be identified for some time by Detroit, was already in full flower. Moreover, it was flowering courtesy of FoMoCo, whose engines were not only the ones to have, but the *only* ones to have.

This, in part, prompted Iacocca at Ford to seek "excitement" since Chevy's V-8 in 1954 (the 1955 model) had suddenly replaced Ford as the *sine qua non* for all American performance chasers wherever they were and whatever they were doing. As we will see, the V-8 engine powered Chevrolet to a quick reputation on the late-model stock-car circuit and put Ford further in the shade.

The Mustang was born to revive Ford's performance reputation. The only wonder was that it arrived so long after Ford had originally captured the franchise.

A good many of Southern California-developed mechanical improvements in aid of higher performance became known to the engineers in Detroit—who were far too preoccupied in postwar years with simply designing and planning ordinary automobiles to worry about having to invent extraordinary automobiles. Detroit's laserlike look at what was being done in California began in earnest only when midwestern stylists began to look around for inspiration. Not only had Californians been urging their cars ever onward with modifications to the innards, they were spending inordinate amounts of time and money making them *look* different.

Standard procedure was to take off all or most of the chrome, and fill in the

1961 Ghia
An effort by a Detroit entrepreneur to combine American componentry with Italian coachbuilding panache, the Ghia was built on a Chrysler platform that was sent overseas for its body, then returned to the U.S. for its mechanicals. This car belonged to Frank Sinatra, and the few that were ever sold went originally to other members of the "Rat Pack," including Sammy Davis, Jr. It is still a car with significant performance despite its enormous size.

Really, there were a few points to all this activity. Americans were developing an automotive sport of their own; California was the home ground for that sport, and something called the "youth market," which, as we have seen would not be identified for some time by Detroit, was already in full flower. Moreover, it was flowering courtesy of FoMoCo, whose engines were not only the ones to have, but the *only* ones to have.

This, in part, prompted Iacocca at Ford to seek "excitement" since Chevy's V-8 in 1954 (the 1955 model) had suddenly replaced Ford as the *sine qua non* for all American performance chasers wherever they were and whatever they were doing. As we will see, the V-8 engine powered Chevrolet to a quick reputation on the late-model stock-car circuit and put Ford further in the shade.

The Mustang was born to revive Ford's performance reputation. The only wonder was that it arrived so long after Ford had originally captured the franchise.

A good many of Southern California-developed mechanical improvements in aid of higher performance became known to the engineers in Detroit—who were far too preoccupied in postwar years with simply designing and planning ordinary automobiles to worry about having to invent extraordinary automobiles. Detroit's laserlike look at what was being done in California began in earnest only when midwestern stylists began to look around for inspiration. Not only had Californians been urging their cars ever onward with modifications to the innards, they were spending inordinate amounts of time and money making them *look* different.

Standard procedure was to take off all or most of the chrome, and fill in the

1961 Ghia
An effort by a Detroit entrepreneur to combine American componentry with Italian coachbuilding panache, the Ghia was built on a Chrysler platform that was sent overseas for its body, then returned to the U.S. for its mechanicals. This car belonged to Frank Sinatra, and the few that were ever sold went originally to other members of the "Rat Pack," including Sammy Davis, Jr. It is still a car with significant performance despite its enormous size.

1977 Jerrari
William Fisk Harrah, owner of the 1,400-car collection, had a jeep wagoneer fitted with a Ferrari Daytona engine and transmission, which would make 130 mph.

gaps with lead. Fenders were smoothed, headlamps got eyebrows ("Frenched headlights," they were called), cars were lowered in front and raised in back or perhaps the other way around. That was the easy stuff. Some custom shops did catastrophic plastic surgery: entire sections of the middle of cars were cut out, and the cars rejoined to the top, losing a 6-inch width of beltline in the process. Passenger compartments were sawed off at their bottoms and reattached, half of their original height gone forever, and then covered with some exotic material. The best known of these treatments even got its own name: the Carson Top. Nor were interiors ignored. Upholstery was rolled and tucked; carpets were made of angel's hair, angora, sometimes mink. There was nothing too bizarre for the "Kalifornia Kustomizer."

Before we look briefly at how seriously Detroit came to take all this, here is a word from Tom Wolfe, whose title piece of his book *The Kandy-Kolored Tangerine-Flake Streamline Baby* speaks to the very point we have been discussing. Trilling the history of the setting of tastes through the centuries—and attributing style in every epoch to the whims of the aristocracy—Wolfe gives the background of his piece on "Kalifornia Kustoms" in terms of discovering quite the opposite effect at work in the United States. "What has happened in the United States since World War II . . . has broken that [aristocratic trend and taste setting] pattern. The war created money. It made massive infusions of money into every level of society. Suddenly classes of people whose styles of life had been practically invisible had the money to build monuments to their own styles." Next we are presented with a list of behaviors taken on by the newly rich young: "Practically nobody has bothered to see what these [new behaviors] are all about. . . . Nobody will even take a look at our incredible new national pastimes, things like stock car racing, drag racing, demolition derbies, sports that attract five to ten million more spectators than football, baseball and basketball each year.

"Part of it is built-in class bias. The educated classes in this country . . . are all plugged into what is, when one gets down to it, an ancient, aristocratic aesthetic. Stock car racing [and] custom cars . . . still seem beneath serious consideration, still the preserve of . . . people with ratty hair . . . and so forth. Yet all these . . . people are creating new styles all the time and changing the life of the whole country in ways that nobody seems to bother to record, much less analyze."

But, at last, Detroit was analyzing it and analyzing it a lot. First came the stylists, hanging out at the Art Center in Pasadena, where industry reality and California craziness were combined into an extraordinary automotive design curriculum. It was no accident that Ford's 1955 styling leader, the Thunderbird, appeared with Frenched headlights. Pontiac's understanding of understated trim came from the California custom shops. Needless to say, there were also people in Detroit who tried to impart Kalifornia-ism into their products and failed miserably. AMC's Marlin is a perfect example of Wisconsin stylists' peering across the nation into sunbelt souls and deciding that what was happening in California was nothing more than a slight variation on trends visible throughout the rest of the country, requiring nothing more than a special color of paint and slightly reworked roofline to satisfy.

No, it took car people of talent to understand the new values. Bunkie Knudsen, Pete Estes, and John DeLorean at Pontiac understood. Lee Iacocca at Ford understood. In an age of drab cars, the Goat and the Mustang, followed by a slew of imitations, stood tall.

To the American inch-brow, which is how car lovers were seen at the time, they were true monuments.

CHAPTER 17

Battle on the Interstates

The Goat was a marvelous idea, good for Pontiac, good for the industry. It was so good, in fact, that it was not long alone as a Muscle car. DeLorean had taken a compact and made a formidable demiracer out of it. Everyone else would follow the pattern. By the 1969 model year, every company in the industry was making what had come to be called an Intermediate, available with the largest engine in the inventory and a four-speed floor shifter. Best of the lot, in the minds of the connoisseurs, was a little number from Chrysler Corporation called the Plymouth Road Runner.

It was based on a body shell (the corporate "B" body) called the Belvedere. It used a Mopar (an acronym for the Motor Parts Division of Chrysler) four-speed transmission with a Hurst shifter—the product of a specialty aftermarket company catering to America's speed crazies. The best part was its engine, the famous Hemi, a last-minute addition when Chrysler came to understand it needed a Muscle car and had the parts lying around to build the engine. There remains some black magic about engine design. Nobody at Chevrolet could have foreseen that in its 1954 V-8, the division was introducing an engine that would last two decades or more and, better still, veritably ache to have its size and power increased again and again. When Chrysler's engine people laid out the Hemi, they knew what the goal was—a high-performance monster motor—but they could not know how stunningly successful they would be in achieving it. It was 426 inches in piston displacement—very large indeed. It had hemispherical combustion chambers, which is where a good deal of the black magic came in. Much of the power an engine makes depends directly on the efficiency of combustion of the air/fuel mixture, which depends on the kind and degree of flame produced when the mixture is lit off in the combustion chambers. The flame does not produce an instantaneous explosion. The mixture is lit, but if what happens then is viewed very carefully, a progressive fire can be seen to travel across or around the chamber. It has long been felt that a hemispherical shape to the chamber promotes the quickest-spreading fire and hence the most efficient one. So a hemi is what Chrysler's engine men decided its new engine would be, and what a hemi it was!

Used on the National Association for Stock Car Auto Racing (NASCAR) circuit—the great races for late-model stock cars—it was an absolute terror and hastened Chevy engineers into production of something called a Porcupine-head engine, and sent Ford people scurrying to design what they named the Tunnelport, or Highriser. The hemi design would later be recast all in aluminum by a famous builder of engines for drag racers, Keith Black, and would make incredible horsepower when fueled with alcohol and boosted by the use of a supercharger.

Chrysler Corporation wasn't interested in such exotica in the 1969 model year; all the company wanted was a Muscle flagship. That its product was so seen by the young buyer was proved in 1968, when Plymouth sold almost 45,000 versions of a

Plymouth Road Runner
By 1968, Chrysler Corporation was full into the Muscle car wars, producing perhaps the ultimate street ripper of them all, the Road Runner. Like the Pontiac GTO, it began life as a weak kneed Intermediate, but with the addition of the famous Chrysler 426-cubic-inch "Hemi" (for hemispherical combustion chamber) engine, it became the darling of the street racers.

single model within a model—remember, the Road Runner was not a distinct car to the company, it was a variation of the regular intermediate.

What Chrysler, and Plymouth in particular, understood was that the Muscle car buyer wanted something *purposeful*. Plymouth did not doll the thing up with gadgets; it was starkly plain except for a couple of tiny cartoon emblems on its sides and a shaker hood, an air intake on top of the hood (cold air, which is denser than the air that generally circulates around a running engine, makes the air/fuel mixture more potent).

The Road Runner could be ordered with fat tires (F-70s, almost as wide as they were tall), disc brakes on the front, and a low numerical axle ratio, which improves gas mileage (since the engine doesn't have to work so hard at low speeds) and *also* allows increased speeds (the lower the numerical ratio, theoretically, the higher the top speed that is available within the limits of the engine's power). And it came with a limited slip differential, which allowed the driven wheel to spin only a little before transferring power to the *other*, nondriven rear wheel, which made them both work. This was a handling option. It was also very useful in getting away from stoplights and in accelerating suddenly at *any* speed on the highway.

Of all the Muscle cars—Plymouth's competitors were the Dodge Super Bee, the Chevelle SS396, the Ford Torino Cobra, and the Lincoln Mercury Cyclone CJ, along with the founder of the genre the Pontiac GTO (now with a version called the Judge, complete with deck lid wing)—the hemi Road Runner went the fastest, accelerated the quickest, stopped in the shortest distance, and handled almost as well as the best of the others. One contemporary observer, comparing the cars, said the rest seemed

to be "hotted-up" passenger cars, the hemi Road Runner like a very slightly domesticated race car.

To drive the car is to forget about notions of seating, temperature, visibility of instruments, accessibility of controls. Ergonomics simply don't apply. The thing just takes your breath away. It accelerates so quickly that if the driver isn't absolutely prepared, the rear wheels will just spin. Worse, they will twist the back end right off the road. Even if the driver is prepared for letting all that power loose, he still can't believe what's happening. The world turns into a blur. The nose of the car climbs toward the sky, the rear paws just squat down and dig. Fighter pilots talk about accelerative "G" forces and what they do to intestines and spleens, and even how they cave in cheeks, lips, and second chins, but fighter pilots don't have the ground right outside to measure the speed of travel. You can lose a passenger to faintheartedness within 50 feet; you can lose your lunch if you haven't ordered wisely; you can lose all decency and respect for the rest of the world.

It is a loud car—the sound of power. When the engine is cold, the driver hears the impact-extruded pistons clattering around inside the cylinders; when it warms up, the driver hears the roar of cold air coming in, the two four-barrel carburetors sucking and screaming, and the exhaust bellowing an immense, continuous, and arrogant flatulence at the world.

The car's suspension was as stiff as a diving board. It used torsion bars, the size of Big Bertha's barrel, in front and elliptical springs in the back that were about as yielding as Mt. Rainier. For those interested in pure numbers, a good hemi Road Runner would get up to just over 105 mph in the standing quarter mile, reaching the electric eyes at the end of the strip in just over thirteen seconds. With the Hemi option (a 383-cubic-inch engine was standard), costing $813, the Road Runner was $4,200 in 1969. About the only other $4,200 investment you could have made that would have gotten you through the air as quickly would have been the equivalent in fireworks strapped to your tail. It was an absolutely *awful* car to take on a trip. Very shortly after departing, the thrill wore off along with much skin from the buttocks. Worse, at every little town there appeared the local gunslinger with *his* Muscle car, waiting to take on the Road Runner.

In fact, the car was best suited for that absolutely extraordinary scene of the late 1960s, the street race. Take a suburban road, any road that had at least one drive-in movie. Add darkness. Fill full of grumbling, snorting, heaving Muscle cars, each with a pair of Ricky Nelsons in the front seat. Surround the whole scene with the ominous shadow of the local police. Stir in some balm from the San Fernando Valley or grit from the Bronx. Mostly, add the crisp fall air of suburban Detroit. For it was Woodward Avenue, a highway that bore the great managers of the industry in and out of their offices from the rarefied atmosphere of Bloomfield Hills, that was the major scene, the holiest place, of street racing.

There was a very good reason for Detroit to be America's street racing capital. Nobody would ever accuse factory engineers of going out to Woodward Avenue and running the kids. But some very famous names in the industry seemed to pop up now and then in cars that were suspiciously fast and that went home frothing at the mouth and with flanks heaving.

The rituals were strict. So was the social stratification. The kids in their blatantly striped cars with mag wheels would sit at a curb or in a parking lot or near a drive-in *whumping, whumping,* as they stabbed the throttle. Except for the prepubescent girls in their parents' commuter cars, nobody paid much attention. Then there were the serious guys who would actually park at the drive-ins. You couldn't always tell much about them by looking at their cars. Of course, the cars were from the Muscle stable, but sometimes they looked so shabby it seemed they would barely be able to chug out of the parking lot. Often, these were the meanest cars in town. Under their hoods lived monster motors. When they were Mopars, their drivers were often not content even with the wonderful engine from Chrysler. In its street version, the motor was down about 200 hp from the racing, or NASCAR, engines. The technology of retuning an engine was well known. A full race engine might not live for more than an hour or two before it needed a complete rebuild. But that didn't make very much difference to the young men who lived to rumble out to Woodward Avenue and get it done.

When a couple of these predators found themselves close to one another, there was a required period of mutual ignoring, then a casual turn of the head and a lifted eyebrow. Slowly, slowly, the two cars would leave the drive-in, and as they burbled down Woodward toward I-75, the kids in their counterfeit racers would suddenly look up, switch on, and begin a parade of spectator cars.

Street racing was something of a misnomer, for it was not a drag race down a boulevard from stoplight to stoplight, except for a few raw amateurs who didn't know better than to challenge the cops. No, street racing was a flat out race on an interstate highway with the cars running side by side right up to their maximum speed.

The pair from the drive-in might by now be over an interchange and running through the darkness alongside one another, at perhaps 60 or 70 mph, windows open, trailed by a school of spectator cars. One of the drivers would suddenly yell "Go" at the other, and they were off—all the way off, pegging the speedometer needle to the far end of the instrument, beyond the ability of even the fastest spectator car to

distinguish between those disappearing taillights. One hundred twenty, one hundred thirty, one hundred forty. That was about where the good, crisply tuned Muscle cars peaked out.

Then there was a third variety of racer—even more serious than those who ran for $20 or $50 on the interstates. At least it was *rumored* they were there. The factory engineers, who in that era of numb passenger cars but screaming rockets on the track, felt some small obligation to find out what the kids were really doing. Who had the hot setup? Who, in the shade of his backyard tree, was making modifications to stock parts that improved them? What were some of the styling gimmicks that made slugs look fast? Better still, how did the engineers' modifications—carefully designed and done by hand during the day in the back shops of executive garages or R&D departments—prove out in the real world of street racing?

It is true the Muscle car did not have a long life. The times supportive of such a strange genus of car were brief and strange in themselves. But when they thrived, the econoracers from Ford and GM and Chrysler brightened the lives of a generation. Doubtless, they also killed their share of the members of that generation and maimed perfectly innocent bystanders. California police had realized early the dangers of allowing this kind of behavior on the public highways, which is why they supported and encouraged organized drag racing as a sport.

The moral question aside, this was the age of performance that lives in the memories of many American drivers today. Not many of us got to sit in an MG, much less own one, and even fewer than that to take it out on a road racing circuit.

No, for Americans now of responsible age, motor sport was the drive-in, the street racer, and cars like the Road Runner.

As this is written, even in this age of limitations, street racing continues. There is almost no town in the nation without its back road, the lake highway or the wrong-side-of-town stretch of interstate, or the industrial park thoroughfare, where today's much different versions of the Muscle car square off against each other. There are huge pick-ups with great engines and roll cages. There is the occasional foreign roadster with a small but powerful motor. There are still the cosmetic darlings, by now in the majority, the new Mustangs and Firebirds, with more decals than a school could use at Halloween.

Every once in a while, there is also a bright, shiny, beautifully preserved Road Runner, sitting somewhat apart, as is only proper, shaking rhythmically to the rumble of its Hemi engine, waiting for a time that will never come again.

VII
PERSONAL CARS

CHAPTER 18

Forecast: Gloom

Sometime in the late sixties, the searchlights disappeared. Suddenly, almost without our knowing it, new-car introduction day was just another Monday or Thursday. There were no more balloons, no more soapy windows, no more hoopla.

Perhaps it was that the ills of the decade kept nagging at us. "Millions of Americans still lived in poverty," Robert Kelley reminded us. "Black Americans made up 29% of the poor. Factory and automobile pollution increased. The Vietnam war produced massive protest and disillusionment. The cult of success, pride in industrial growth and joy in technological achievement that had inspired earlier generations gave way to a reluctant belief that such ideas had had much to do with propelling the nation into grave crisis."

We were becoming a land of disbelievers in industrial manifest destiny. People were beginning to question the heretofore unspoken premises of our national life, the verities on which the Detroit automobile industry was founded: Do we want to drive modules that foul the air with hydrocarbon pollutants? Are we prepared to continue to subsidize Bruce-Briggs's auto-highway-driver mass transportation system? How much is auto-mobility really costing us? The people asking all the questions—not yet booming across the land in one national voice but nonetheless beginning to annoy the automotive establishment—were war babies. They constituted a huge age cohort just beginning to move as adults through the population, about to become the "new consumers," at the leading edge of the demographic buying group that formed the juicy target for marketers of hard goods—particularly hard goods with four wheels and an engine. It was the first generation of Americans brought up from diapers to Nehru jackets under the threat of war. They were indeed skeptical, and militant skeptics at that. The social militants coalesced into the consumerist movement. The political militants were destined to staff an as yet uncreated cluster of regulatory agencies that would build up around our tripartite transportation structure.

This was a constituency prepared to accept still anonymous Ralph Nader's condemnation of Detroit's callousness about auto safety, to sympathize with the Club of Rome's plea for an end to the profligate use of fossil fuel, to applaud the Sierra Club's insistence that not a molecule of oxides of nitrogen be permitted to issue from automotive tailpipes.

Its collective attitude toward the automobile was summarized by a California futurist (and former car enthusiast) who—all his life conditioned by the availability of car-granted mobility—junked his automobile cold turkey. David Miller, as quoted in *Driven: The American Four-Wheel Love Affair,* gave up his car because he decided it was no longer cost-effective: "When you start adding up the time you spend in a car, not just behind the wheel but the time looking for parking places, and paying parking tickets, and getting the damn thing serviced,

LEFT AND OVERLEAF:
1957 Cadillac
Cadillac began using tailfins in a modest way in 1948; their use reached a crescendo by the 1957 model.

329

and getting it maintained. . . . I'd just much rather have the time at my disposal to use as I see fit." What's more, Miller thought that the entire consumer economy was coming to an end in the United States. "It was a basic culture theme from 1946, fueled by the ambitions and the expectations of people whose parents had bitter memories of the Depression. In a world of plenty, these are the people who constituted what we called the 'Flatulent Consumer Society.' There was material affluence; people were discovering more discretionary time.

"These people, who used to rejoice in [suburban living] have been forced to become realists enough to be able to say, 'That was a good trip, but it had some high prices. . . .'

"Even if they didn't say it, even if they didn't feel it, the trip is over anyway. It's simply less and less possible, and we're going to feel more and more inhibited about flatulent consumer behavior as well, so what next?"

One answer, particularly disturbing to Detroit, came from David Miller's former place of work, SRI International (originally the Stanford Research Institute). In the normal course of outlining policy choices for the several transportation studies one of its groups had done for a variety of federal agencies, SRI has posited the existence of a bifurcated society: Seventy percent of us will remain "materialists"—members of Miller's flatulent consumer society. But 30 percent of us will have embraced something SRI's sociologists and economists call voluntary simplicity—the David Millers of our nation, turning their backs on huge-screen televisions and video cassette recorders and automobiles, because all these *things* encumber their lives.

According to Kelley, "The tone of those who were critical of American society had grown bitter.... Using a combination of wit, realism and fantasy...writers such as Kurt Vonnegut and pop artists [like] Andy Warhol portrayed American culture as not just being in trouble but as being beyond repair or wildly and insanely ridiculous."

At the very least, many of us were becoming skittish and questioning buyers. At the very most, we were turning into a people wondering about the worth of some of the achievements we had previously thought of as our crowning accomplishments, and the auto-mobiling of America was a particular focus of the new unease.

Paralysis on the 14th Floor

Most of this rising discontent was going unnoticed by Detroit's managers. In the mid-sixties, sales of passenger cars reached an all-time high of 9.3 million units. And sales stayed high: 8.6 million in 1966; 7.4 million in 1967; back up to 8.8 million in 1968; only half a million less in 1969. There was a big drop in 1970 to 6.5 million, and then a steady climb back up to 9.6 million in 1973.

Detroit was still reveling in flatulent consumerism. It was also suspended in time. Had it wanted to understand what was happening to its bright new generation of buyers, it would not have been able to lift itself out of its own mind-set to ask questions. Sloanist management, so productive in its time, had turned even GM into an arteriosclerotic company. And what was bad for General Motors was bad for the entire industry.

By the early seventies, one of the bright young car men who had turned Pontiac Division around a decade earlier, John Z. DeLorean, had been pushed out of GM's line management and into a policy-making position — the coveted promotion to the 14th-floor offices of the people who ran what was still the largest corporation in America. DeLorean was appalled by what he found there.

DeLorean's discontent had begun at the operational level: "Sometime in the late '60s...a nagging suspicion about the philosophy of General Motors and the automobile business began to overtake me.

"My concern was that there hadn't been an important product innovation in the industry since the automatic transmission and power steering in 1949. That was almost a quarter-century of technical hibernation. In the place of production innovation, the automobile industry went on a two-decade marketing binge which generally offered up the same old product under the guise of something new and useful [DeLorean is being a little harsh on the GTO here]. Year in and year out we were urging Americans to sell their cars and buy new ones because the styling had changed. There really was no reason...except for the new wrinkles in the sheet metal."

Now here was a man already questioning the essence of Sloanism as an heir apparent to the presidency of a company built by Sloan. DeLorean did not articulate his feelings at the time. He waited until he left GM to write a book with J. Patrick Wright called *On a Clear Day You Can See General Motors*, which he later disavowed, so that Wright had to publish it himself. The book was an enormous success. It was the first uninhibited account of how the exemplar of the American corporation had evolved, of what flatulent consumerism had done to the best and the brightest of our executives. A good deal of what DeLorean said is self-serving, certainly those last words represent hindsight, but at the same time they suggest that the then general manager of Chevrolet Divi-

OVERLEAF LEFT:
1964 Chevrolet Impala Convertible Model SS
In some cases, the efforts to build cars with a performance image stumbled, or were half hearted. Chevy put a wonderful 396-cubic-inch displacement engine in a medium-sized car, but it concentrated more on the use of the logo "SS" for Super Sports than it did on engineering development.

OVERLEAF RIGHT:
1967 Chevrolet Camaro Convertible
Chevrolet was late getting into the Pony car field; when it did the result was the Camaro, at first a simple, relatively unexciting car. When famous race-car entrant and constructor Roger Penske was given a contract to develop the car for the TransAmerican Road Racing Series, the car became a marvel, and much of what Penske's people did found its way into the car available to the public.

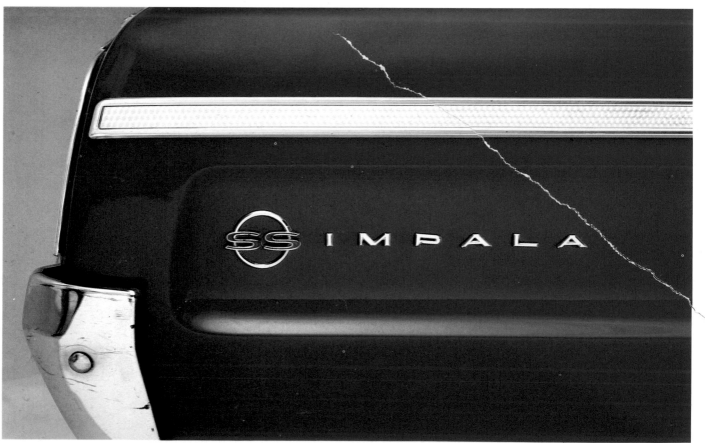

sion was feeling the waves of discontent that were washing over his constituents, even if he didn't know exactly why they were there or how quickly they were building into a real sea.

DeLorean's real unhappiness came when he was removed from daily operational tasks and sent upstairs to think, to help set policy. There he discovered a cadre of decision makers who, when they looked out of their windows, still saw the calm of the 1950s. John DeLorean found himself in a time warp. He had finally ascended to the temple of Sloanist management, to join the keepers of the shrine. But once there, he discovered they had so misread the Book of Sloan that it had been turned into a disaster tract. Said DeLorean: "The success of General Motors in the past had come from a finely tuned balance between . . . centralized control and decentralized operations. I found the fine tuning had gone out of control. I watched GM's operations slowly become centralized. The Divisions gradually were stripped of their decision-making power.

"Men rose in power who did not seem to have the capabilities or broad business outlook necessary to manage the business. They had gotten into power because they were part of a . . . system which for the most part put personal loyalties from one executive to another, and protection of the system above management skills, and put the use of corporate politics in the place of sound business management.

"The committees and subcommittees which were methodically set up during the '20s, '30s and '40s to plan and guide General Motors' growth were not doing that. They spent little time looking at the big picture, instead occupying themselves with minuscule matters of operation."

DeLorean and Wright's book is a horror story of mismanagement. It tells of rampant sycophantism, arrogant misuse of power for personal gain, and imperious disdain for test results condemning prospective products as inefficient or unsafe. Above all, it is a repeated criticism of the incredible provincialism of an earlier generation in Detroit, a provincialism that had been codified to form the philosophical basis for GM's purpose in life: to make a profit and to be cost-effective.

DeLorean wrote: "The undue emphasis on profits and cost control without a wider concern for the effects of GM's business on its many publics seemed too often capable of bringing together, in the corporation, men of sound, personal morality and responsibility who as a group reached business decisions which were irresponsible and of questionable morality." DeLorean's example is chilling: "Charlie Chayne, vice-president of Engineering, along with his staff, took a very strong stand against the Corvair as an unsafe car long before it went on sale in 1959. He was not listened to but instead told in effect, 'You're not a member of the team. Shut up or go looking for another job.' The car was approved even though serious questions were raised about its engineering."

The paralysis striking Detroit was far from confined to General Motors. At Ford there was real turmoil. The company had hired Semon Knudsen from GM as its president. He had barely settled in when he was fired for not getting along with the boss, Henry II, who was becoming very like his grandfather. Lee Iacocca would feel the same breath of fire not long after, but first came Harold Sperlich's curious adventure.

Sperlich was a product man, a *Ford* product man whose horizons were domestic until he was posted to Europe. There, his eyes were opened to the advantages of both the small, sophisticated car and a buying public that was educated not only about the product but about the industry that produced it. "I was flabbergasted at the minutiae printed in every little newspaper about Euro-

1966 Oldsmobile Toronado
This car was a breakthrough for a relatively staid division of GM, with what is now considered a lovely body with clean lines.

pean cars and car companies," he said later. It was his introduction to a consumer body that had had to educate itself very early, given the high cost of the European product and the constraints on its use due to the high price of fuel. Sperlich spent his European tour learning—unwittingly—about things that would stand between him and disaster when he became president of Chrysler: the customer's need for high quality and good fit and finish as the basis for longevity and low maintenance costs.

When Sperlich came back to Ford's headquarters in Dearborn—called the Glass House—he pushed for a small car to meet what he was convinced was the new world of limitations. He further understood that the car was becoming a discretionary item in a world in which ownership was no longer a transcendent achievement; in fact, it was becoming an encumbrance and even an embarrassment. Henry Ford II wanted no part of Sperlich's arguments; in fact, he wanted no part of Sperlich. Off went the small-car advocate to Chrysler Corporation, followed by Lee Iacocca, who also disagreed too much with Henry II.

Prior to their arrival at Chrysler, things were just as bad there. Lynn Townsend (succeeded too late by John Riccardo) had been elevated to emperor of Highland Park. A prototypical accountant, he had neither a feel for the product nor a particular interest in it. Chrysler Corporation cars of the late sixties and early seventies were reflections of Townsend's attitudes. They were huge, dull, inefficient, costly, and badly built. A company that had earned a reputation for engineering excellence was squandering it through indifference. Its management was not just hidebound, it had atrophied. The products plan at Chrysler was a blueprint for disaster. Nobody in the executive suites seemed to understand that the world was changing and that Chrysler's customers were changing with it.

Auguries and Entrails

Much of the disaffection that galvanized the car-buying public and went unnoticed by Detroit's managers coalesced around a consumer advocate named Ralph Nader. Nader's broad-brush indictment of the industry was devastating: "For over half a century the automobile has brought death, injury, and the most inestimable sorrow and deprivation to millions of people," he said in the opening to his now-famous book *Unsafe at Any Speed*. His prosecutorial opening statement concluded: "A principal reason why the automobile has remained the only transportation vehicle to escape being called to meaningful public account is that the public has never been supplied the information nor offered the quality of competition to enable it to make effective demands through the marketplace and through government for a safe, non-polluting and efficient automobile that can be produced economically.

"The consumer's expectations regarding automotive innovations have been deliberately held low and mostly oriented to very gradual annual style changes. The specialists and researchers outside the industry who could have provided the leadership to stimulate this flow of information by and large chose to remain silent, as did government officials.

"The accumulated power of decades of effort by the automobile industry to strengthen its control over car design is reflected today [1965] in the difficulty of even beginning to bring it to justice."

The specific object of Nader's book, indeed the fulcrum of his argument against the industry, was Chevrolet's Corvair, whose design and production he called, "one of the greatest acts of industrial irresponsibility in the present century." He examined the conception, gestation, and birth of the car with great care. He concluded that its design was faulty, primarily as a result of an undue emphasis on low cost, that GM management had known about the car's faults and had done nothing, and that while the Corvair's specific engineering deficiencies might not be endemic to the industry, all of Detroit shared GM's cavalier attitude toward its buying public. It was only a beginning. *Unsafe at Any Speed* defined the automobile as a hazard to the nation's health. And it gave prescriptions for the cure—ranging from occupant protection to emission controls.

Nader's book enraged Detroit. The scene on the 14th floor at General Motors can only be imagined during those days—a hall of terror filled with outraged men in dark suits grabbing their phones and yelling at their secretaries, holding meeting after meeting to decide how the power of the mightiest company on earth could best be used to crush this impertinent nobody who had questioned the morality of a great American institution. It is a pathetic footnote to the degree of executive degeneration at GM that its managers decided Nader could best be handled by clandestine and illegal reprisal. The company hired private detectives to investigate his past for the inevitable black mark. The aim was to publicly embarrass and discredit him. A discredited Nader would mean a vindicated Corvair, and a vindicated Corvair would mean an innocent Detroit—business as usual.

There were a couple of problems with GM's approach. First, Nader's past was spotless. Worse, he discovered the investigation, sued GM (settling out of court), and the *company* was discredited and embarrassed. Nor was that all. Ralph Nader, it turned out, was right about the Corvair.

"The whole Corvair case is a first-class example of a basically irresponsible and immoral business decision which was made by men of generally high personal moral standards," said John DeLorean, who was sickened by GM's

decision to attack Nader personally instead of defending its product and who mercilessly criticized his then colleagues for their methods of dealing with Nader.

"Furthermore," said DeLorean, "The Corvair was unsafe as it was originally designed." He described the inherent instability of the design in almost the same way Nader did. "These problems...were well documented inside GM's engineering staff long before the Corvair was ever offered for sale," he went on, adding that a top-level engineer actually flipped over in a prototype on a GM proving-grounds road and that "others followed." DeLorean did not stop there. "The questionable safety of the car caused a massive internal fight among GM's engineers over whether the car should be built with another form of suspension. At the very least...within General Motors in the late 1950s, serious questions were raised about the Corvair's safety. At the very most, there was a mountain of documented evidence that the car should not be built as it was then designed." DeLorean's division at the time, Pontiac, was slated to build its own version of the car. "As we worked on the project, I became absolutely convinced...that the car was unsafe. So I conducted a three-month campaign, with [Pontiac General Manager] Knudsen's support, to keep the car out of the Pontiac lineup." He was successful and no doubt later very thankful that he had taken this stand. In sum, he blamed the system, the perversion of Sloanist management: "There wasn't a man in top GM management who had anything to do with the Corvair who would purposely build a car that he knew would hurt or kill people. But, as part

ABOVE AND OVERLEAF:
1960 Chevrolet Corvair Sport Coupe Corvair was the car made infamous by Ralph Nader in his book *Unsafe at Any Speed.* It was an experiment that was undercut by cost-saving design techniques. According to GM engineer John Z. DeLorean, the car was recognized as unsafe before it was marketed. The model produced in 1965, the penultimate year of the Corvair's production, incorporated suspension redesign—which eliminated the Nader/DeLorean criticisms but failed to save the car.

337

1960 Chevrolet Corvair Sport Coupe

of a management team pushing for increased sales and profits, each gave his individual approval in a group to decisions which produced the car in the face of the serious doubts that were raised about its safety, and then later sought to squelch information which might prove the car's deficiencies."

The Corvair's tendency to flip over was corrected in 1964 through the use of a compensating bar. That bar—insisted upon by then Chevrolet general manager Bunkie Knudsen (over from Pontiac)—cost $15 per unit to install, and Knudsen's initial request for its inclusion had been rejected by GM management as "too expensive." Only after Knudsen threatened to resign unless the bar became part of Corvair's suspension did management back down for "fear of the bad publicity that would surely result." In 1965, the car got a complete suspension redesign, which virtually eliminated its hazardous behavior. It was far too late. The Corvair had been rightly identified as an example of Detroit irresponsibility; it was a dead issue and dead as well in the marketplace.

The next year, 1966, Nader watched from a Senate cloakroom as the National Highway Traffic Safety Act was passed—a law that curbed forever the freedom of the industry to design and sell what it chose and that mandated most of the safety suggestions that Nader had made in *Unsafe at Any Speed*. It was the first in a series of legislative acts that brought Washington squarely into Detroit boardrooms and, some said, brought Detroit design studios inside Washington regulatory agencies.

We will look at the components of this legislative revolution later. For now, we remember that another of Nader's criticisms had to do with auto pollutants. In California, something was already being done about that.

In the same year that the Corvair was introduced, 1959, California biochemist Dr. Arlie Haagen-Smit finally discovered the link between auto exhaust gases and photochemical smog. The Los Angeles Air Pollution Control District had long been at work on the smog problem, for even if the district hadn't known exactly what caused it, smog in the Los Angeles air basin was hard to miss. *Something* was producing all that nauseating stuff, and the pure-air police had identified the car as the culprit. But they were having trouble proving it. It is highly likely that Detroit had had more than a hint about the problem considerably earlier but had chosen to ignore it. A Ford engineer had written a Los Angeles supervisor in 1953: "The Ford engineering staff, although mindful that automobile engines produce exhaust gases, feels these waste vapors are dissipated in the atmosphere quickly and do not present an air pollution problem. Therefore, our research department has not conducted any experimental work aimed at totally eliminating these gases."

What brings us full circle with the Corvair incident and the question of Detroit negligence and mismanagement is the discovery that our current solution to exhaust emissions—the catalytic converter, a kind of scrubber fitted to cars' exhaust systems near the end of the tailpipe—was known to the industry seven years before Haagen-Smit's linking of automotive pollutants to photochemical smog. "In 1952, the catalytic converter existed but the industry decided it wasn't feasible to use," a later technical director of the California Air Resources Board (CARB) said. "In the early '60s, our predecessors at CARB decided catalytic converters could be mass produced."

It's hard to imagine that Sloan and Chrysler—and especially Henry Ford the Original—would ever have allowed their companies to come under such criticism. Perhaps Sloan—who did, after all, postpone the use of safety glass in GM cars for a few years on the basis of its high cost—would have listened with impatience to the engineering staff's complaints about the inherently unsafe

1954 Ford Crestline Skyliner
This car had Ford's first overhead-valve V-8 engine and transparent plastic roof insets. It was a splendid example of what was becoming Detroit's pattern in model evolution: Begin with something simple and make it larger and fancier.

design of a new product. But he was tough-minded enough and businessman enough to understand the potential effects on the profit and loss statement of allowing an unsafe car to be let loose on American roads with a GM logo on it.

Walter Chrysler's people would never have brought the design to him in the first place; he would have fired them on the spot.

Ford's engineers were not allowed to change very much at all, much less start from a blank sheet of tainted paper, so a Ford Corvair-equivalent would have been out of the question from the beginning.

Something had happened to Detroit, and that something wasn't good.

Getting the Word Around

That the Corvair was generally well received when it saw the light of day was due in some measure to the enthusiasm of what had come to be called the "buff books," the auto-enthusiast magazines. Speaking about that reception, and at the same time giving full credit for the criticism of the Corvair design that some magazines had made, Nader said, "Critics are not necessarily crusaders. They never [he was talking specifically about the buff books here] indulge in commentary about the kind of engineering and management operations within General Motors which led to such an unsafe vehicle in handling. In the automobile magazine world such commentary is considered poor taste. It may also be indiscreet. One concentrates on the vehicle, not on its makers.

"Most of the auto-buff magazines are run on a shoestring by a small group of car-infatuated, articulate people editing or writing the copy. The general tone is laudatory, but to hold their readers, there are substantial amounts of crisp criticism concerning vehicle deficiencies. However, an unwritten rule is that you never 'straight-arm' a vehicle or its manufacturer, nor enter the territory of muckraking.... These magazines need the automobile company advertising, but probably more important, they require the technical assistance of company liaison men for pictorial materials and the loan of cars which they test-drive and write about each month."

When cars first arrived on the scene, there were a handful of magazines devoted to their characteristics and use. Later, the so-called workbench magazines, *Popular Mechanics,* for example, took their place as overseers once the excitement of the new device had faded. But after World War II, there was a coming together of a variety of interests—some of them already catalogued by Tom Wolfe—and desires, including the hunger for cars and information about cars, that gave new life to car magazines.

In the late sixties, one of those very magazines took a look at itself and at its competitors and rendered judgment in an article, for by then the magazines had already asserted themselves as important influences on buying and driving

habits. Moreover, there was considerable unease within their editorial staffs about the kind of criticisms Nader was making about them. The piece was called "Road Testing the Road Testers." It was written by Brock Yates, a youngish automotive journalist who fit Nader's description—car infatuated and articulate—to a T. It profiled the major magazines devoted entirely to the car: *Road & Track, Sports Car Graphic, Motor Trend, Hot Rod* (the largest in circulation), *Car Craft, Car Life,* and itself, *Car and Driver.* The profiles of the magazines were interesting and are interesting still about the Big Four that survive: *Hot Rod, Motor Trend, Car and Driver,* and *Road & Track.* More interesting yet are the things Yates discovered the magazines did and did not say.

"By 1947 it became evident to a number of people that a market existed for magazines that could reach the guy with the '32 Ford 5-window coupe in Downey, California or the advertising executive from Fairfield, Connecticut with a shiny new Jaguar Mark 5."

1955 Ford Crown Victoria
By the mid 1950s, the great car thirst engendered by the Second World War had been slaked, and Detroit's car companies understood they needed to build cars that could be sold instead of cars for which people had stood in line to buy. Ford's response was typical: do a car that *looked* all new and was particularly flamboyant.

Of the major magazines, *Road & Track* tried first. It was founded in new York but was soon transferred to California, where it was taken over for a printing debt by its technical editor, John Bond. He was a graduate of General Motors Institute (one of the toughest automotive engineering schools in the world) and an alumnus of Oldsmobile Division, Studebaker, Harley-Davidson, and supercharger manufacturers McCulloch and Paxton. Under him, *Road & Track* became the magazine of record for the sports and foreign car enthusiast. It was "probably the most stable of all automotive magazines," said Yates in its profile. "By appealing directly to imported car enthusiasts and the fanciers of exotic machinery, the magazine has become a prestigious monthly, perhaps at the cost of some vitality. [It is] practically devoid of editorial commentary on important issues...rely[ing] heavily on statistical data." Called "an extremely prosperous property," by Yates, *Road & Track*'s readership had a median age of 27.1 years and 68.9 percent of them had attended college.

Yates continued: "In the meantime, a pair of California war veterans named Robert Petersen and Robert Lindsay were gathering $400 each to attempt the publication of the first issue of a magazine they called *Hot Rod* which, by 1949, had produced enough surplus revenue to permit Petersen and Lindsay to take their second major plunge into publishing. *Motor Trend* was a magazine aimed at a more general automotive audience than either *Hot Rod* or *Road & Track*, with an emphasis on road tests of domestic cars (a story format originated in the U.S. by Tom McCahill in the January, 1946 issue of *Mechanix Illustrated*)." Yates called *Hot Rod*'s editorial policy "non-exploratory for much of the magazine's history." He described *Motor Trend* as "a car magazine with more car than magazine" and lacking in a "contemporary editorial stance."

Intermixing history with profile, Yates described the breakthrough into the big time of his own magazine, *Car and Driver*. "By 1955 acceptance of the automotive magazines had lured major advertisers in the automotive field—car manufacturers, tire makers and petroleum marketers—into grudging support of the car enthusiasts and their magazines. In early 1956, Ziff-Davis Publishing Company of New York purchased *Sports Cars Illustrated*," and renamed it *Car and Driver* in 1961 after operating as "a rather pale imitation of *Road & Track* for seven years." Yates gave himself and his magazine full marks: "Operating as an outspoken, often controversial commentator on the entire automotive scene [the magazine] rattled the foundations of the traditionally timorous automotive journals with a combination of candor and iconoclasm unheard of in the industry.... Coverage is general, with strong emphasis on road tests, competition news, and social commentary relating to the automobile." The median age of its readers was 27.6 years, and 62.5 percent of them had attended college (the numbers for *Hot Rod* and *Motor Trend* were slightly higher for median age and slightly lower for college attendance).

Now, what did all this mean to the industry, the American car, and the American car critics? Yates said that primary (unduplicated and not including pass-along) readership of the major magazines was 4 million persons. That represented a big chunk of American car buyers, a particularly important group since they were well educated in general and specifically knowledgeable about the automobile. Those 4 million could have had profound influence on what the industry did and on what it produced.

With the exceptions of the Muscle and Pony cars, they did not. They *were* largely responsible for the growing respect among American buyers for the products from overseas. They *did* encourage Detroit's conviction that what was needed was not new product but "excitement" through racing. They *were* supportive of the magazines' product criticisms. But Nader was right: They and their magazines kept very far away from the totems of the industry. Nader was wrong in saying that the magazines did this because they operated on a shoestring, but his underlying analysis of their terror of alienating advertisers was correct: They weren't poor, they were rich; and they wanted to stay rich, and get even richer.

A number of things are of interest here. That the car magazines were so large and so healthy meant there was a significant constituency ready to read about and celebrate the automobile—even during an age of engineering hibernation. The audiences were quite willing to accept criticism of cars, so it can be assumed that they were equally willing to hear about the ills of the industry. But they never got the chance—or at least not until quite late in the history of the buff books. Finally, no matter how critical the magazines were and no matter to what degree their audiences agreed with their objections, Detroit paid almost no attention.

Detroit's arrogance and provincialism finally irritated the editors of *Car and Driver* so much that they sent the very man who had been laudatory about the car magazines out to Detroit to examine attitudes there. Yates came back with a piece entitled "The Gross Pointe Myopians," which detailed most of the skews in points of view of the industry's managers. It was a landmark article, and it was followed by deeper examinations, including one by *Road & Track*, that, in the magazine's carefully documented, dry way, simply dismantled the VW Beetle on the basis of its unsafe fuel tank and insecurely mounted driver and passenger seats. Nobody but the magazines' readers paid attention to those criticisms either.

Management disaster at GM, growing dissatisfaction in consumerland, the Corvair fiasco, identification of the automobile as polluter of the atmosphere, delineation of a clear group of auto buffs learning about cars and listening to criticism of them—none of this seemed to faze Detroit.

CHAPTER 19

Detroit Goes to Play

At first Detroit had viewed the immigrant cars with contempt. Perhaps rightly so. Europe chose to grace us with the Lloyd, Messerschmidt three-wheeler, NSU, Renault-Dauphine, and Austin A 30 and 35. The builders of Impalas and Galaxie 500s could well afford to laugh at a lineup like that.

They also laughed at an inverted soup bowl that looked variously like a turtle, an "angry overshoe," and an entomologist's nightmare (which finally prevailed as the popular image): they laughed at the Beetle. They ignored MG, Triumph, Austin-Healey, Jaguar, Alfa-Romeo, and Porsche. They considered them to be cars for the harebrained, cars for the silly rich. Finally, they considered Rolls-Royce and Mercedes to be the same automotive aberrations they had always been: land yachts, rolling necklaces and bracelets for people with more money than sense.

Detroit was wise enough to recognize the end of the classic era when it saw it. Surely this was no time to go back simply because some German and English eccentrics were trying to revive the epoch.

The newly influential car magazines howled and clawed the air at Detroit's apparent refusal to recognize a design philosophy—represented by the imports—that had so much more to offer an enthusiast than Detroit's typical vanilla-barge image of a car. And the magazines were right to complain, considering their audience's predilections. Although their understanding of the suitability of the American product to American conditions left something to be desired, they were right about one kind of car Europe was sending us, and Detroit should have been far quicker to understand their enthusiasm. Beginning in the early 1950s, *Road & Track* in particular was touting the sports car. Sports cars would never gain a large segment of the market, never produce the kinds of profits GM was making with its station wagons and standard sedans. But when the company threatened to stop production of the Corvette, its in-house parent, Zora Arkus-Duntov, offered to buy the rights to the car and produce it himself. Not for love, for money. There was gold in those two-seaters. In 1963, when the time came for Detroit to go looking for excitement, its managers finally understood the importance of sports cars. The GTO was a sports car in pure American terms. So was the Mustang.

Not that a few people hadn't tried earlier. But the ones who could have pulled it off built cars that were simply dreadful. They had a strong American accent, a strong American flavor; the senses of people attuned to European sports car—European cars in general—were offended by their personalities. The American automotive persona had long since taken a divergent path from that of cars built everywhere else in the world. American cars were bigger, fatter, thirstier, more solicitous of their occupants' comfort. Nowhere was this gulf in automotive philsophies more apparent than in our sports cars.

In the middle fifties, Hudson, Kaiser, and Nash tried—and failed—to build

LEFT AND OVERLEAF:
1953 Chevrolet Corvette
Corvette began life as a General Motors show car, an industry version of a trial balloon. Reaction was marvelous, and in 1953, Chevrolet Division introduced the production version with a six-cylinder engine called Blue Flame. Whatever else the early Corvette was, it was not flamingly fast. But very soon Chevy recognized that sports-car owners wanted high performance, and one wonderful car followed another in the Corvette series, starting with the V-8–equipped car in 1957, going on to the next year's Corvette Super Sports, a full-on race car, and beginning its end in 1967, when —in the purist's view— emissions control equipment strangled the engine. Still, Corvette is America's only sports car—in the absolute sense—and its owners continue to be completely devoted to it.

sports cars of the European kind. Hudson had an Italian coachbuilder do a body on its small car, the Jet, that was in many ways reminiscent of some of the worst mistakes seen at the annual car shows in Geneva and Turin. It was a great, bulbous thing called the Italia. One senior Hudson official attributed its disastrous midriff bulges and arched eyebrows to interference by Hudson's chief stylist after the overseas coachbuilder had executed a relatively pleasing design. Perhaps this was so. In any case, plans to produce the car faded after it was designed. Reaction to the model was not good.

Kaiser retained Darrin—of Packard fame—to do a two-seater. It was a decent-looking car despite a grille that seemed to belong in the kitchen and the peculiarity of its sliding doors. It was a failure. One reason given for this was that it was an extreme car from a company that had yet to establish itself. It was too risky to own for fear of never being able to resell it.

Nash's sports car was the most successful. In its first edition, it was a combination of Nash suspension and powertrain components and a useful if low-style wraparound body done by Donald Healey in England. It was later regowned by the Italian coachbuilder Farina, which improved its looks but endowed it with a mouthful of a name. Nash-Healey-Farina.

All of these cars were interesting; the automotive archeologist of today finds them fascinating. Their failure is likely due to a pair of causes in addition to their inherent deficiencies. First, they looked and felt American, a considerable problem in view of the irreconcilable design philosophies of the American and European industries. European sports cars—think of how naturally the words go together—were the original creations, the genuine thing. They were taut, agile,

quick—the merest mechanical liaisons between driver and road. American sports cars—which many thought a contradiction in terms—were large, soft, comfortable, and faster than most European cars, but they insulated their drivers from the highway in the best Detroit tradition. The second problem was the same as existed with the Springfield Rolls-Royce. Americans who were going to buy sports cars wanted the real thing, and the real thing came from England or Italy or Germany.

There were a handful of sports-car constructors in the United States who probably never intended to sell the cars they produced in any quantity—with the possible exception of Earl "Mad Man" Muntz. We saw Muntz hawking Kaisers and Frazers, a cutting-edge promoter in Los Angeles, one of the early shamans of the cult of late-night television sales. He built a strange coupe named for himself—complete with snakeskin or lizard interior—which he almost certainly hoped would be clutched to the American bosom. Luckily for all of us, it never caught on.

Frank Kurtis, constructor of the best Indianapolis race cars available, tried his hand at a racing sports car and a garden-variety sports car. The road racer could have been a contender based, as it was, on the Indianapolis car; but the boulevard sports car was far too large and somewhat difficult to drive, with its heavy steering and startling acceleration. Worst of all, it was even uglier than the Hudson Italia.

An Eastern aristocrat, Briggs Cunningham, brought together some of the finest independent craftsmen in America and built both roadster and coupe, first as an American effort to race against the Europeans primarily at Le Mans, and

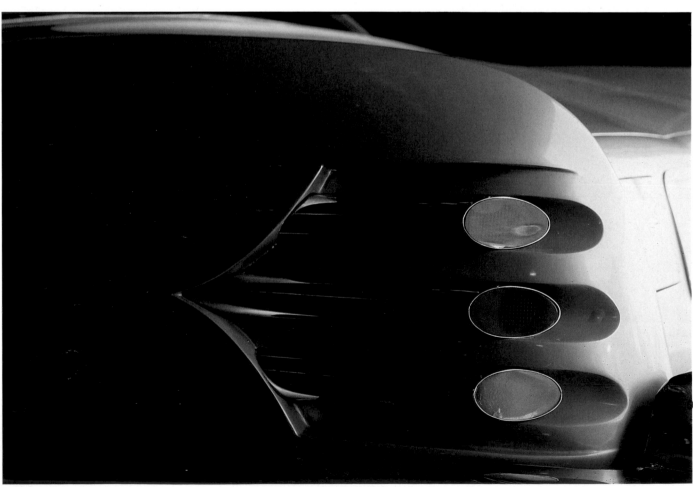

then to sell as limited-edition road cars. Cunningham's cars were marvelous. They were large. They were also immensely powerful. Their buyers got a choice of a Cadillac or a Chrysler engine.

Cunningham was relatively successful as a race-car constructor, successful too in his own terms as builder of limited-edition grand touring cars. But he was not a man driven to empire. He was a "sportsman" in the best sense of the word. Had Cadillac Division or Chrysler put his car into production, who knows what might have happened? Very likely neither was offered the chance. There were a few others—the Edwards, for example, built by a wealthy San Franciscan—but they were mere blips on the sales oscilloscope.

Early post–World War II American sports cars are not to be dismissed lightly. They gave tacit recognition to a phenomenon the industry would eventually pursue with vigor. They taught American dealers who handled them that a new buyer was coming into existence, one who walked into showrooms with at least as much technical knowledge of automobiles as the seller, one who, furthermore, had been educated by the foreign-car retail establishment that there was a set price for a car and that that was what it would be sold for. This was entirely different from the haggling that went on in the sedan bazaars. In the way it was sold, the foreign car, in particular the foreign sports car, would show American dealers the difficult, upward path from the disgraceful pit that they had dug for themselves.

These primitive American attempts—particularly given the companies that attempted them—revealed that there *were* those in the domestic industry who, if desperate enough, could defy convention and try something different. In that, they were following a grand tradition.

PRECEDING OVERLEAF, LEFT AND ABOVE:
1953 Cunningham
The Cunningham was produced by Briggs Cunningham, an American auto racing hero and yachtsman. The Cunningham had an Italian body—an attempt to bring high quality European styling to American sports cars.

The Sporting Americans

"Seldom had so much machinery been covered by so little sheet metal." This was said by Griff Borgeson and Eugene Jaderquist in *Sports and Classic Cars*, celebrating the stark loveliness of our greatest early sports car, the Mercer Raceabout, built from 1911 to 1915. "[It] had a wire-wheeled chassis, a hood strapped over the engine and a dashboard from which a brass steering column jutted." Yes, indeed it did. It also had real bucket seats and no doors. An enormous fuel tank sat behind the driver and the passenger; atop it perched one of those distinctive "eared" fuel caps that is the mark of the demiracer. The controls were large, brass, and right out there for the world to see: shifter, hand pumps for fuel and oil, hand brake. "The total, practical effect of this nakedness was that these cars had little more than their own chassis weight to pull, and they did it in hair-raising style." Finlay R. Porter designed this Type 35 Raceabout, which at first was powered by an ordinary engine, a four-cylinder Continental T-head of five liters' (302 cubic inches) displacement, slow turning (1,700 rpm), and not very powerful (50 hp). Then, when the Model 35 was replaced by the Model 22, designed by E. H. Delling, a new, more powerful engine was used, but gone were many of the uncompromising sports-car attributes, for example, the monocle windshield.

The American who was willing to own and drive a far more civilized MG-TC in 1947 was considered a man of courage and stoicism. More than forty years earlier, the Raceabout required an automotive equivalent of John Fremont, at least a Buffalo Bill Cody. It gave no quarter to comfort, except for wrapping the driver and passenger in a supportive seat. It may have later been thought of as a mediocre performer, but with almost no weight to pull, it attack-

1913 Mercer Raceabout
Lower and more lithe than its principal American sports car competitor, the Stutz Bearcat, the Mercer Raceabout was a young man's dream, with its minimal body work consisting mainly of a bolster tank, two bucket seats and a monocle windshield. It did not have a long life, but it was considered the quintessential example of the breed when it was new, and it is thought of that way still.

ed the primitive roads of pre–World War I America with a savagery that only the Stutz Bearcat would match. There are no contemporary accounts of a Raceabout (nor of a Bearcat) doing a drive as perilous as the Ridge Route, the goat path that passed through the Tehachapis and represented the only northern egress from Los Angeles to the Great Valley of California, but it must have been done. Besides, such roads existed wherever there were hills, and a trip in a bucking, heaving, straining sports car with only the wheel to hold, and drop-offs of 2,000 and 3,000 feet on either side of the rutted path must have tried the pioneer courage of the handful of young men who owned Mercers and Stutzes.

The Mercer's founders died, passing the company into the hands of Emlen Hare, who also acquired Locomobile and Crane Simplex. There were a number of sports cars, the early ones remarkably tough and good, the later ones getting more conventional by the model. That is not to say that they were boring. Although the exhaust cutout was dropped by 1922 ("the last vestige of undisciplined violence"), Mercer used a 331.3-cubic-inch engine with an aluminum crankcase, tried dual ignition, and even stiffened the chassis. By then, Americans were turning to classics or pure transportation. Mercers, with their "monumental low-speed torque, their terrier-like responsiveness . . . the growl of their gears and the virile bark of the exhaust" were far too uncivilized for a nation in pursuit of comfort. Mercers were European. We would not welcome that approach for some time to come.

Stutz we have already examined. It was advertised as "the Car That Made Good in a Day" after one placed eleventh in the first Indianapolis 500 of 1911. But this was not a Bearcat, which did not appear until three years later. The first Bearcat had a bigger engine than the Mercer and was the Raceabout's only com-

1912 Stutz Bearcat
This is the car that defined a type—the sports car—in the American idiom and was associated with the era of the flappers.

1926 Stutz Two-Passenger Speedster Series AA2
Not a car most of us think of when we hear the name Stutz, this was nonetheless an extremely interesting car. The body was by American. The car's weight was enormous at 4,175 pounds. Its advertised speed was "75 plus"—a very decent figure for 1926.

petition. Harry C. Stutz left his company, founded another, and tried building his own sporting car, called the H.C.S. Neither the company nor the car lasted.

We have noticed that Duesenberg as a classic was considered unrefined because of its race-bred engine. It was too noisy, too vibration-filled. What else could the world expect of a car that came from a line of distinguished American sports and racing cars? Fred and Augie Duesenberg's early engine has been described as a "radical, weird powerplant." But the strangeness of its rectangular combustion chambers and integrally cast head and block, and its two valves per cylinder and "walking beam"–actuating mechanism (the valves were horizontal and they were actuated by foot-long vertical rocker arms), didn't detract a whit from the Model A's performance—they enhanced it. In fact, the Duesenberg

engine was used by a whole slew of arcane cars, including Biddle, Shad-Wyck, Premocar, and Wolverine. Roamer used the engine until 1927.

Duesenbergs did reasonably well in racing—as we shall see shortly—but it was not the all-conquering car it is thought to have been.

There were a few real American sports cars in addition to the well-known ones, including DuPont—from the very same family that did in Billy Durant—a car with a boattail, cycle fenders, and knock-off wire wheels. It was entered at Le Mans in 1921, but it was vastly underpowered and finally broke. A later model was aesthetically appealing, but it was a racing disaster at Indianapolis.

Purists may disagree, but some would insist that a lovely car from a tiny company in Wisconsin qualifies as a noteworthy early American sports car. The Kissel Gold Bug never raced anywhere, but it was short-coupled and sporty; better yet, it was *sporting*. Like so many other independents, Kissel was hard hit by the 1920-1921 recession and never really recovered. The company was gone a decade later.

Before World War I, there was little choice among cars; they were big or small, almost all were open, some were stark (sports cars), some were not. Some were outright race cars (Ford's 999, for example), but most were derivatives, and often it was hard to tell a racer from an unorthodox production car.

After the war—between the wars, really—American sports cars were produced by specialist manufacturers many of whom were mainly concerned with

ABOVE AND PRECEDING OVERLEAF:
1933 Duesenberg Speedster Model SJ
This is a boat-tail speedster with Weymann coachwork, making it one of the few open Duesenbergs not bodied by Murphy of Pasadena. The siren and red light were fitted for its former owner, George Whittell, a famous collector and an honorary fire marshal in California.

high-priced classics and whose clientele was more interested in elegance than in performance. This, of course, did not inhibit E. L. Cord. His company produced a supercharged sedan in its penultimate year that set many records at Bonneville.

While the American sports car was taking a turn back to its passenger-car progenitor in the late twenties and thirties, European sports cars were becoming more and more a distinct genre. But just as Bruce-Briggs made it clear that to define an American passenger car by European standards was to ignore uniquely American driving conditions, we must look to our national character for some clue to what our kinds of sports cars were. They were largely the cars being chopped, channeled, hopped up, and stripped down in California, for if the point to a sports car is to enhance usable performance so that a car can be taken to its maximum and enjoyed for what it can do, top speed was to Americans what handling was to the English, the French, and the Italians.

After World War II, we came closer to reconciling the American and European points of view. By then, we were world citizens interested in world sports. One of these sports was pure road racing, which required the attributes developed overseas while we were still concentrating on making our cars straight-line terrors. The reconciliation between *our* point of view and *theirs* comes in the history of racing, a fascinating chapter in the development of the American car.

1920 Kissel Gold Bug
Kissel did not manufacture many cars, but the tiny company did turn out a truly sporting sports car, the jaunty Gold Bug.

Racing: Detroit's Lighter Side

Racing in Europe developed in nice, orderly fashion. There were races to prove the worth of early cars; there were races from city to city (very bloody and early abandoned); and then there were races held on public roads shut off for the occasion. It made sense to develop cars suited to the conditions, so whether European race cars were large or small, open or closed, they were road racers with road-racer gears and suspensions. They evolved in Darwinian fashion, becoming more and more specialized to cope with the very special conditions under which they competed. All roads led to one car, really: today's Grand Prix racer—a needle-nosed marvel good for going around corners to the left and to the right, for accelerating from a 20 mph hairpin turn to a 200 mph straight. Lesser cars, touring, sports, sports/racing cars, do the same things, only not quite so well.

We were never a cohesive enough people nor did we live in a sufficiently compact area to achieve such consensus on what a race car should or should not be. In consequence, we have drag racing, in which cars go from a stop to the end of a quarter-mile strip; we have stock-car racing, for cars with shells that resemble buyable cars with real names like Buick and Thunderbird; we have Indy car racing for cars that look like European needle-nosers but that are meant to run on high-speed oval tracks, and only now and then race on tracks with different kinds of turns and elevation changes; we have sports-car racing, which may or may not mean average, ordinary cars available to average, ordinary folk who take them out on race courses to see how fast they can go. Sports cars can also be single-seater monsters that weigh 1,400 pounds, have 600 hp Chevy engines stuck behind the driver, and race for $100,000 purses on circuits that are all but identical to the simulated city-to-city tracks of Europe. We have demolition derbies. We have the extremely popular short oval track racers—midgets or sprint

ABOVE:

Prudhomme Engine
This engine began as a Chrysler Hemi. When racing engine builder Keith Black began to cast them in aluminum and supercharge them, they became virtually unbeatable.

ABOVE RIGHT:

Prudhomme Funny Car
The Funny Car was so called because its body was meant to resemble a production car, while underneath it was pure drag racer.

RIGHT:

When street rod customizing meets short-track race-car design, this is the result.

FAR RIGHT:

1954 Lincoln Custom Coupe
This car won in category and represented Ford Motor Company's awakening interest in racing.

368

HAL Sprint Car
When most people think of a race car, this is the kind of short-track screamer they have in mind. Sprint cars—"sprinters"—are fierce and dangerous. They have engines as large in cubic-inch displacement as Indy cars but are much smaller and lighter cars. They run on dirt and pavement and have served as training equipment for such superstars as Parnelli Jones and A. J. Foyt, Jr.

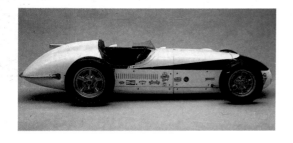

1955 Kurtis Roadster Model 500D
The Indianapolis racing car has always represented some of the best of American design and workmanship. Frank Kurtis's cars dominated the Speedway during the 1950s and 1960s precisely because of his superb craftsmanship.

cars or "modifieds" or late-model sportsmen (*old* late-model stock cars, often)—that run on "bull rings," 3/5- or 1/2-mile dirt or asphalt tracks with grandstands for perhaps 3,000 that sit in the semi-industrial slums of almost every city in America and draw crowds every Friday night. These crowds are so large that when their number is combined with the number of people who go to the big, glamorous events (a far smaller figure, by the way), the total audience makes up the second- or third- or fourth-largest spectator sport in the nation (horse racing is first).

We've seen how drag racing developed. While the postwar baby boom was in its adolescence and early twenties, drag racing was a huge sport. Lately, it has tapered off, probably because it's not much fun to watch even though it's fun to do.

When we talk about racing in the United States now, we generally mean the NASCAR (National Association for Stock Car Auto Racing) circuit, which has the highest attendance of all competitions in this country, or we mean Indianapolis, or we mean the "fruitcuppers." This is a derogatory term coined by the hard cases of the short tracks and Indianapolis that originally referred to the amateurs who raced sports cars on road-racing circuits not for money, but for trophies. Hence, "Fruitcup." The short-track races have been the birthplace of many of our great drivers, their training grounds not only for the techniques of racing, but also for their manners off the track. That makes a good many of them very hard-nosed citizens, for you do not come to stardom through the bull rings without stubbornness, perseverance, and raw courage; and you don't come up without having to fight your way. Few people are willing to challenge Anthony Joseph Foyt, Jr., to a discussion, much less a fight.

After Ford's invasion of the Indianapolis Motor Speedway, race car technology in this country soon became as advanced as that of European cars. This is an Indianapolis McLaren, powered by an American engine and built in England by a company owned and operated by Americans.

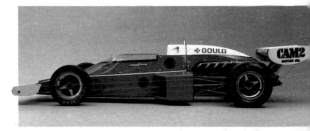

TOP:

Novi Indianapolis Car
This car—hard to drive, lovely to hear—was an artistic, but not a racing, success.

ABOVE AND RIGHT:

Lotus
This English racer has an American turbine engine. Outlawed because it was too quick, the engine was also quiet, which racing fans hated.

Although we ran a few Grand Prix races prior to World War I—notably one in Savannah, Georgia, in 1908 and a short series (revived later) of Vanderbilt Cup races on Long Island that began in 1904—the proper vision of American racing between the wars is at Indianapolis, built as a proving ground in 1909 and scene of the first great race in 1911, won by a Marmon Wasp.

"There were too many races [in the United States] for most of them to matter [so the promoters at Indianapolis] decided to concentrate their efforts on one big race to be held on Memorial Day. Eventually they decided on a distance of 500 miles (so that it could be concluded during daylight) and thus was born the richest, brightest, most ballyhooed, and occasionally most frightening, motor race in history, a race almost as long in span as motor-racing history itself." That is the view of the most prominent motoring writer in England, L. J. K. Setright, who is not known as a fan of American motor sports and owns nothing but very sharp pens. That his comments are so generous is due to the recent history of the

372

1922 Ford Model T Speedster
The Model T was the basis for most of the so-called aftermarket industry: manufacturers of special equipment for production cars. This speedster has an overhead valve Frontenac Model R cylinder head and an Ames body.

Speedway. (Nobody in racing calls it "Indianapolis" except at the beginning of a discussion—and there is, of course, only one "Speedway"—even though Daytona and Talladega are newer and better, and an Indianapolis replica was built in Ontario, California.) Early races at the Speedway were run and won by famous American cars and drivers, but Europeans came over too, for the event was becoming known worldwide and was beginning to pay out large purses.

From modified production cars (Duesenberg) to race cars based on production cars (Fronty Fords) to out-and-out racing cars (Millers), Indy developed into a competition for the toughest racers in the world.

When V-J day came, the Speedway was a decrepit place, waging a war against collapsing buildings and thriving weeds. It was refurbished and eventually sold to Indiana businessman Anton Hulman, who ran it like a feudal

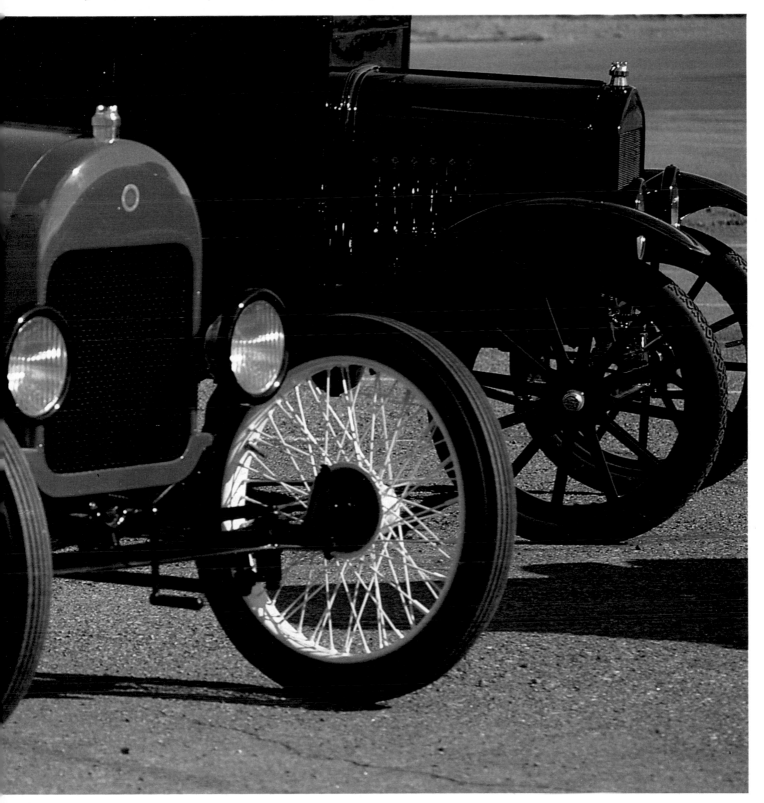

1948 Tasco Prototype
American Sports Car Company built this Gordon Buehrig–designed car with the body executed by Derham. It is based on a 1948 Mercury, its body discarded, frame modified, and wheelbase shortened. The fiberglass front fenders turned with the wheels, and the semigullwing doors are among the first of their kind. The car was never produced.

manor: one race a year, no attendance figures given out, the most ancient and rigid administrators hired to keep the thing going, dueling with the variety of sanctioning bodies that staged the races and never yielding an inch to anyone. Indianapolis Motor Speedway was bigger than racing organizations, and it was bigger than the competitors who ran the race.

Even when the Ford Motor Company, plunged by Lee Iacocca into a frenzy of worldwide competition in the sixties, built a special engine and hired Lotus designer Colin Chapman to construct the rear-engined chassis and blew away the Indy establishment, the Speedway managed to assert its superiority over the Ford battalions so that they felt oddly treated. Ford's top driver, Jim Clark, who won in 1964, decided that even though the money was better than anywhere else, he was weary of being treated like a novice.

That was the point to the Speedway, really; it was the home of the American racing establishment. There were few innovations after the war and great inertia. Whatever we told ourselves about what a marvelous car country we were, about how intense our love affair with the automobile was, in the heart of that love was a technological lassitude; we were not building cars that were the equals of those being constructed elsewhere. That was a sad measure of our failure to keep the flame. Not until Ford arrived at the Speedway did contemporary racing design arrive there too. At first, the high priests of America's premier racing event rejected Ford and everything it tried to do. When the company proved itself and its product, everyone instantly made copies of Lotus-Fords.

In fact, we needed to look to the South for vigor in racing. There, a former gas station attendant named Bill France had started racing on the hard, flat sands at Daytona, thought enough of the future of that kind of racing to form an organization, and eventually became the toughest, most successful race promoter in the world.

look like cars everyone could buy so that everyone would pour into the stands at his tracks and "identify" with one or another competitor, stock-car racing became enormously interesting to Detroit. We have seen what it did for Pontiac when Knudsen, Estes, and DeLorean decided they needed to give the car an image. That sort of thing had been going on ever since France had established his circuit, and it absolutely boomed when promoters all over the South began building great concrete ovals on which the cars could race.

Hudson made wonderful use of stock-car racing after the war, with its fine-handling "stepdown" car. Oldsmobile was successful in establishing a reputation with its Rocket 88. Then, Chevy took to the track with its bright new V-8 engine and blew the doors off its competitors. This was deeply troubling to the Ford people, who thought that all the activity in California, which had spread to a good deal of the nation (albeit underground), gave the company an undying reputation for building performance into its product.

Watching Chevy clean up in NASCAR and Chrysler doing almost as well, Ford finally had had enough and began a stumbling effort to catch up. At the very moment that things began to look good for Ford—in 1957—the Automobile Manufacturers Association decided its members could no longer go racing. To this day, Ford people believe the ruling was meant to discriminate against them and was at least encouraged if not instigated by Chevrolet.

Nonetheless, the deed was accomplished. Chevy had wrested the national vision of performance from Ford. Nobody was racing, so nobody could challenge Chevy for the title. Ford people were discouraged and angry. But not for long. Three years later, Ford, defying the Association's ruling, was back with an immense racing program, almost simultaneous with the introduction of the Mustang. The company had a wide series of objectives. It had to win Indianapolis, which it did in 1964. It had to win at Le Mans to prove to the world that it could and would build performance cars that were the equal of any. It had to win the TransAmerican Road Racing Championship for Pony cars. It had to win the world manufacturers' title, a task that would require racing on two continents in events (including Le Mans) from six to twelve to twenty-four hours long against the likes of Jaguar and Ferrari.

All these things it managed to do, its overseas victories coming with a family

BELOW AND OVERLEAF:
1967 Ford Mark IV GT
Of all automobiles produced in the United States, the Mark IV has the most awesome performance. Conceived and built during a time when the Ford Motor Company had decided that racing on road circuits worldwide would enhance its domestic and international sales, the Mark IV was the culmination of a long development program at Ford Special Vehicles. The company hired the finest road-racing and oval-track drivers, including A. J. Foyt, Dan Gurney, Bruce McLaren, and, to race this car, Ken Miles and Mario Andretti.

of cars that are still considered among the most formidable ever built. The Ford GT-40 was a low, sleek coupe, highly aerodynamic and very strong. It was run by the company and then by private entrants, and it was driven by some of the finest drivers ever to set hand to wheel, including Mark Donohue and Peter Revson. The GT-40, which was powerful but not powerful enough to overwhelm its opposition, was followed by a slightly stronger version. But this was still not enough for Ford, which thereupon produced the Mark IV, a brute. It won at the twelve hours of Sebring in the hands of Mario Andretti and Bruce McLaren. It won at Le Mans, where the Mark IV Ford team was made up of the greatest names on the list of postwar Americans: Dan Gurney and A. J. Foyt, who teamed up for the victory in 1967.

None of this is to say that Chevrolet sat back and watched. Perhaps the greatest racing wars between manufacturers in the United States took place on the TransAmerican circuit (which had a car named after it—the Pontiac Trans-Am), where Mustang (Parnelli Jones, team leader) raced against sibling Cougar (Dan Gurney), Chevy Camaro (led by Mark Donohue), and Pontiac (Jerry Titus), with Sam Posey's Dodge Charger and George Follmer's AMC Javelin

occasionally sticking their noses into things. When Chevrolet hired the legendary racing driver turned entrant/constructor Roger Penske, whose driver was Donohue, the tide turned in Chevy's favor.

At the same time, Chevy was helping Texan Jim Hall, who was competing in a North American series for unlimited sports cars. With Chevy's help, he built a remarkable car called the Chaparral, on which, as a test bed, Chevy developed an automatic transmission efficient enough to last in racing and quick-shifting enough that it didn't give away any time to the manual-shift cars. Chevy also experimented a great deal with aerodynamic devices, including wings mounted at the rear of the car and fans enclosed in plastic skirts to suck down on the ground and improve road holding. Eventually, things got to be so Flash Gordon-like with the Chaparral that the organization putting on the racing series outlawed the car. It was simply too good.

How could anyone blame those ordinary, everyday passenger-car engineers in Detroit for not building wonderful cars to put into showrooms when they were playing with marvelous toys like the GT-40 and the super sports Corvette and the Chaparral?

CHAPTER 20

American Motors Goes Racing

With so many varieties of auto racing to choose from, what could a little company like American Motors afford if and when it decided its product line needed adrenalin?

It could go drag racing, but its median buyers would never notice; they were far too old. The very young racing audiences who spent their weekends at Fremont or New York Raceway were not likely to be converted from their hard-held views that AMC made Ramblers and that Ramblers were suitable for the halt, the lame, and the aged.

Stock-car audiences were good bets: right age and income, good part of the country, and one of AMC's component companies, Hudson, had made a fine reputation with the stockers—not forgotten by the car buying burghers of the South. But stock-car racing—*competitive* stock-car racing—would require an enormous budget. Still, it would be nice to put a car out there that was very much like the ones the company sold. The point, after all, was to move metal. Racing was just a marketing device.

So American Motors compromised. It had a Pony car called the Javelin—a weak-kneed car ordered mainly with the company's sinusy six-cylinder engine. But you could never tell about these race car constructors. Maybe they could get the thing to work. Better still, maybe American Motors could acquire for Javelin a race-track reputation that would carry over onto showroom floors. The place to race was in the most competitive circuit in North America—the Trans-American Sedan Championship.

In a sense, to think of the factory as racing was to misunderstand the process. The marketing and sales departments might meet first with engineering to make the initial decision, but usually within marketing there was a racing chief—a sort of track master. His budget went to the professional racing operation that bid on the job and that, to him and the company, seemed to offer the most by way of organization and panache. Frequently, the racing group had a driver already in the stable. Sometimes the factory racing man would express a preference for one or another person. This was important, for auto companies in racing needed a driver with not only the ability to push the car around the track ahead of everyone else but also with the right look and voice—a spokesman, a Roger Staubach, a John Houseman, in a Simpson fireproof racing suit.

When AMC decided to field a team of Javelins against Camaro, Mustang, and Cougar, it picked a man from Wisconsin to run its racing team: Jim Jeffords. Jeffords, a former racer himself, had a partner named Ronnie Kaplan, another racing veteran. Their two drivers were George Follmer, even then (the late sixties) an experienced hand, with the reputation of civility off the track and savagery on it, and Peter Revson, a wonderfully controlled, highly disciplined man who became an outstanding Grand Prix driver.

1972 AMC Javelin
With the success of Ford's Mustang and Chevrolet's Camaro, all Detroit had to compete in the personal-car segment of the market. AMC built the Javelin, a sad effort until it was developed on the race track, where it became an interesting marketing device for the company, but where it was also a loser. Nevertheless, the racing program convinced the company that some higher performance had to be brought to the everyday version of the car, and the result was a good street car, if not a great one.

The car they were to drive was a moderately weird piece. It was large and lumpy. Its high-performance version used a 315-horsepower, 390-cubic-inch engine with a floor-mounted, three-speed shifter. This was butterfly stuff, lightweight. Not only wouldn't the car be competitive in the TransAm as it came, it wasn't close to legal. Rules specified that the largest engine that could be used was a five-liter, or 302 cubic inches.

The Javelin group set out to make a car that would run with the best of them, but it was too inexperienced. For example, Roger Penske, one of the Javelin's competitors, was virtually constructing his own car. In his shops, Penske received what were called "bodies in white" from Chevrolet. A body in white meant a Camaro body without any civilized junk at all: no seats, no hardware, no paint, no glass—just a shell. Penske's people would dip the Camaro body in Chem-Mill, an acid used mainly in the aircraft industry. The acid would eat away at the body until it was as close to paper thin (and therefore as light as paper) as it could get. Meanwhile, across the country in California, Jim Travers and Frank Coon, partners in an engine-building company called Traco, were hard at work on the engine. Traco was taking the small-block Chevy engine (which had been introduced in the 1955 model) and making it raceworthy. One of the problems was that it had to be able to run at 8,000 rpm for perhaps six hours. That's a very high figure for a large engine. The Chevy engine wasn't designed to turn anywhere near that fast, and it wouldn't at first. But after running on a dynamometer for weeks on end (and blowing up with regularity—the problem was the connecting rods), the thing was finally made reliable. By the way, producing a more reliable engine was one of the few real contributions to passenger-car design that racing could make. The engine people at GM paid attention. They liked what they saw, and they made modifications to the standard unit. As a result, everybody who bought the Chevy 302 got a better motor.

Anyway, Jim Travers and Frank Coon finally had an engine that would "live" for six hours and make a reliable 400 horsepower. The pistons were special, the connecting rods were made to order, the crankshaft was doubly balanced, the valves and valve springs were all created by racing shops, the camshaft was ground to order. Traco's motors used the Chevy block but they were Chevy by grace of manners, not specific content.

Back at the Penske shop, the body was no longer in white. It had been placed on a very special frame. The original frame was virtually discarded; a substitute of far lighter material was tied to a "roll cage," a descriptive term indeed. Imagine that you have a ladder lying on the floor and you want to build a sturdy house using the ladder as the foundation. The first thing you'd do is find some kind of framing; in the instance of the race car, this was rolled tube made of Chrome Moly steel. You'd bend the tube around in the shape of your house, and you'd weld it to the ladder, so that the whole thing could support an enormous weight. Penske's chassis and body people didn't want enormous weight—quite the contrary. But they wanted great strength, both because the car would be taking a beating and because it might go off the track at high speed, roll over, or flip end for end, and the driver needed protection.

Over this frame-cum-cage, Penske's shop would place the lightened body. Then, because the rules also specified that the car had to carry all the clips, pins, buckles, zippers, handles, latches, and knobs of the showroom car, Penske would remove a stock Camaro from his showroom (he had a Chevrolet dealership nearby), strip it of all its external trim, and transfer the trim to the racer. However odd this might seem, it was less expensive than buying the parts separately. So now Penske Racing had a Camaro ready for the track (three actually, a race car, a backup car in case something happened to the racer, and a "mule," which was a race car used for testing and experimenting purposes). Did Javelin, Jeffords, Kaplan, Follmer, and Revson have anything comparable?

The answer is no. They had no acid-dipped body and no real roll cage. They had an engine turned out by a specialist engine builder all right, but it couldn't match the Chevy engine in kind or quality. When small factories went racing for the first time, they invariably went in naive.

A small New England dealer invited to Lime Rock Park in Connecticut, just at the edge of the Berkshires, for Javelin's battle with the giants would know nothing of this. AMC might not know how to find someone to build a successful race car, but it did know what it wanted from its racing budget. It wanted sales. To get sales, it invited dealers from all over the area, gave them each a red, white, and blue nylon shell racing jacket with patches all over it, stuffed them into a green-striped tent, and served them Bloody Marys in the morning, beer at lunch, and bourbon in the afternoon. Some time after the Bloody Marys, the marketing man would stand up in front of them and talk like Knute Rockne. Then Jeffords or Kaplan would drag the drivers over to wave to the 200 or so dealers and then get them back to their cars.

Camped by the tens of thousands around the lovely green hills overlooking Lime Rock were people the dealers wanted to see in their showrooms but rarely did.. They were young, single, very likely in college, and had money to spend.

Many of them were sophisticated race watchers, some of them even raced themselves—in purely amateur events, however. But no matter how much they might know about racing or the specific series or even the specifications of the cars, they were totally innocent of the enormous trouble and expense of Penske-type preparation. (Even Revson was an innocent. He tells the story of the time, a few years later when he drove for Ford, that he walked over to help move some tires only to be warned not to touch *anything*. The Mustang team owner had a special set of wheels filled with concrete that he used on the car when it was taken to the scales to be sure it came up to the required weight. Of course, when the race was about to begin, the wheels and tires would be changed.)

All this was unknown to the dealer, who was probably impatient by this point, a little drunk, and wondering why he had left his home and television set on a Sunday to watch all this folderol. It didn't take long for him to get the picture, however, once the cars lined up on the grid for the race. On the front row might be the Penske Camaros (Penske had gone to enough trouble, God knows, to see that they were fast enough to qualify first) and behind them the Mustangs. Somewhere in the first six might be a Javelin, not much more than a highly tuned street car, up against pure racers. When the flag fell, the roar of those big V-8s screaming up to 8,000 rpm shook the ground; the pack was off in a clump, dust everywhere, tires spinning, the stench of burned rubber floating over everything, the crowd barely audible although it was screaming in a single voice.

Then, even insulated by all the alcohol, the AMC dealers began to feel the excitement. The pushing and shoving in the pack of cars was unbelievable: good thing Penske's people had put in a roll cage and stiffened the frame; good thing too the racing Javelin was at least as strong as the street version. Think of a subway car at rush hour, a department store the day after Thanksgiving, and you begin to have a notion of the traffic out on the race track. Then contemplate the noise level. There's no sound like the roar of twenty or thirty great racing cars coming off the line. (Some people are so addicted, they go to Indianapolis—where the sound, because of the kinds of engines used, is higher and shriller—just to hear and see that first charge into the first turn, and then go home, totally satisfied.)

Meanwhile, at the wheel of the Javelins, Revson and Follmer would be hav-

ing their problems—again, totally unknown to the dealers in their AMC jackets. Steering was heavy, the four-speed special shifter might be binding—worse still, a gear could have gone away in that first banzai charge. It was screamingly noisy inside. Even though the driver had earplugs under a balaclava inside a helmet, his ears hurt. He could see through a mandatory visor or goggles, although the car had a complete windshield, but it might already be splattered with dust or oil. The track had right and left turns, high speeds and low speeds, uphills and downhills. And then there was the traffic. In addition to the three or four factory teams driving cars with big engines, there were less well prepared cars run by privateers who were bog slow. Behind *them* came a second patch of racers with engines of 120 cubic inches or less (2 liters). Although more agile than the big cars, they were far slower—particularly accelerating out of the corners.

Very soon, Revson and Follmer would begin to lap these slower cars. Now a road race track is not wide. It duplicates secondary roads on which the early machines here and abroad had to drive, and it replicates those cambered two-laners with a smug vindictiveness. With their monstrous Goodyear tires (as wide as 15 inches), their relatively light weight, and their great horsepower, the big coupes were a handful, particularly for getting by slower cars. Even though Revson, like his teammate and every other driver, was strapped in by a six-point restraint, a harness that came over both shoulders, across his lap, and up through his legs (to keep him from submarining), he was thrown around in the car in its violent heaves across the road. And braking was sudden and vicious—even without traffic. Approaching a Dodge creeping into a corner under the control of a virtual novice, Revson might find he had to brake as if to avoid a darting child. Then he would be back mashing the throttle and upshifting in controlled anger.

Without any doubt, he would run out of brakes about three-quarters of the way through the race, and then he would have to use his gearbox to slow the car down. Stab the brake in vain hope, roll the front over onto the throttle to bring up the engine revolutions, and jam the gear lever down into lower and lower gears, coming off the throttle each time, to the growl and burble of the decelerating engine, snorting and backfiring in protest. Sometimes too—more often than any driver wanted—the clutch would simply give up. That meant shifting by sound and feel and using only the throttle, the gearshift, and the steering wheel to control the car.

By now the race was almost over. The Penske cars would be—almost certainly—out in the lead; the Javelins, if they had been lucky, would be fighting for third or fourth. To keep up the faith of the AMC dealers inside the tent, the marketing man had told them that there had been engine trouble in both cars. Despite this "trouble," by this time an amazing number of those middle-life entrepreneurs were captivated by racing, not knowing exactly why, except that the cars were colorful; they could hear the crowd scream; and in some mysterious way they had come to feel a part of it all.

When Revson and Follmer pulled in after a cool-off lap, their hands were raw and bleeding under the racing gloves. Their heavy, fireproof suits were drenched with sweat. Their helmets felt as though they weighed at least 100 pounds. But they had spent a day at the office for which they were being paid about $1,500. This would go up during the history of the TransAm and other road-racing series in the United States, so that today a topflight road-racing professional—there are only about eight in the whole country—gets a retainer of as much as $150,000 a year, endorsements, and perhaps 40 percent of his winnings.

Anyway, the sun was beginning to set, the race was over, beer was flowing down in the pits, and the clogged spectator traffic was slowly making its way out of the track. If the AMC dealers really cared, they looked very carefully at the traffic because it carried their target market. And if the dealers were very good at marketing, they put up banners and signs and racing patches in their own showrooms. Although it helped, you didn't have to win on Sunday to get people to come in to look on Monday. You just had to be ready to talk optional rear-end ratios and available four-speeds and after-market camshafts when the enthusiasts came in.

When the Javelin first appeared, it went to what we would now call the lease market—single women and route-driving salespeople. It needed only its flaccid six-cylinder engine and a three-speed shifter as along as a fancy radio came with the package, and a good air conditioner if the car were sold in the humid Northeast. Now, though, the AMC dealers who had spent a Sunday in a tent at the races knew that there was a whole different market for a Javelin. It wasn't just another Rambler; it was (they had to draw a breath to say it with conviction) a sports car.

The dealers had learned this from Peter Revson and George Follmer the Sunday they had let the Red Sox and the A's go it alone on TV to go off and take in a TransAm at Lime Rock.

VIII
WORLD CARS

CHAPTER 21
The Age of Limitations

It is unlikely that even Ralph Nader foresaw the explosive effects of his book *Unsafe at Any Speed*. Granted, he was an adviser to Senator Abraham Ribicoff's Senate Subcommittee on Executive Reorganization. Agreed, when Ribicoff was governor of Connecticut, Nader had been friend and counselor in Ribicoff's avowed campaign to eliminate speeders from his highways. Given, Ribicoff was fully committed to the taming of the automobile. But bring Detroit to heel with one massive piece of legislation seemingly modeled on his tract—legislation that included almost everything he had recommended? It is unlikely that even Nader anticipated this.

But it was even more unlikely to industry managers who hadn't been paying attention and who still lived in a world bounded by Bloomfield Hills Country Club and the Detroit Yacht Club. Yet, the explosion had been building for years.

"Love affairs rarely survived the brutality and infidelity to which the public had been subjected by the auto industry for a decade," wrote automotive journalist Morris S. Cooper after passage of the National Highway Traffic Safety Act of 1966, hoping he might be heard in the uproar of protest that followed it. It was a point decently taken. Since the selling of the first new postwar car with an under-the-table bribe twenty years earlier, the American public had been ripped off, or ignored, or told to mind its own business by Detroit. All the while that industry managers were gushing about their products, there had been a rising chorus of complaints about service, about longevity, even about Detroit's failure to build cars to suit its customers instead of building cars to suit itself.

The enormous increase in the size of the Detroit standard car and the proportionate increase in the size of its engine were due to GM's philosophy of planning product at the top of each model line and filling it with money-making accessories. A big car carried a big gross profit; a big car with air conditioning, power everything, and push-button stereo radio carried an even bigger profit. It was all very simple. Considering that the more austere the car, the smaller the profit in it, there was no reason for GM to build anything smaller than the *Queen Mary*. GM, the largest company in the industry, with by far the largest market share, set prices. Hardly anybody announced new-car sticker prices before GM. A company that did opened itself to the embarrassment of having to make rollbacks or increases when GM's prices were made public.

GM set the market, and its market was for big cars. "In its high handed sales methods, its arbitrary exercise of power of life and death over supposedly independent dealers, its monopolization of the market, its ignoring solid worth in pursuit of more car per car and therefore more profits, Detroit was pushing the clock to high noon," wrote Cooper.

There were a lot of unhappy consumers out there. There were also a lot of consumers who had been unhappy but who could no longer complain: They had become part of the automobile fatality statistics. By the middle sixties, the

photo by Joseph Kugielsky

1958 Chevrolet Impala
Stagnation in the engineering departments of Detroit produced cars of minimal competence and exterior vulgarity. Chevrolet Division was not immune, although it did not plunge to the styling depths of its competive divisions within GM, in particular Oldsmobile and Buick.

number of accidents had grown to an extraordinary 16 million a year. This is not the fatality figure—about 50,000 people died on the highways each year. But with an estimated 4 million injuries, and both injuries and deaths including a large number of pedestrians, the auto constituted what one physician, William Haddon, who became the first head of the new National Highway Traffic Safety Agency in 1967, called "the nation's number one health hazard."

So the industry was busy not listening to its buyers, and the buyers were becoming restless and were beginning to listen to the voice-of-doom criers about a very real and tragic problem that was killing and maiming a very alarming number of citizens.

During the Lyndon Johnson presidency and with the activist mood of Congress in the middle sixties, the federal government was only too happy to act. Senator Ribicoff certainly was, and in the chief counsel to his committee, Jerry Sonosky, he had the perfect point man. "Sonosky was a New Frontiersman. Nothing seemed strange to him in assaulting imperial Detroit," read a later Sonosky profile written by William Jeanes in *Car and Driver.* The same piece wondered why the drama of the hearings never saw print, for certainly it was the stuff of which tabloids were made. Early on, the Ribicoff troops were easily rebuffed. Detroit was used to attack, and it had barrels and barrels of snake oil to rub all over itself, so punches slipped harmlessly off. Then, in desperation, Ribicoff and Sonosky decided to summon the heads of the auto companies. At the meeting, Nader was in a cloakroom passing notes to Sonosky; the TV cameras were finally on the scene because of the publicity worth the Great Detroit Emperors. The late Senator Robert Kennedy was a member of the board of questioners—Kennedy's dropping by the hearings for a moment was the result of a chance reminder. A famous dialogue took place between Kennedy and the president and the chairman of GM, James Roche and Frederic Donner, respectively. Kennedy walked in more or less at the moment that Roche confessed that his company had spent "about one million dollars" on safety during the previous year. Kennedy asked about GM's profits for the same period, which annoyed Roche. That, in turn, infuriated Kennedy, and he insisted on an answer, which brought Donner into the melee. There was considerable temporizing, and then Roche, who had turned to an associate replied: "One billion, seven hundred million dollars." Kennedy appeared flabbergasted. "What?" he said. Answered Donner, "About a billion and a half, I think." Said Kennedy, "About a billion and a half." To which Donner said, "Yes." Robert Kennedy knew blood when he drew it. TV cameras grinding, he repeated the question: "You made one point seven billion dollars?" And Donner had no choice but to repeat his answer, "That is correct."

The Kennedy-GM encounter took place in midsummer. Nader's book was published in the fall. It became the *Silent Spring* of the automobile industry. The hearings were bad enough for Detroit, but up to this point the paladins of the industry had been doing battle with only a silent majority of consumers allied with an obscure Senate subcommittee. GM thereupon sealed its own fate and the fate of its competitors by bringing the president of the United States into the battle on the side of the Ribicoffians. "One night," wrote Jeanes, "as Sonosky was working late in his office . . . a security guard knocked deferentially on his door. The guard told Sonosky that he had noticed someone . . . following the by-now out-of-the-closet consultant to the Committee, Nader." It was, of course, the GM detectives and it was this, more than the exchange in the committee room, that infuriated President Johnson.

Nor was this to be the end of Detroit's mismanagement of the problem. Still

photo by Joseph Kugielsky

photo by Joseph Kugielsky

unwilling to understand that a bell was tolling, the industry representatives let it be known that everybody could go home now; Detroit would clean its own house. To Ribicoff, Sonosky, and, ultimately, Johnson, that was the capper. With the evidence in and the arrogance observed by the nation, clearly something had to be done. If Detroit's legislative experts had realized that the sanctity of the industry would inevitably be invaded just as the sanctity of the railroads, the meat packers, the financiers, and the drug manufacturers had been invaded, they might have been willing to draw up a model bill that would have represented some compromise between industry freedom and government intervention. They did not. Instead, they patted the committee people on the head and told them to go home to bed; everything would be all right.

Ribicoff's committee was out of allotted time, and its members had returned to their everyday assignments. But the moment Sonosky heard Detroit's response, he threatened to request the committee chairman to reconvene, at which time, he said, the committee would demand recall records—the most private of all private papers in industry sales—for all cars built between 1960 and 1966. Jeanes quoted Sonosky as saying that when the industry man heard that, he "turned *white*." There were a couple of interesting things about that threat. First, nobody really knew whether Detroit was keeping recall records or not, much less whether they pointed to any egregious engineering errors by the industry. Second, the threat was a desperate bluff. Sonosky later admitted that there was no power he had that might have compelled Detroit to respond to such a demand. Nonetheless, the bluff worked. When the records were produced—they existed after all—they showed that almost 20 percent of the cars Detroit had built during the sixties had been defective. Ribicoff and Sonosky had no trouble getting the National Highway Traffic Safety Act of 1966 passed.

The Taming of Detroit

Although the industry howled and moaned, it later said through a new generation of leaders that the act was beneficial to everyone. The real purpose of the act—in fact, what it accomplished—was occupant protection. Nader and Dr. Haddon had talked about "the second collision," which was not that between the car and another large object but rather the one that followed this, when the occupants were thrown forward onto the interior sheet metal inside their own cars. The act mandated that occupants be protected from the second collision in a variety of ways, many of them involving removal of projections from auto interiors, others mandating increasingly protective restraint systems. From simple seat belts to seat belts that buzzed when unfastened to automatic seat belts to air bags, the act required the industry to provide protection for the people who rode in its products. Actually, the air bag, or passive restraint, standard was the 208th requirement in the act. When the time came for its implementation, both government and industry decided that the purposes of the legislation had been served—particularly since an earlier step, the so-called interlock, which set off a buzzer when seat belts were unfastened and which prevented the engine from being started, enraged car-owning senators and representatives enough to strike it down.

There was a lot of grumbling about standardizing automatic-shift quadrants and installing collapsible steering columns, but there wasn't full revolt until Congress, having discovered the heady pleasures of regulating the auto industry, passed the Clean Air Act of 1970. This act required that three pollutants be 90 percent removed from automobile exhaust by the middle of the decade and the rest by a couple of years thereafter.

The Otto Cycle (internal combustion) engine, which makes its power by mixing oxygen with certain hydrocarbons, is not a particularly efficient device. Much energy is dissipated in heat, and much is lost through incomplete combustion. The gases that were fouling the air were in part the product of this inefficiency. There were two ways of handling the Clean Air Act so far as Detroit was concerned. It could improve the output of its internal combustion engines so that they were nearly totally efficient—a little difficulty that had eluded engineers ever since Karl Benz and Gottfried Daimler's first patent. Or it could hang scrubbers, washers, brushes, filters, catch-bags, screens, recirculating valves, and mops and brooms on the insides and outsides of its engines to catch all the carbon monoxide, oxides of nitrogen, and unburned hydrocarbons that were spewing out.

The first solution certainly could not be adopted immediately, nor even soon, according to most industry engineers. The second solution was the only practical course, particularly since no alternative to the internal combustion engine was on the horizon despite endless experiments in almost every industrial country in the world. And so Detroit began—whining and whimpering all the way—to clean up the air by cleaning up automotive exhausts. Over and over again, the same phrase was heard about what Detroit considered an impossible deadline: "They're holding our feet to the fire." It echoed in the R&D halls in Michigan; it was mouthed in Washington by pages, aides, and congresspersons.

Indeed, the complaint was somewhat justified. There was no question but that the car polluted the atmosphere; likely it was the principal polluter. But the automobile and its larger siblings, buses and trucks, classified as "mobile source" polluters, were not the only foulers of the air; there was also a category for "stationary source" atmosphere foulers, and they—the factories and mines of the nation—were to have a period of relative freedom before they too would be subjected to the strict measures imposed on the automobile.

Another cause for Detroit's outrage was Washington's seeming failure to understand that things took *time*. Redesign was not a simple matter. Tooling for redesigned products was equally complicated. And then there was the matter of cranking up production.

Strict tests had been defined in the Clean Air Act to be certain that cars complied with the increasingly severe standards. There would be no fudging if the feds had anything to say. Detroit reacted reluctantly but on the whole responsibly to meet the requirements—there were huge penalties awaiting if they didn't. At the same time, there was at least one amusing sidelight to the whole, tumultuous affair. The engineers who had been assigned to Detroit's racing programs—by definition the most clever, inventive, and creative engineers—were set to solving the emission problem, believed by many industry experts to be a task that was very possibly beyond the state of the art. Now one of the reasons these engineers had been in racing departments all over the city was that they had a fine ability to read rule books and bend whole paragraphs out of shape. There is absolutely no proof of this—although Ford was caught fudging on its compliance tests—but industry insiders would smile crookedly after the sixth or seventh round of drinks at the Ponchartrain bar and suggest that anyone who wanted to write the real story of Detroit's "creative engineering" might get in with the former racing engineers now charged with meeting government emission standards.

Whether there was any edgework going on in the early days of the industry's efforts at cleaning up exhaust is not the point. The work was done—not perfectly but to a sufficient extent that the people who manufactured cars could argue reasonably that an effort to reduce pollutants by more than 90 percent would require exponentially increased expenditures. Furthermore, they could say accurately that so far as the car was concerned, clean air could be achieved only if owners of automobiles already on the highway were required to keep their cars in tune. That meant periodic motor vehicle inspection programs funded by the federal government and implemented by the states. The ball was back in the legislative courts, where it remains.

The Amazing Shrinking Car

Not much of what happened between 1966 and the early seventies was to Detroit's liking. Still, it was hog heaven for the industry compared to what was to follow. First, the Organization of Petroleum Exporting Countries shut the oil tap. Simultaneously, Congress passed yet another law that really put Detroit's feet in the fire. It was called the Energy Policy and Conservation Act of 1973, and it told the industry to stop building large, gas-guzzling cars.

There were two problems with this. First and worst was that the large car was the profit maker for the industry—do away with size and you did away with accustomed return on investment. Second, to design and tool up for a whole

new breed of small automobiles would cost billions of dollars. Once again, in addition to cost, Detroit was given a deadline, and if the clean-air deadline was bad, the downsizing (as the expression emerged) deadline was catastrophic. It was put in terms of what legislators called "corporate average fuel economy" (CAFE), which meant that all cars built by any one company had to average a given fuel economy standard. The standard was in miles per gallon, and it became stricter and stricter from the moment the act went into effect (1977) until the end of the decade, when the fleet of cars of all sizes built by anyone marketing in the United States had to average 20 miles to the gallon. Between 1981 and 1985, mileage would have to be improved to 27.5 mpg. Detroit found the Safety Act bad enough, the Clean Air Act worse, the Energy Policy and Conservation Act the worst yet.

The industry got very little sympathy from the public, who were by now waiting in gas lines as a result of the first great embargo by OPEC. Perhaps the public's callousness was somewhat inappropriate. We have seen that Detroit's products were, on the whole, satisfactory for a nation with huge expanses of highway and cheap fuel. They were not well built, and they were sold in execrable ways. Now suddenly, Detroit, which had gone its own way since it had adapted the European automobile to the very special requirements of an enormous nation, had to follow the European example and build cars suited to a fuel-short world. Moreover, the manufacturers had to do this in less time than they had been given to clean up mobile source pollutants, and if they didn't, the

1977 Chevrolet Caprice Classic
With the passage in 1973 of the federal fuel conservation act, it was clear to the automobile industry that if their products were to meet the fuel economy standards the act mandated, they would have to be brought down in size. This represented the first generation of "downsized" cars from Detroit, a shock to the public. The Caprice Classic had been the top of the line Chevrolet standard or big car. The whole breed has disappeared.

penalties for failure were even higher.

By now, Detroit had a couple of additional problems: The automobile had gathered around it a host of formidable critics; not only was the love affair with cars coming apart, it was being called illegitimate in the first place. And gas was running out.

"People who dislike the auto-highway system prefer to denigrate or disregard its obvious benefits and concentrate instead on its costs. Almost all public literature produced in the United States during the last 20 years has been hostile to the automobile." And who would say such a thing but B. Bruce-Briggs? Point by point, he listed the criticisms and put forth refutations in *The War Against the Automobile,* published in 1975.

Just who was doing all this criticizing and why? According to Bruce-Briggs, the culprits were Northeastern "elitists." Said Bruce-Briggs, "Major social movements—like the anti-auto crusade—do not happen unless they are in the interest of powerful elements. No one can honestly claim that there is a widespread *public* benefit in screwing the average American. . . .

"Those who are opposed to the automobile and who have been howling about its 'faults' for a generation are the same people who are trying to block suburbanization, halt the production of new energy sources, and promote measures to run up the cost of driving. As the Marxists say, 'It is no accident' that they will profit as individuals, and as a class, from the curtailment of auto use. . . .

"The class aspect is the foundation of the war against the automobile. . . . Depending on the national density, the optimum situation for an automobile [meaning being seen as a societal benefit] is roughly when half the households have it. The U.S. is up to 85%—and that is a killer for the people on top." Bruce-Briggs went on to say that it was when the middle class had to begin sharing the road with the workers that complaints against the automobile grew loudest. "It is no coincidence that both the agitation against the automobile and the promotion of mass transportation began when the urban workers switched from mass transit to the car."

To attribute anticar sentiments to an elitist conspiracy goes a little far. More likely and more reasonably they were due to pent-up dissatisfaction with shoddy products and arrogance in the face of consumers' complaints about them and also to what seemed to be a very real problem with fuel availability and what a permanent world shortage might do to a nation so utterly dependent on the car.

Down to a Quarter Tank

Running on Empty is the title of the Worldwatch Institute's 1979 report predicting dire consequences for those of us who count on auto-mobility. "The global automobile fleet now consumes about one-fifth of all the oil produced in the world," said the report. In a far less dire fashion than some forecasters, it suggests that peak production of oil in the world might well come in the mid-nineties. A couple of other reasonable sources—a U.S. Geological Survey and a study by the International Energy Agency—suggest the same thing. Others go as far as to suggest an end to fossil fuel availability to the Western world around the turn of the century, preceded by a series of sharp interruptions in the supply much like the one in 1973 and the later one that accompanied the fall of the shah of Iran in 1979.

It would be comforting to think that even if the predictions are accurate, our

TOP LEFT:
1981 Chrysler K Car
Part of the program to save the Chrysler Corporation was the building of the so-called K car, a small, front-wheel–drive series bearing both Plymouth and Dodge nameplates. It has become the basis for all other cars manufactured by the company, and if Chrysler Corporation survives, it has the K to thank.

BOTTOM LEFT:
1982 Chevrolet Cavalier
Down, down, down they came in size as the industry entered an era of limitation and competition from overseas. This is Chevrolet's Honda competitor, the J car, a thoroughly good automobile that will surely become an even better one as it is developed over its lifetime.

future is filled with either alternative fuels or new kinds of engines that will keep our population scurrying across the face of our nation. But such thinking is not realistic. The most promising—and immediately available—alternative fuel is produced from biomass. It is called ethanol, an alcohol, or it can be produced as methanol, which powers all the cars at Indianapolis. Although obviously there is no doubt that it works, there are other doubts. Said *Running on Empty,* "A Department of Energy review of the potential for alcohol fuels in the United States, published in mid-1979, suggests that if all the land idle under farm programs were brought back into production, if large quantities of organic wastes such as cheese whey, citrus pulp, and municipal garbage were used to make ethanol, there would be sufficient raw materials to produce 4.8 billion gallons of ethanol per year. That works out to less that 5% of current U.S. gasoline consumption."

There is also a cost problem. Ethanol and methanol are expensive to produce. "Gasohol," which we have already seen sold in gas stations in the United States (and is required fuel in Brazil for everyone) is subsidized. It's like pouring champagne into beer," someone once said about using expensive alternatives to stretch our gasoline. But it is perfectly possible that crude oil will reach the $62 a barrel that ethanol now costs. Unfortunately, even if we were willing to pay three times the current price for gas at the pump, we have discovered that we won't be able to buy very much, particularly since the primitive calculations that we've just made don't include the *energy* cost of producing energy.

If ethanol and methanol won't work, what about "syncrude," the synthetic petroleum made from coal liquefaction or extracted from bituminous sands or from the kerogen in shale? There are even bigger problems here. First, only about 2 percent of the oil-bearing sands on the North American continent are in the United States. A great deal of these sands are in Alberta, Canada, and no

matter how much we have in common with the Canadians, when fuel gets short, so will tempers. Coal liquefaction is useful and possible. There is even a plant in South Africa producing the fuel commercially. But it too is expensive. As for oil-bearing shale, we have lots and lots of it in the United States, mostly in the West. But extracting oil from shale is a difficult process that takes a great deal of water. We have all the shale we need in the western states, but we are short on water.

The syncrude solution depends on still another factor. We must have plants up and operating by the time the petroleum runs out. That, according to a Stanford Research Institute International study, is already impossible. So what do we have to look forward to? "In the United States the government's priorities in fuel

402

allocations became clear in the spring of 1979 when there was a shortage of diesel fuel, which is used both in trucks and in farm tractors. The Department of Energy had little choice but to give the agricultural sector first claim on the scarce fuel supplies. As a result, farmers were able to plant their crops on schedule, but truckers . . . went on strike." The Worldwatch Institute's summary statement is succinct: "Two fundamental trends are shaping the future of the automobile. The first is the leveling off of world oil production. The second is the projected increase in all the most essential uses of oil—to produce food, to heat homes, to run factories, and to power trains, trucks and buses. As these expanding demands press against fixed supplies of petroleum, there will be less and less fuel for cars."

Can we sleep easily anyway, calm in the knowledge that Detroit will come up with something to eliminate the problem of a world shortage of oil? No. Not only Detroit but Stuttgart and Cologne and Gothenburg and Osaka and Coventry have been trying to solve this one for some time now with no success.

Recall that right after the war, Chrysler Corporation began experiments with the Brayton Cycle (gas turbine) engine for passenger cars. The turbine's advantages are many: It works; it can be made small enough to fit into the engine compartment of a car; it has a great deal of power; and best of all it runs on almost anything. Chrysler and the rest of the industrial establishment just can't produce the engine at a reasonable cost. The trouble is that to function, the engine has to turn incredibly fast, on the order of 60,000 rpm. If we don't want it to tear itself apart or to come through the firewall and tear *us* apart, it has to be made of very lightweight, highly exotic metals. Materials other than metals have been tried—ceramics, for example. The problem there is that the structure of ceramics is crystalline, and crystals have undetectable random flaws. There is no turbine engine in our future.

There are no electric motors in our future either, despite some highly optimistic projections from General Motors. We don't have the battery technology or the fuel-cell technology. Nor is it likely that we will before the turn of the century. The same holds true for almost every motor or engine except the good old Otto Cycle. Very shortly we will find out that therein lies our best hope for preserving all we hold dear—as far as the automobile is concerned anyway.

1963 Chrysler Turbine Experimental
For almost four decades, Chrysler Corporation has been experimenting with the turbine engine as an alternative to the internal combustion Otto-cycle engine used in almost all cars built in the world (the successful alternative is the diesel). Those who hope that a silver bullet solution to a world fuel shortage will come from the R&D shops in Detroit in the form of a wonder-engine are due to be as disappointed as the Chrysler engineers who have been trying to get the turbine to work in a passenger car for all this time.

CHAPTER 22

Miniature Cars

Twenty-seven-point-five miles per gallon by 1985, *are you kidding?* Not at all, and maybe after 1985 (as suggested in the Energy Policy and Conservation Act of 1973) the Secretary of Transportation will require an even better figure for passenger cars. After all, we're almost there, and we haven't had much trouble reaching the goal so far as most people can tell—that is, people *outside* Detroit, for the industry indeed suffered in its downsizing programs.

Visitors to the Chrysler plant at Highland Park during its days of conversion to small cars (required by the act for all of Detroit at huge cost to the industry) would not have taken the wartime atmosphere of the place for anything but what it was: indication that a huge institution was on the edge of disaster. Nor would they have made any mistake about where they were. The parking lots were filled with company products. Workers and management were loyal—in particular, there wasn't a Japanese car to be seen, unless it had the Chrysler Pentastar emblazoned on it. Chrysler faced the same problems as the rest of the industry; problem really, for it was one intertwined, complex conundrum. At the very time the government was mandating the spending of $50 billion, business was falling through the floor.

In 1973—with the coming of the first oil embargo—9.5 million cars were sold; in 1974, more than 2 million less; in 1975, almost a million less than that. The pattern continued in 1979, 1980, and 1981—only it was even more extreme.

In Chrysler's case (and later Ford's) a good deal of the blame could be laid at corporate doors. But Chrysler's was the perfect example of management numbness. Cars normally take three years to plan and produce. Since all companies have several car lines, each going through a three-year design cycle, lines are renewed on a staggered basis. In 1970, the forward planners at Highland Park decided it was time to take the 1973 big cars in hand. Thus, just when the tap was closed and people were beginning to turn their interest to fuel efficiency, Chrysler introduced a whole fleet of battleships. It was a clear case of management myopia. Nor had Ford made substantial changes. Even GM, which had plans for shifting production to smaller cars, was generally unprepared.

Not so Japan, Inc., which is what the U.S. industry was beginning to call its Japanese counterpart. Detroit was shocked to see import sales penetration rise to 20 percent in the late seventies (it was almost 50 percent in California), hover there for a few years, and then climb again. The invaders this time were not Europeans, but Japanese—who had tested this market as early as 1959 with an execrable product, withdrawn for redesign and study of American methods and then returned with an increasingly attractive group of cars.

There was a further attribute Detroit did not notice for a long while—particularly during the time prior to the first embargo, when Japanese penetration

1976 Cadillac
In the heyday of the ocean liner, Cadillac ruled the roost, building cars with all the superficial luxury of the *Queen Mary* and of almost her size.
photo by Susan Wilson

amounted to 15 percent and total import sales were still noticeably under a fifth of the market. It was perhaps the most important, the least visible to short-sighted industrial managers, the least believable to them, and therefore the most scorned: quality control. Since the Japanese industry was relatively new, its factories were better equipped for both productivity and quality. Its workforce adhered to a very different ethic, one more conducive to disciplined labor. From its so-called just-in-time method of accepting subcontractor orders—which eliminated the costs of holding inventory—to its willingness to reject parts that were in any degree out of tolerance, the Japanese industry was more efficient *and* more dedicated to producing high-quality products.

That moment at Chrysler in Highland Park after the federal government had agreed to consider an enormous loan to bail out the company was indicative of how U.S. legislation, in combination with consumer attitude shifts, was affecting Detroit: New products were being rushed to completion; Mustang Lee Iacocca was finally sitting in the chief executive's chair; Harold Sperlich, whom Henry Ford II had thrown out of his company for advocating small cars, was Chrysler's man responsible for hardware. Those were times nobody in the industry will forget. To walk around any factory—but especially one belonging to Chrysler—was to soak up DeLorean's or Iacocca's feeling of excitement. The same sort that must have existed in London during the Battle of Britain. But still it was excitement.

Everyone involved knew that the industry had to solve its problems by building cars people wanted. This required a change of attitude by industry executives who had been convinced that the barges they were producing were what America craved. They were for a while. But then—for very good reasons and with Japanese examples to follow—Americans changed their minds. Despite all the motivational research and all the group discussions, Detroit was

1982 Plymouth Reliant/Dodge Aries
The K car's success prompted Chrysler to build variants with Chrysler nameplates as well as a luxurious version with the Dodge nameplate called the 400. Whatever the name, however, a K car is still a K car.

not a good listener. Even the progressive Sperlich, at his desk in the K. T. Keller Building at Chrysler, marveled over a report from an outside market research firm that listed "high quality control: fit and finish" as the number 1 criterion among car buyers and "styling" way down in eleventh place. Skepticism about the importance of quality control could not last. In Dearborn, at GM's proving grounds at Milford, in Highland Park, a counteroffensive according to the newly scouted market battleplan was being mounted.

Small cars, well built, honestly marketed was the new Detroit strategy, and about time too. With the straightforward approach to its buyers, an enlightened Detroit decided to let America in on an ill-kept secret. Instead of calling cars golden Comets or angel-skin Petrels or crouching Panthers, the industry came right out and started selling cars by their engineering designations: GM built the X body, its first small, front-wheel-drive platform, and didn't even hide the fact that there was an X Chevrolet, an X Pontiac, an X Oldsmobile, and so forth. Chrysler did the same with its two K cars—nearly identical Plymouth and Dodge twins. It was refreshing—as were the cars.

Pulling Toward the 21st Century

In fact, the first full family of downsized, energy-efficient cars, mandated by Washington and costing so much to build and design, appeared from General Motors in 1978. These were the X cars, approximately a third smaller than the cars they replaced but far roomier and, on the whole, much better automobiles. The design concept was European. They were what German, French, English, and Italian product planners called "three-box cars." The new notion—new to the United States—was that one box should contain the entire powertrain, engine

1982 Chevrolet Citation X-11
While the 1977 Caprice Classic was the first downsized car from GM, the series called the X cars represented the breakthrough in engineering. Chevrolet's first contemporary design in memory featured a two-box design (one compartment for passengers and luggage, the other for all mechanical devices), made possible by mounting the engine sideways over the front, driving wheels. The X-11 version is a high-performance option package, an attempt to revive the muscle concept with about half the calories.

ABOVE:

1954 Buick Skylark
Buick would eventually build a model named Skylark that was crisp, small, and efficient. But the early Skylark, pictured above, was a visual and an engineering disaster.

ABOVE RIGHT:

1978 Buick Apollo
On its way to basic reason, the Buick compact, nee Skylark, changed its name, its size, and its relationship to other cars built by GM. This is the "A" in a series of four known as the acronym cars: Chevrolet Nova, Pontiac Ventura, Oldsmobile Omega, and Buick Apollo.
photo by Joseph Kugielsky

BELOW RIGHT AND OVERLEAF:

1982 Buick Skylark
It took a while, but Buick finally got its compact right. The Skylark is one of GM's X cars, and as such is a member of a highly respectable family.
photos by Don Hamerman

and transmission, one should be reserved for passengers, and one for luggage. This meant front-wheel drive and a "sidewinder" engine: the X cars came with newer, smaller powerplants turned east-west in the engine compartment instead of north-south. This reduced the amount of space required for their packaging and made it easier to fit the transaxle—a combination gearbox and differential—to the power unit, now that engine output was going to the front wheels. In addition, the transaxle removed that annoying hump from the floor of the passenger compartment. Packaging was the trendy word in Detroit. The industry was packaging the power source up front, separate from the packages containing people and luggage. In Europe and Japan, most manufacturers of small cars were building two-box cars—engine and transaxle combined up front, people behind it, and a hatchback *cum* luggage compartment behind the people in the same box. Detroit would follow this configuration in its next round of even smaller cars. In fact, Chrysler had already done this with its Omni and Horizon, twin VW copies using Volkswagen engines and transmissions that had actually preceded the X cars from GM.

Imagine an X car—a Buick Skylark, say. Now imagine the owner of a new slick 1955 Chevy being transported over twenty years into the future and set down beside the Skylark. What does he notice?

Standing back from the car and looking at its silhouette, he sees it is considerably smaller than his Chevy and that the proportions are very different—no more long hood, very little overhang front or rear, a much squarer shape (although the 1955 Chevy was not among the swoopier cars of its era).

Inside the Skylark, he is impressed by its plushness. ("They're ahead of us all in interiors," a competitor's president would say after his first ride in a Skylark.) The seat materials are much softer—and more durable. The Chevy owner notices the straightforwardness of the instrument panel despite a flock of new dials and numbers. Detroit has gone back to instruments—instruments that are easily visible and easy to read. The pods and lights of the 1955 Chevy are gone. In their place are white-on-black instruments with real numbers in front of the driver. The shift quadrant is a small surprise—it is incorporated in a rectangle containing the speedometer, easy to read and use. The Chevy driver is puzzled by a speedometer that only goes up to 85 mph. This is part of the 1966 Safety Act. The Skylark is capable of considerable top-end speed, but its driver will never be able to take the car out on the road and see what it can do because the speedometer doesn't register anything higher than 85 mph.

From the moment he sets sail in the Skylark, the Chevy driver notices dramatic differences. The first comes from a series of design improvements attributable to the normal course or refinement since 1955. For example, the power steering in the Chevy was limp and mindless. The steering in the Buick has been redesigned. It is called variable ratio, and its efficiency increases as the wheels are turned.

There aren't many devices to baffle the Chevy driver in the Skylark except perhaps the climate control, with which the occupant sets a completely automatic heater/air conditioner at the desired temperature and then ignores it forever. The Chevy owner doesn't see a variety of startling mechanical improvements, but they are there: microprocessors controlling the air/fuel mixture, tailpipe emissions, fuel injection, and disc brakes.

He does notice something known as torque steer. Since an engine has a tendency to revolve (and is held in only by its mounts) when it makes power to turn its crankshaft, it transmits a brief twisting inclination to the front, steering wheels (in a front-wheel–drive car) when the driver steps down on the ac-

celerator. The car tends to take a momentary turn toward the wheel onto which the power is being put. The twisting motion is called torque. And torque steer is the term for that instant's pull on the wheels. The driver finds that a puller handles somewhat differently from a pusher, particularly in emergency conditions, but it doesn't bother him since the way to avoid terminal understeer in a front-wheel–drive car is to come off the throttle, and that is the instinctive reaction of most panicked drivers anyway.

When the Chevy driver gets his Skylark out on the highway, he notices a few more strange things. First, with its smaller engine and lighter weight, the car performs well but not as well as a car of this advanced time might have been expected to perform. That, of course, is because performance has been redefined to mean fuel efficiency. The Skylark does not accelerate as fast as the 1955 Chevy, particularly if the 1955 has the new V-8. But when the Chevy owner takes the Skylark out on some back roads, it does surprise him. First, it feels as soft as his car, but it doesn't roll quite so much in the corners. Second, it tracks better. Front-wheel–drive cars have, by definition, better directional stability than cars that are pushed through the air. This is particularly noticeable in a high crosswind.

If a child or a dog runs out in front of the Skylark, the Chevy driver, mashing the brake petal to the floor, will be astonished by how quickly the Buick comes to a stop. Front-disc brakes have become standard since the 1955 model year. Not only are they more efficient, but they do not have as great a tendency to fade. So if this is the second or third dog to dash in front of his car, the Chevy owner is even more impressed.

If our Chevy driver is a young blood, he nails the throttle on the back road and is absolutely amazed at how well the Buick handles, almost as well as European grand-touring contemporaries of his 1955 Chevy and far, far better than his Chevy's American competitors. He can't tell how much over 85 mph he's going, but if a highway patrol officer is following him, he'll know soon. Flat out, the Buick with a V-6 (the larger of the engine options) makes a little over 100 mph. The Chevy driver will be surprised and shocked to learn he has almost doubled something called the "double nickle," for by this time we have instituted a national maximum speed limit of 55 in order to save energy. He will also be saddened to learn that our wartime expertise with radar has turned it into a weapon focused on the motorist.

The best surprise comes when the Chevy driver has done perhaps 200 miles flat out in the Skylark and pulls into a gas station. There he discovers that even with the throttle wide open, the car gets about 25 miles to the gallon, at least 7 more miles per gallon than his 1955 Chevy. But he forgets that pleasure the moment he looks at the numbers racing across the face of the pump. Perhaps it reads in liters, perhaps in half-gallons; in any case the dollar amount sends him into shock. In many places in the nation—particularly on the back roads—the price of gasoline has quadrupled since 1955. It would be unlikely that his windshield will be washed, for almost certainly he has pulled into the most accessible lane in the gas station without noticing that it is labeled "Self-Service." He is disappointed if he expects trading stamps or National Football League glasses with his gasoline purchase.

He probably wants to check the tires, for to him they look very low. Bias-ply tires have been replaced with radials, for more mileage and lower rolling resistance, but since they carry less air, to someone unfamiliar with the new tire technology, radial tires always look low. He may have wondered about the tires earlier, particularly if he got into the Skylark first thing in the morning. Radials tend to fall into odd shapes when they sit for a while; they feel "square" until they warm up.

Still, the 1955 Chevy driver is impressed. If his family is with him, they find as much room in the Skylark, particularly head room in the back seat, as in the Chevy. The ride is as smooth, the car quieter.

The car, then, is a pleasure—as long as the Chevy driver hasn't seen its price. In the year of introduction of the X cars, GM prices averaged something over $8,000. Much of this was due—if the manufacturers were to be believed—to federally mandated equipment for emissions and safety. But a lot of it came from the fact that Detroit had to spend a great deal of money to build a new kind of American car, and somebody had to pay, and it wasn't the factories.

The World Car

In a sense, the Skylark was a new concept not only for Detroit but for the world. We had always competed by exporting industry, plants, and expertise. Foreign invasion of our market, combined with a world problem in the shortage and cost of fuel, was pointing us in a new direction. If the American car were redefined in terms of the Skylark, its smaller J car successors, and the other variations, were we not suddenly in the same position as the Japanese? Did we not now have a car of internationally appropriate design that could meet universal competition?

Indeed, we did—indeed, we do. Now that cars built in France cannot be distinguished from those made in England, Italy, Germany, Japan, or even the United States, the world has become everyone's market. The Japanese, with their high-tech auto establishment, their work ethic, and their government support, have an advantage over most of the rest of the world in exporting cars. We have an advantage in the existence of manufacturing facilities in most developed nations.

The Germans and the Japanese are beginning to build plants in the United States. And very shortly they will be able to assemble cars, if not actually manufacture them, in as many places as we can.

Moreover, the world industry is beginning to coalesce. General Motors owns a significant part of the Japanese company Isuzu. Ford has a part of Toyo Kogyo (Mazda). Chrysler is partners with Mitsubishi in Japan *and* Peugeot in France. Volvo, Saab, and Peugeot are partners in an engine plant that makes motors for all of them—plus small-volume cars like the DeLorean, which is built in Northern Ireland. Renault, a nationalized French company, has a very large interest in American Motors (the combination is called—facetiously—Franco-American Motors). Daimler Benz manufactures Freightliner trucks in Portland, Oregon. And on it goes.

Many observers see the industry shaking out once again, this time on a worldwide basis. There will be, according to them, perhaps eight megacompanies by 1990.

And what will these companies be building? Why the "world car," of course. The VW Rabbit (called the Golf in Europe) is the exemplar. In the shape of the Rabbit, a two-box hatchback, design distillation takes its ultimate form. From a distance, not even the most sophisticated car person can tell a VW from an Omni/Horizon from a Chevy Chevette from a Ford Fiesta. The Rabbit is made in Wolfsburg, Germany, and Westmoreland, Pennsylvania. Ford has taken this even further, designing a car called the Escort, which is made in every country that has a Ford plant. The German Escort is slightly different from the English

Escort, which varies somewhat from the American Escort. But they all look the same and use the same engine, transmission (Japanese for the manual, American for the automatic), wheels, and body panels. Franco-American is about to manufacture a French-designed car in Kenosha, Wisconsin, and Leyland Cars is on the verge of building a Japanese design (Honda) in Abingdon-on-Thames, England.

At first, there was a good deal of complaining about this, particularly by car lovers, who saw the future as an unrelieved line of identical boxes stretching from Manhattan to San Francisco and then picking up again in Peking and going to Paris.

Nonsense, said Bruno Sacco, chief stylist for Daimler Benz, and he showed the world what he meant with the introduction of a variety of new sedans in 1981 that were fuel efficient and very (teutonically) individualistic. What's more, he said, we can still have big cars and fuel efficiency too. He was talking about his company's wide use and refinement of the diesel engine, another German invention, which uses a middle distillate of petroleum (the same oil we heat houses with) but has more energy by volume than gasoline and is more fuel efficient. Diesels are internal combustion engines. Instead of a spark, they use very high pressure to ignite the mixture of air and oil; compression ignition, this is called. Since a diesel must accommodate enormous pressures inside it, the bottom end of the engine—the crankshaft and bearings—has to be immensely strong. This enhances longevity. Properly maintained diesels can last three times as long as gasoline engines. Diesels are also heavier. But what the diesel does for the passenger car is to allow it to be larger, to accommodate more people, and at the same time—because of the engine's fuel efficiency—to deliver the same high mileage in a big car as a much smaller gas engine powering a far smaller and lighter car can give. So, according to Sacco, if we use diesel engines, we won't

1982 Chevrolet Chevette
When Chevy came around to building a real subcompact, it used a seven-year-old design first put into manufacture by GM's Brazilian subsidiary. In a sense, the Chevette was and is a world car; it has equivalents in Japan, England, Germany, South America, and Australia. Sales were slow early on, but by the year of this model it had become the best selling single car in the U.S.

1975 Cadillac Seville
Even Cadillac had to bow to the mandates of the Energy Policy and Conservation Act of 1973. Building on the acronym cars, the NOVAs, already in manufacture by GM's less prestigious divisions, it produced the Seville, which was meant to compete with foreign cars, principally Mercedes.

have to look at that long line of little boxes on the road.

We won't have to do this anyway, according to Georgetto Giugiaro, the Italian designer who styled the Rabbit. That was only one solution, he says, pointing to a slick, four-seater design exercise he calls the Medusa. Notice the low drag coefficient, he says, and indeed the relative "slipperiness" of the Medusa is as good as many racing cars designed to cheat the air. Giugiaro wants the world to know that efficient cars need not be ugly or afflicted with sameness. The problem is to make the best use of fuel. The solutions are many.

He is right. Detroit is working as hard as Giugiaro—harder, probably—on aerodynamics. It takes an enormous amount of energy to push a box through the air. The smoother the box, the smaller its frontal area, the less energy it takes. A great deal of practical knowledge about aerodynamics comes from race tracks. If two cars have the same power, weight, and handling, the faster car is the one that slides through the air better. Race-car designers have been experimenting with aerodynamics since the first stripped Model T body was made.

And the shape of the car is not the only solution being pursued. The communications revolution has given us a tiny computer called the microprocessor. The size of a pack of cigarettes, it can perform miracles. Today, we are using microprocessors and sensors to measure emissions in the tailpipes of our cars and then to "instruct" the mechanism that mixes the fuel to correct the proportions. It is a closed-loop system overseen entirely by the microprocessor. And this is only the beginning. On Lincolns and Cadillacs, there is an information center instead of a series of instruments. It can give the driver: average speed, estimated time of arrival at destination, continuing average miles per gallon, hours or minutes left to travel—all sorts of marvelous data. Again, the microprocessor is at work. Very shortly, microprocessor black boxes will be reading out to drivers the state of tune of their engines, their tire pressures, their oil consumption, the number of miles to go before spark plug replacements, and so forth. It is a very real revolution in control—and therefore efficiency—of the Otto Cycle engine.

These developments have provided some relief from the pressure of developing alternative power sources and alternative fuels. Many engineers all over the world feel that the improvements we are making in our garden-variety powerplants will take us through a period of fuel shortage until we find other ways and resources to power our cars.

SRI International thinks the automobile will be our principal mode of transportation through the year 2025.

Bruce-Briggs's alma mater, the Hudson Institute, thinks the fuel-shortage problem is much overstated, and, therefore, the car will be with us (almost) always.

Car companies all over the world and particularly in Detroit feel the design revolution of the last decade has been so profound that it has defined a vehicle that will be in use for a very long time.

Not much planning for a nation bereft of auto-mobility has been done. The prospect is too awesome to contemplate. A whole slew of people, from Frank Duryea to Ransom Eli Olds to Roy Chapin to Henry Ford to Alfred Sloan to John DeLorean to Lee Iacocca have seen to that.

ing "influence groups." He saw to it that word spread. Soon, the Rabbit was seen on road-racing tracks, running as a "showroom stock" car—almost unmodified—and doing very well against its competition: Opel, Pinto, and Datsun.

In substantial contrast to its Japanese competitors, the Rabbit was showing off its European heritage, which pleased the former Porsche owner no end. It came standard with a 1.5-liter engine, about the same size as the engine in a comparable Toyota, but in a far lighter overall package. Interior trim, sound conditioning, and accessories were fewer and lighter than those on the Japanese car. This encouraged the Los Angelino, who had been one of the first to buy a Rabbit, to enjoy its performance. It didn't do much for people who wanted tiny replicas of American cars; and they were the increasing part of the market. Moreover, the Rabbit suffered another disadvantage. To give it such marvelous handling qualities, VW had specified rather stiff springs and pretty hefty shock absorbers. The Rabbit used something called "rack and pinion" steering—a term very descriptive of the cogs and wheels inside the steering box—which is very precise but a little quick, perhaps too definitive, for people used to the vagueness characteristic of Detroit cars, which meant most Americans. The Rabbit's standard tires were European radials. They were tenacious pavement grippers, but they gave the car a somewhat harsher ride than most cars not so equipped. All in all, the Rabbit was well within European design practice: a cannily crafted piece that would pull away from most small cars at a stoplight and tear up the side of an Alp with some of the better of its betters. But it was not soft (the ex-Porsche

owner was particularly pleased about this—overcompliant cars are often sluggish handlers). The Rabbit did not coddle its passengers. It demanded attention at speed. Going fast around a tight, hard corner prompted the car to lift an inside rear wheel perhaps 5 inches off the ground. It was spectacular to watch, strange to feel at first, but in no way dangerous—just characteristic of front-wheel–drive cars being driven to their maximum.

Although small cars were becoming a standard, many Americans, perhaps even Rabbit owners from Los Angeles, could not imagine the car as a cross-country transporter. The problem was a lack of interior plushness—the Rabbit owner had a neighbor who had opted for a Datsun on the very grounds that it was so much more hospitable on journeys, with its deeply padded seats, push-button radio, and infinite dash gadgetry. For those who did not share the ex-Porsche driver's sophisticated appreciation of vehicle dynamics, this unease with a Rabbit was (and is) understandable. It is no fun to endure a Rabbit on a trip up Interstate 5 from Los Angeles to Portland, as even the Rabbit owner might have discovered. The road, which is variously six to eight lanes wide, climbs the Tejon Pass parallel to the old Ridge Route that would have been so demanding of a Mercer driver in the 'teens, arcing up a steep five-mile stretch and then swooping around a variety of hills, thereupon dropping into a great valley.

Climbing the Grapevine, as this whole section of I-5 is called, the Rabbit driver would be careful to stay in the outside lane. Neither laden nor empty trucks can come within 30 mph of the speed of the Rabbit can attain on the upgrade, nor can most American cars built after 1973, burdened as they are by smog-control equipment that chokes down the breathing ability of their engines. Rabbits whoosh by most foreign cars on the Grapevine too. The Japanese competition is not interested in building cars with hidden performance, so Subarus, Hondas, and Toyotas fall behind. Even if our new Rabbit owner, at 6 feet 4 inches tall, had had to crouch just a little in his Porsche, he sits upright in the VW. The car's seats, in keeping with the design approach of the whole piece, are firm. There is lumbar support, although it is not adjustable, and some fore and aft movement, enough so that, combined with the enormous amount of head room, the car can accommodate his height with little trouble.

If our man's Rabbit is a "high line" model—fully trimmed and outfitted, these days costing almost $8,000—he watches not only his speedometer but the tachometer in his car going up the hill. People accustomed to watching revolutions per minute turned by the engine (as the Rabbit owner was from his Porsche days) have a better sense of optimum shift points. The Grapevine climber, though, is concerned only in an academic way. He could go right up in top gear in a four-speed Rabbit. However, he probably bought a car with a five-speed option, a "long" overdrive fifth, so he has kept his car in fourth, knowing it would work too hard in high, losing revs. The steering is a particular pleasure to him. It feels very positive in the big sweeping turns. But if he chooses to go off the road at Gorman, near the summit, he might find the steering getting heavy. A front-wheel–drive car with the weight of its engine over the steering wheel, tends to demand well-conditioned forearms. What's more, VW does not come with power steering.

It will be like the good old Porsche days when the new Rabbit owner streaks down the other side of the Tejon Pass on the Grapevine. Top speed on a good Rabbit is about 103 mph; mashing the throttle to the floor and pitching down a 6-percent grade should get you 110 easily, although the speedometer, mandated by federal law to stop at 85, will never show it.

But then, as the great concrete apron of I-5 points north, never deviating from

its path, never offering a moment's entertainment, the Rabbit will begin to wear not just on its driver but on his family. After a few hundred miles of this kind of work, the joints between concrete slabs begin to feel like motorcycle jumps, the steering wheel jerks at every bump, as the steering/driving wheels feed back the road to the driver's hands. The car is geared for fuel economy, which means a low numerical final drive, best taken advantage of by driving at constant speed. So if our driver is turning the engine 3,500 rpm and getting 63 mph, very soon the road sound becomes a constant resonance in his brain.

Unless the buyer ordered an expensive, nonstandard radio, he hears almost nothing but static coming from the dash. The VW-supplied unit picks up from only short distances, and its fidelity of reproduction is poor. Nor will its new owner find his car comfortable on a hot day. The Rabbit uses outside-supplied air-conditioning equipment, and it is less effective than the factory units in American-designed cars.

In many ways then—particularly those Americans put great value upon—the Rabbit seems unduly austere, especially when one has to live inside it for long periods of time. This is the very austerity that appealed to our ex-sports car man, for he wanted to experience the sensations of driving as opposed to sitting behind a wheel and waiting for his car to bring him to his destination in some mysterious, almost automatic fashion. In addition, this austerity is a kind of hair shirt of distinction for the Rabbit owner, setting him apart from Buick and Mazda drivers, who have opted for marshmallow transport, which became the norm for our products in the easy days of available metals, cheap gas, and a consumer body that turned its cars over with regularity every two or three years and therefore was not concerned with inherent design, finish, and fit—only comfort.

One more thing about this new Rabbit, now churning up I-5. It is a true world car. VW followed American practice in exporting—not product—but factories to build it. It is assembled in almost all industrial and some Third World countries. It can accommodate itself to every kind of weather and road condition. It is simple to maintain. It is economical to operate. VW parts depots dot the globe.

With its American bumpers, American lighting system, American color-

keyed interior; with all the concessions and compromises VW has made with the Pennsylvania Rabbit to bring it into conformity with U.S. safety, fuel economy, and emissions laws, the company is making clear that it can build the same basic car to a variety of national requirements. It can build a world car. Driving up I-5 is a long trip. Philosophically, this car has already taken a far longer one.

Without a doubt the American car has contributed to our cultural development. It has helped us make the transition from an agrarian to an industrial age; it has moved our population into concentrated centers of production; it has encouraged our consumerist behavior; and it has contributed to the rise of the middle class.

What we are as a nation, then, good and bad, we are in large measure because of the car, the automobile manufacturing establishment, and the people who set it on its course.

And the journey isn't over yet. Until well into the next century, nothing looms on the horizon that will do what the car can do for us. It has given us a measure of independence, mobility, and, through its ownership, a feeling of achievement.

More than that, it's taken us on a great trip.

Afterword and Acknowledgments

A museum supplied the cars for most of the photos in this book. The man who established, assembled, and owned the museum saw the automobile as both an object of beauty (or strangeness or wonder or delight or humor) as well as the manufactured centerpiece of our national life. He was William Fisk Harrah, and when he died, one automotive magazine said of him and of Harrah's Automobile Collection: "Henry Ford built the car; Bill Harrah built its monument." Indeed, the collection is monumental. At its peak it contained almost 1,400 cars, the largest array in the world, and its emphasis was on American cars because they spoke clearly to Bill Harrah about himself. He was a gambler, a landholder, a hotelier, an immensely successful businessman, and the quintessential American car addict. He bought one (a 1911 Maxwell) and then another and another and another. Harrah never saw his collection as the stunning cultural contribution that scholars and car enthusiasts all over the world recognize it to be. Bill Harrah died in 1978, unaware that he had assembled the most marvelous historical tour through our industrial age outside the Smithsonian Institution.

American Cars was conceived and begun just as the announcement of the sale of the Harrah's Automobile Collection was made. In accordance with Harrah's wishes, after his death his company, and with it his collection, were sold to a large hotel chain. But the hotel's accountants could not justify ownership of a 1,400-car non-income-producing asset (worth perhaps $75 million). To its enormous credit, the new owner responded to a tidal wave of concern over the loss of such a cultural treasure as the H.A.C. by setting up a nonprofit foundation to which it hopes to donate $50 million worth of cars and a research library over the next five years. The rest of the cars will be sold.

This solution was arrived at only after delicate negotiations led by Nevada's governor, Robert List. His efforts and those of his chief of staff, Greg Lambert, were strongly supported by Nevada Senators Howard Cannon and Paul Laxalt and Representative James Santini.

Harrah's management, led by Chairman Mead Dixon, President Richard Goeglein, and General Counsel Phil Satre, was immensely cooperative and even instrumental in the solution.

But principal credit for the salvation of the core of the collection goes to an elegant Reno-ite, George Charchalis, architect, scholar, fifth-generation Nevadan, and auto enthusiast. With Mark Curtis of Harrah's, Charchalis sounded the alarm, and when negotiations flagged, he was forever there maneuvering, cajoling, mediating.

Time pressures in producing this book were enormous under the circumstances. It simply could not have been done without the full effort of the managers and employees of the Collection. They are many; each name deserves a place in an American automotive honor roll, for if *American Cars* gives us our last images of Harrah's Automobile Collection as it once was, it is the result of their work in assembling the museum and then making the cars available so that they and their history could be recorded on film and in print.

Special thanks go to Joel Eric Finn, distinguished collector and author who became president of H.A.C., Inc., and who is charged with implementing the plan to save the core of the Collection.

E. Clyde Wade, Collection general manager; long-time Harrah friend and special services director, Jim Edwards (who was particularly helpful in reading the manuscript); Don Britt, who has conducted all of H.A.C.'s auctions and is immensely knowledgeable about cars of every kind; and Tom Batchelor, technical chief of the Collection, gave their wholehearted support.

To photograph 350 cars under time pressure was no easy matter, even for the talented Baron Wolman and Cindy Lewis. Their splendid work is due in part to the help of a crew, carefully chosen for their understanding of cars, who gently and carefully moved the automobiles to be photographed for this book from in and around the other 1,100. Crew Chief Frank Martin supervised Ted Freeman, John Fuller, Alan Carlson, Bill Papp, Bob Shue, Bill Kuzemchak, Harvey Adams, Dave Jarvis, Dave Carlson, and Mike Earle in this difficult task.

Of the people at the Collection, librarian Ray Borges played an indispensable role, assisted by Pete Grosso on special projects and Linda Huntsman. In addition, Carole Mitchell, Jackie Hawkins, Helen King, Linda Sutherland, Kaye Neal, Frank Harper, and Al Wasilewski were particularly helpful.

Gene Babow, a well-known automobile historian, set me on my way. If I have strayed, it is not his fault. Susan Horton, whose research for my biography of William Fisk Harrah was invaluable, did an equally excellent job of unearthing background material for this book. As always, MaraLyn O'Neal was a dynamo at the typewriter.

Mark Curtis, so early a defender of the faith, cannot receive too much credit. His deputy, Candice Pearce, was also of constant help and support.

During this project, I became friends with the publisher of *American Cars,* Andrew Stewart, whose own fascination with automobiles was sustaining to us both. Art director Nai Chang deserves all the credit for the absolutely marvelous artistic presentation of the work. Editor Leslie Stoker, a friendly adversary, cleared out considerable underbrush in the manuscript. As always, my agent and long-time friend Jacques de Spoelberch saw this project through a number of rough patches. Finally, a very special thanks to Patrick Bedard who checked photo captions for accuracy. He is not, of course, responsible for any substantive errors in the book.

The automobile industry, bloodied on a number of pages in *American Cars,* cooperated with knowledge of the risk. Particular thanks go to Hal Sperlich of Chrysler Corporation and Leo Levine of Mercedes-Benz of North America.

I have dedicated *American Cars* to Lee and Joe Eskridge with a somewhat cryptic explanation. In fact, Lee and Joe were part of Dodge Brothers, Franklin, Hudson, and American Motors. Joe Eskridge was one of Detroit's first body engineers. It is a rare blessing to have parents-in-law who are both charming and knowledgeable.

They produced another bulwark in this endeavor: their daughter, Olivia Lee, my wife of almost thirty years. To her, to our journalist son, Leon, Jr., who gave almost daily help, to our daughter Olivia, who probed the thesis of *American Cars* and thereby strengthened it, my love and devotion.

Genealogies
of
American
Car Companies

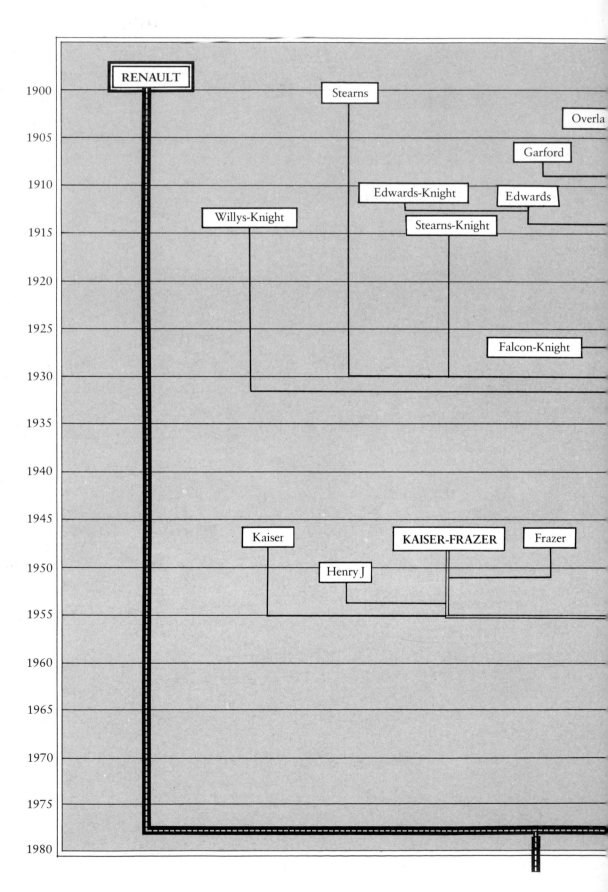

RENAULT

1900

Stearns

Overla

1905

Garford

1910

Edwards-Knight

Edwards

Willys-Knight

1915

Stearns-Knight

1920

1925

Falcon-Knight

1930

1935

1940

1945

Kaiser

KAISER-FRAZER

Frazer

1950

Henry J

1955

1960

1965

1970

1975

¹Name changed to honor
founder, Thomas B. Jeffery.

²Charles Nash bought Jeffery.

1980

426

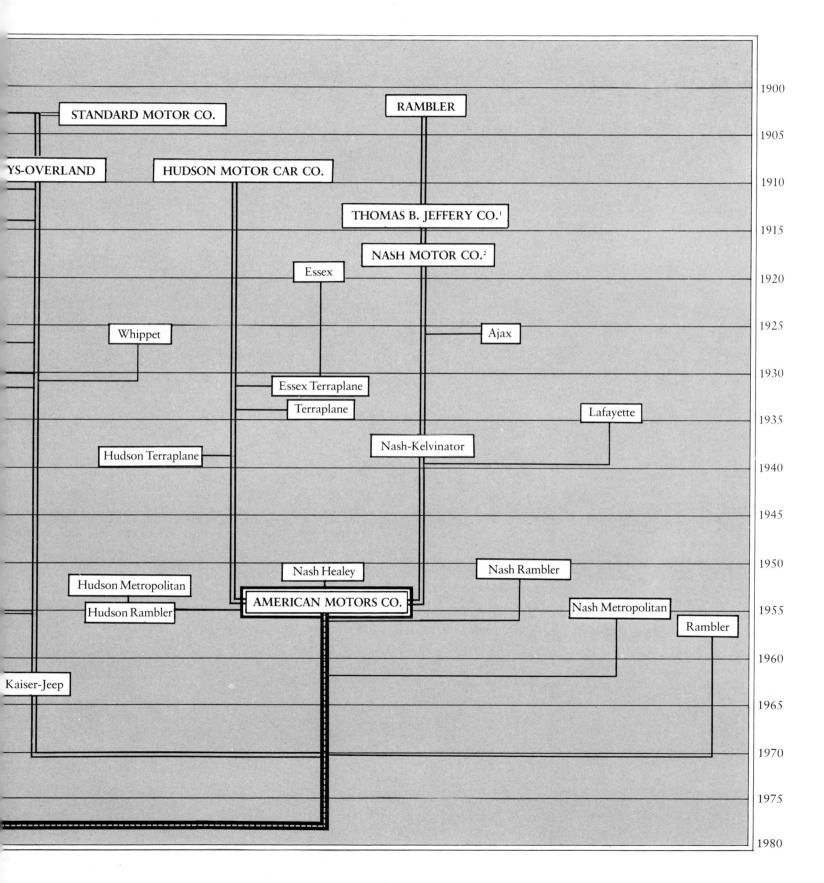

STANDARD MOTOR CO.

RAMBLER

YS-OVERLAND

HUDSON MOTOR CAR CO.

THOMAS B. JEFFERY CO.[1]

NASH MOTOR CO.[2]

Essex

Whippet

Ajax

Essex Terraplane

Terraplane

Lafayette

Hudson Terraplane

Nash-Kelvinator

Nash Healey

Nash Rambler

Hudson Metropolitan

Hudson Rambler

AMERICAN MOTORS CO.

Nash Metropolitan

Rambler

Kaiser-Jeep

1900
1905
1910
1915
1920
1925
1930
1935
1940
1945
1950
1955
1960
1965
1970
1975
1980

Chrysler Corporation

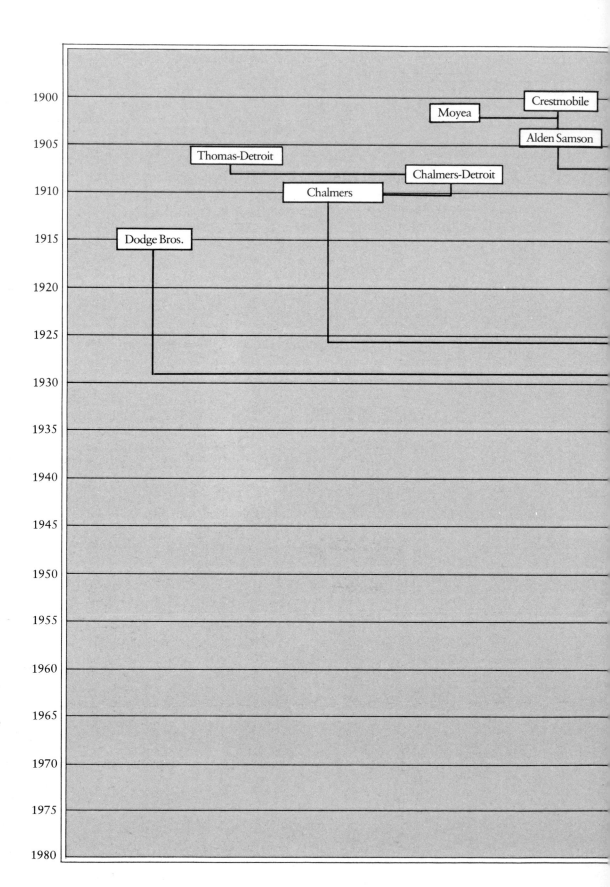

[1] Formed as Standard Motor Co.; then reorganized within a month as Maxwell Motor Co.

[2] Walter P. Chrysler resigned as president of Buick Motor Division to head Willys-Overland and then Maxwell. The Maxwell four-cylinder became the Chrysler four-cylinder and eventually the Plymouth four-cylinder.

[3] Chrysler acquired a majority interest in Simca (France) and Rootes Group (England).

428

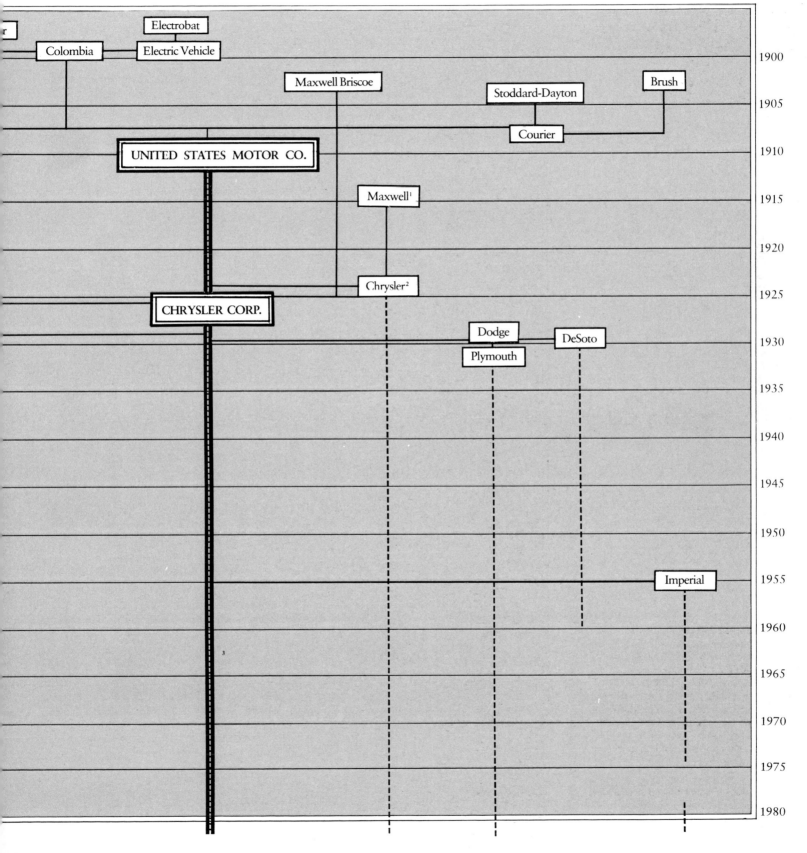

Electrobat

Colombia   Electric Vehicle

Maxwell Briscoe

Stoddard-Dayton

Brush

Courier

UNITED STATES MOTOR CO.

Maxwell[1]

Chrysler[2]

CHRYSLER CORP.

Dodge

Plymouth

DeSoto

Imperial

1900

1905

1910

1915

1920

1925

1930

1935

1940

1945

1950

1955

1960

1965

1970

1975

1980

General Motors Company

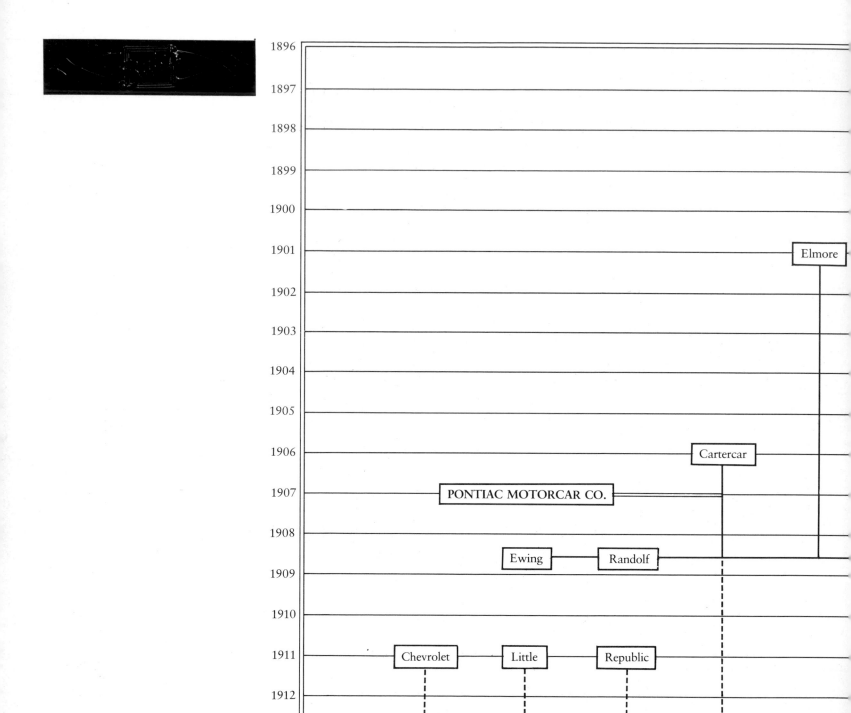

1896	
1897	
1898	
1899	
1900	
1901	Elmore
1902	
1903	
1904	
1905	
1906	Cartercar
1907	PONTIAC MOTORCAR CO.
1908	Ewing — Randolf
1909	
1910	
1911	Chevrolet — Little — Republic
1912	
1913	
1914	
1915	
1916	

[1] Chevrolet under William Durant acquired 50 percent of General Motors Co. stock; Chevrolet was not taken in until 1918.

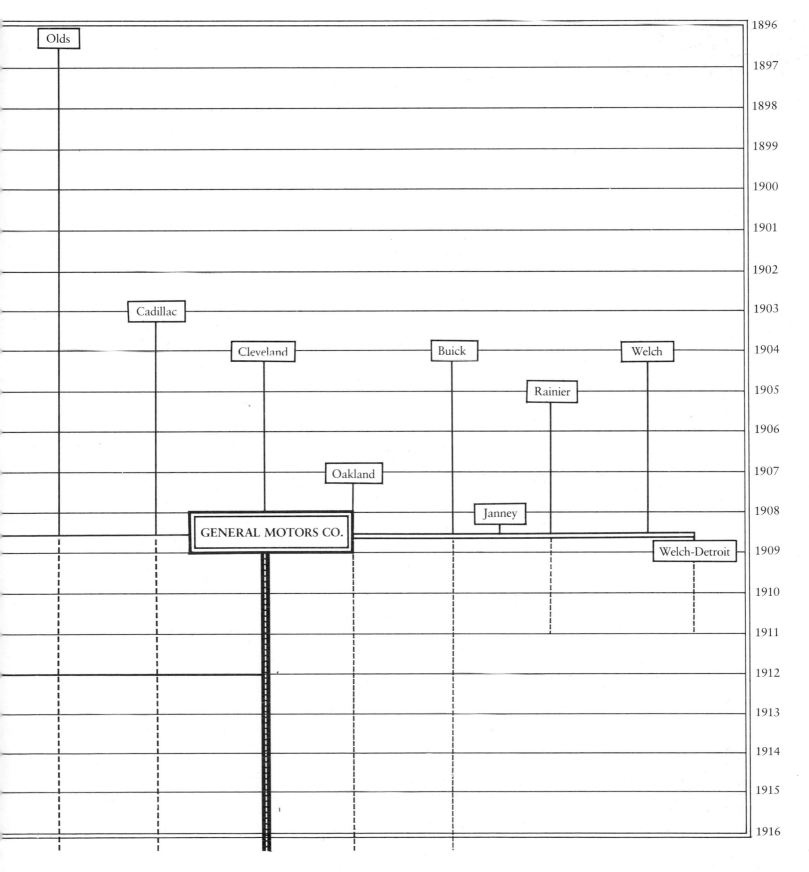

Olds
1896
1897
1898
1899
1900
1901
1902
Cadillac 1903
Cleveland · Buick Welch 1904
Rainier 1905
1906
Oakland 1907
Janney 1908
GENERAL MOTORS CO. Welch-Detroit 1909
1910
1911
1912
1913
1914
1915
1916

431

General Motors Corporation

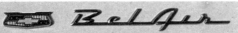

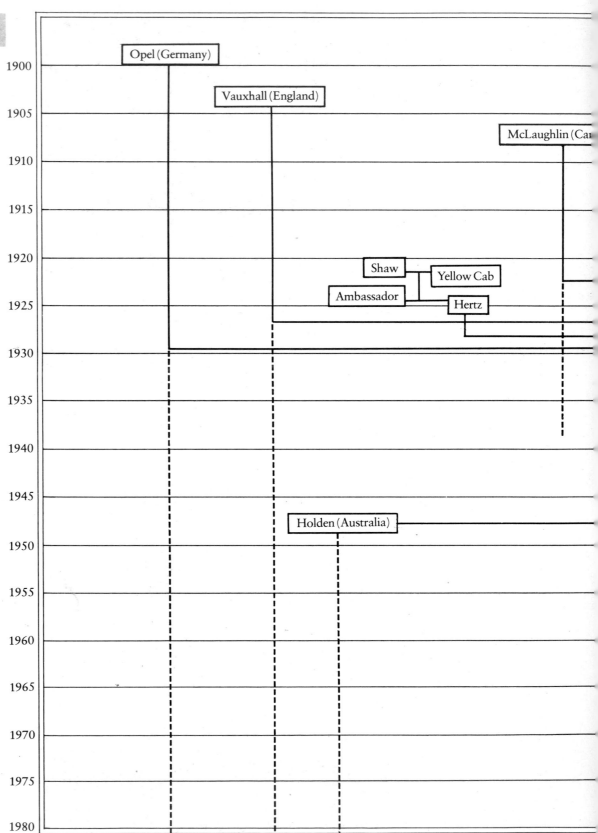

- 1 See genealogy of General Motors Company for details.
- 2 Fifteen-year contract in 1907 with Buick; became General Motors of Canada.
- 3 Cadillac, Oldsmobile, Buick, and Oakland became divisions of General Motors Corporation in 1916.
- 4 Chevrolet became a division in 1918.
- 5 Pontiac became a division in 1932.

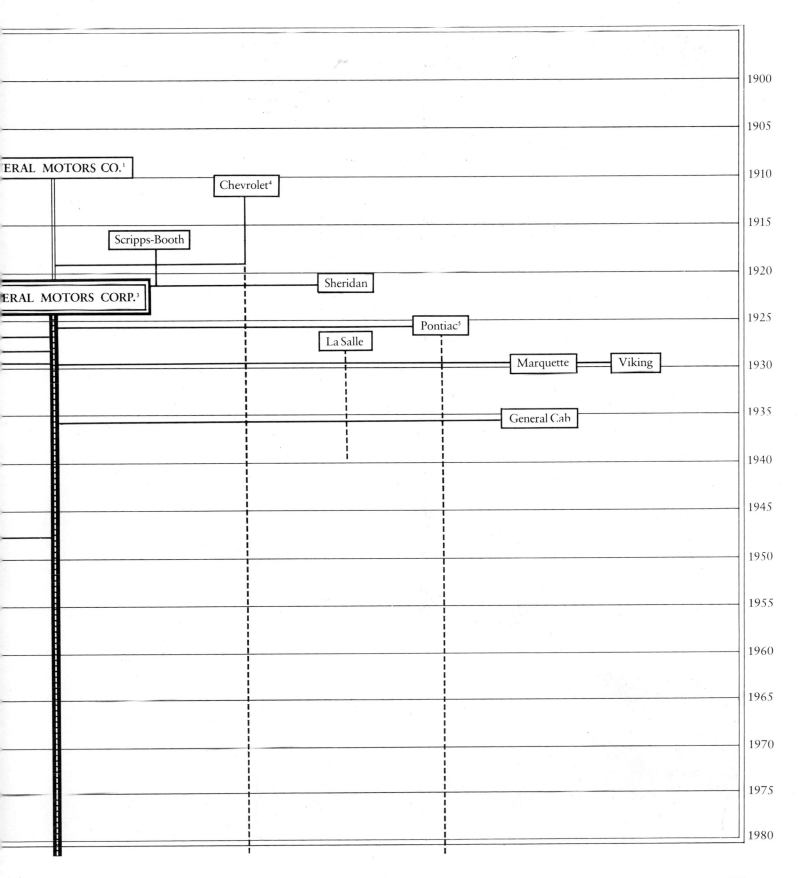

ERAL MOTORS CO.[1]

Chevrolet[4]

Scripts-Booth

ERAL MOTORS CORP.[3]

Sheridan

Pontiac[5]

La Salle

Marquette

Viking

General Cab

1900
1905
1910
1915
1920
1925
1930
1935
1940
1945
1950
1955
1960
1965
1970
1975
1980

433

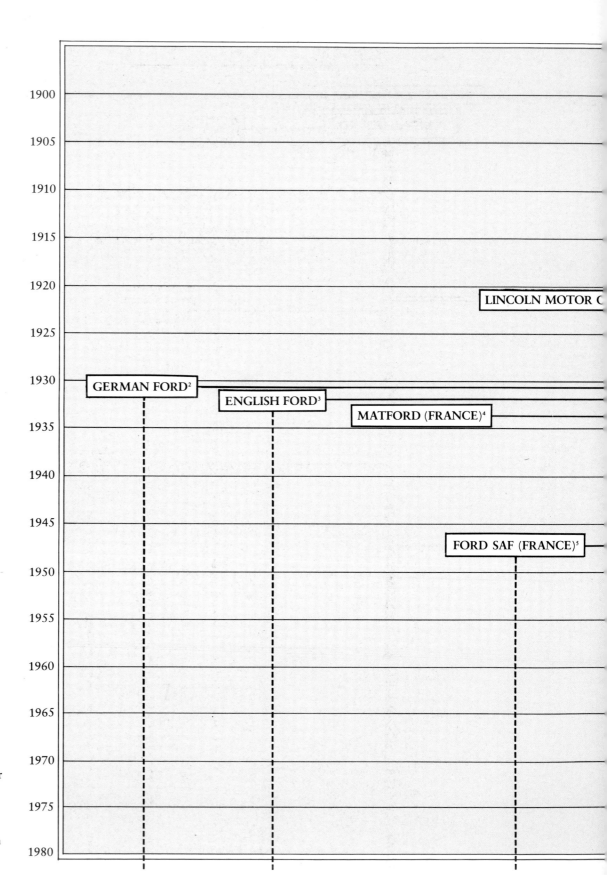

1900
1905
1910
1915
1920

LINCOLN MOTOR C

1925
1930

GERMAN FORD[2]

ENGLISH FORD[3]

MATFORD (FRANCE)[4]

1935
1940
1945

FORD SAF (FRANCE)[5]

1950
1955

[1] Ford purchased Lincoln Motor Co. in 1922.
[2] Actually produced Model T in 1925, but new model in 1931.
[3] Actually produced Model T in 1911, but new model in 1932.
[4] From Mathis factory.
[5] Reorganized after World War II, produced Vedettes; became Simca.
[6] Henry Ford was chief engineer; Henry Leland produced the first Cadillac which was similar to the first Ford.

1960
1965
1970
1975
1980

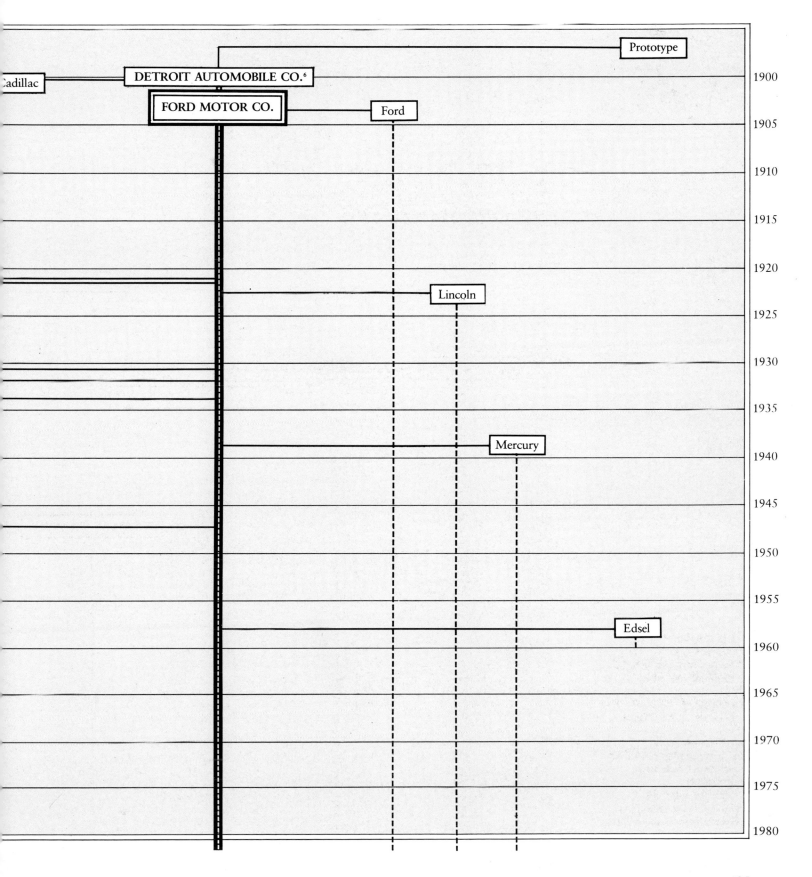

Prototype

Cadillac DETROIT AUTOMOBILE CO.⁶

FORD MOTOR CO. Ford

1900

1905

1910

1915

1920

Lincoln

1925

1930

1935

Mercury

1940

1945

1950

1955

Edsel

1960

1965

1970

1975

1980

Bibliography

Abbott, Ernest Hamlin. "What the Country is Thinking." *Outlook,* vol. 149, 22 August 1928, pp. 665–66, 703; vol. 150, 24 October 1928, pp. 741+.

Aceti, Enrica and Kevin Brazendale, eds. *Classic Cars: Fifty Years of the World's Finest Automotive Design.* New York: Exeter Books, 1981.

Adams, Frederick Upham. "Get Ready for 5 Million Automobiles." *American Magazine,* vol. 81, April 1916, pp. 18–20.

Aldrich, William. "The Automobile & the Railroad." *Harper's Weekly,* vol. 55, 7 January 1911, p. 30.

Allen, Frederick Lewis. *Only Yesterday: An Informal History of the 1920s.* New York: Harper and Brothers, 1931.

———. *Since Yesterday: The 1930s in America.* Garden City, N.Y.: Blue Ribbon Books, 1940.

———. *Big Change, America Transforms Itself, Nineteen Hundred–Nineteen Fifty.* New York: Harper & Row, 1969.

Automobile Manufacturers Association. *Automobiles of America.* Detroit: Wayne State University Press, 1968.

"America Remade in 40 Years: The Story of the Automobile." *Newsweek,* vol. 12, 7 November 1938, pp. 36–42.

Anderson, George W. "Roads—Motor & Rail." *The Atlantic Monthly,* vol. 135, March 1925, pp. 393–404.

"Of Arms & Automobiles." *Fortune,* vol. 22, December 1940, pp. 55–60.

"An Automobile Census." *Literary Digest,* vol. 67, 20 November 1920, p. 29.

"Automobile Fatalities at a New High Mark in 1919." *Literary Digest,* vol. 65, 22 May 1920, pp. 118-19.

"The Automobile—Key to Our Prosperity." *Literary Digest,* vol. 92, 8 January 1927, pp. 52–57.

"The Automobile as a Rest Cure." *The Atlantic Monthly,* vol. 98, October 1906, pp. 575–76.

"Automobile Ups & Downs." *The Nation,* vol. 119, 24 September 1924, pp. 301–302.

Baltzell, E. Digby. *Philadelphia Gentlemen: The Making of a National Upper Class.* Glencoe, Ill.: Free Press, 1958.

Barr, Lockwood and G. A. Kahmann. "Steel in Motion: The Evolution of Automobile Body Design." *Country Life,* vol. 76, October 1939, pp. 52–53.

Beard, George. *American Nervousness: Its Causes and Consequences.* New York: Putnam, 1881.

Bedard, Patrick J. "We Have Seen the Engine of the Future and It's in Your Car." *Esquire,* March 1976.

Blanchard, Harold F. "265 Horsepower . . . 116 Miles Per Hour." *MoToR,* December 1928.

Boorstin, Daniel J. *The Americans: The Democratic Experience.* New York: Random House, 1973.

Borgeson, Griffith and Eugene Jaderquist. *Sports and Classic Cars.* Englewood Cliffs, N.J.: Prentice-Hall, 1955.

Brown, Lester R., Christopher Flavin, and Colin Norman. *Running on Empty: The Future of the Automobile in an Oil Short World.* New York: Norton, 1979.

Bruce-Briggs, B. *The War Against the Automobile.* New York: Dutton, 1975.

Burchell, H. P. "Our Chaotic Automobile Laws." *Harper's Weekly,* vol. 52, 16 May 1908, p. 17.

Byrd, Al. "Let's Hear it for Javelin!—Javelin Who?" *Car and Driver,* September 1968.

California Air Resources Board Bulletin, vol. 7, no. 5, May 1976. Sacramento, California.

"Chauffeur." *Two Thousand Miles on an Automobile.* Philadelphia: Lippincott, 1902.

Collier's Encyclopedia. William Halsey, ed., vol. 3. New York: Macmillan Educational Corp., 1978.

"The Class of Citizens Who Buy Motor-Cars 'On-Tick'." *Literary Digest,* vol. 65, 22 May 1920, pp. 116–118.

Commager, Henry Steele. *The American Mind.* New Haven: Yale University Press, 1950.

Claudy, C. H. "Your $4.65 Worth of Roads." *Collier's,* vol. 67, 1 January 1921, p. 15.

Comstock, Sarah. "The United States on Wheels." *Literary Digest,* vol. 116, 16 September 1933, pp. 3–4.

Conde, John A. *The Cars that Hudson Built.* Keego Harbor, Mich.: Arnold-Porter Publishing Company, 1980.

Conwell, Russell H. *Acres of Diamonds.* New York: Harper and Brothers, 1943.

Crissey, Forrest. "No Parking." *Saturday Evening Post,* vol. 197, 2 May 1925, pp. 32–33.

"Crossing the Continent by Automobile." *Scientific American,* vol. 94, 13 January 1906, p. 24.

Davidson, Bill. "Speaking of Autos: Prominent Americans Talk About the Car and How It Is Changing America." *Saturday Evening Post,* no. 241, 5 October 1968, p. 34.

Dayton, Thaddeus S. "The Motorist & the Law." *Harper's Weekly,* vol. 56, 2 March 1912, p. 12.

Encyclopedia of American History. Guilford, Conn.: The Dushkin Publishing Group, 1973.

"Detroit: A Continuing Crisis." *Business Week,* 4 November 1939, pp. 34–36.

"Detroit's New, New Embarrassed Chariots." *The New Republic,* vol. 139, 10 November 1958, pp. 5–6.

Dianna, John, ed. *Complete Auto Guide for the '80's.* Los Angeles: Petersen Publishing Company, 1980.

Dinkel, John. *The Road & Track Illustrated Auto Dictionary.* New York: Norton, 1977.

Dix, William F. "A Source of Sensible Pleasure." *Outlook,* vol. 83, 26 May 1906, pp. 173–177.

Elgin, Duane, et al. *City Size and the Quality of Life—An Analysis of the Policy Implications of Continued Population Concentration.* Prepared for NSF, Research Applied to National Needs (RANN) Program, under NSF contract GI.138462 by the Stanford Research Institute, Menlo Park, Calif., November 1974.

Faulkner, David. "Staff Report on Methanol Fuels." Sacramento, Calif.: California Air Resources Board, Division of Implementation and Enforcement, September 1975.

Fitzgerald, F. Scott. *The Great Gatsby.* New York: Charles Scribner's Sons, 1925.

Flink, James J. *America Adopts the Automobile, 1895–1910.* Cambridge, Mass.: MIT Press, 1970.

———. *The Car Culture.* Cambridge, Mass.: MIT Press, 1975.

Frazer, Elizabeth. "The Destruction of Rural America." *Saturday Evening Post,* vol. 197, 9 May 1925, p. 39.

Freeston, Charles Lincoln. "The Motor in Warfare." *Scribner's Monthly,* vol. 57, February 1915, pp. 185–200.

"The Future of the Motor Car." *Scientific American,* vol. 77, 17 July 1897, p. 35.

Gardini, Christina and Maria Bugli, eds. *Design Gugiaro: The Automobile Form.* Milan: Automobilia, Societa per la Storia e L'immagine dell'Automobile, 1980.

Georgano, G. N., ed. *The Complete Encyclopedia of Motorcars: 1885 to the Present.* London: Ebury Press, 1968.

Grand, Frank P., et al. *The Automobile and the Regulation of its Impact on the Environment.* Norman, Okla.: University of Oklahoma Press, 1975.

Greene, Howard. "The Possibilities of the Pleasure Tour." *Harper's,* vol. 54, 8 January 1910, pp. 36–37.

Guggenheimer, Elinor. "Can We Live With Our Cars." *The Nation,* vol. 201, 27 September 1965, pp. 164–66.

Gustin, Lawrence R. *Billy Durant: Creator of General Motors.* Grand Rapids, Mich.: William B. Eerdmans Publishing Co., 1973.

Harrah's Automobile Collection: Special Edition. Reno, Nev.: Catalogue, 1975.

Haywood, Charles B. "What is the Seldon Patent?" *Scientific American,* vol. 100, 20 March 1909, pp. 223–25.

Hebb, David. *Wheels on the Road: A History of the Automobile from the Steam Engine to the Car of Tomorrow.* New York: Collier, 1966.

Hemphill, Robert, Jr. and Carmen Difiglio. "Future Demand of Automotive Fuels." Presented at the General Motors Research Laboratories Symposium of Future Automotive Fuels, Detroit, Michigan, October 1975.

"Henry Ford on Autos, 'A Look Down the Road,' Interview with the Chairman, Ford Motor Company." *U.S. News & World Report,* 20 October 1974.

Henry, Thomas P. "The Motorist Pays—and Pays." *The Independent,* vol. 115, 17 October 1925, pp. 437–39.

Hickerson, J. Mel. *Ernie Breech: The Story of His Remarkable Career at General Motors, Ford and TWA.* New York: Meredith Press, 1968.

Hindley, Geoffrey. *A History of Roads.* Secaucus, N.J.: The Citadel Press, 1971.

History of Mercedes-Benz Motor Vehicles and Engines, 5th Edition. Stuttgart-Unter-Turkheim, West Germany: Daimler-Benz Aknengesellschaft, 1972/1973.

Hoover, Herbert C. (Secretary of Commerce). "Your Automotive Industry." *Colliers,* vol. 69, 7 January 1922, p. 5.

"The Horseless Carriage & Public Health." *Scientific America,* vol. 80, 18 February 1899, p. 98.

"How the Automobile Has Altered Our Lives." *New Scientist,* 24 May 1973.

Jerome, John. *The Death of the Automobile*. New York: Norton, 1972.

Kahn, Helen. "Large Cars, U.S. Models Safer, Insurers Report." *Automotive News*, 18 January 1982.

Katz, Michael, Robert Levering and Milton Moskowitz. *Everybody's Business: An Almanac: The Irreverent Guide to Corporate America*. San Francisco: Harper & Row, 1980.

Keats, John. *The Insolent Chariots*. Philadelphia: Lippincott, 1958.

Kelderman, Jake. "Serviceability Wins Popularity for Imports, Survey Says." *Auto Week*, 14 December 1981.

Kelly, Robert. *The Shaping of the American Past*, 2nd ed., Englewood Cliffs, N.J.: Prentice-Hall, 1978.

"Killings and Accidents as Threat to the Whole Motor-Car Industry." *Literary Digest*, vol. 80, 12 January 1924, pp. 60–64.

Kraft, J. "Annals of Industry: The Downsizing Decision." *The New Yorker*, vol. 56, 5 May 1980, p. 134.

Labatut, Jean and Wheaton J. Lane, eds. "The Highway and Social Problems." *Highways in Our National Life*. Princeton, N.J.: Princeton University Press, 1950.

"Legislation for Pedestrians." *Literary Digest*, vol. 92, 5 February 1927, pp. 61–64.

Leighton, George R. and Joseph L. Nicholson. "Has the Automobile a Future?" *Harper's*, vol. 185, June 1942, pp. 63–73.

Leland, Ottilie and Minie Dobbs Millbrook. *Master of Precision: Henry M. Leland*. Detroit, Mich.: Wayne State University Press, 1966.

Lewis, H. Bertram. "The Economic Status of the Passenger Motor Car." *Outlook*, vol. 118, 27 March 1918, pp. 508–509.

Long, J. C. *Roy D. Chapin*. Presentation Copy, 1945.

"The Lost Liberty of the Road." *Living Age*, vol. 258, 25 July 1908, pp. 249–52.

Lowry, Helen Bullitt. "Woman's Place is in the Tonneau." *MoTor*, November 1923.

Lynd, Robert Staughton and Helen M. *Middletown: A Study in American Culture*. New York: Harcourt, 1929.

———. *Middletown in Transition: A Study in Cultural Conflicts*. New York: Harcourt, 1937.

Macauley, Alvan. "Our Servant—The Passenger Auto." *Outlook*, vol. 127, 6 April 1921, pp. 556–57.

McComb, F. Wilson. *Veteran Cars: The Formative Years of Motoring*. London: Hamlyn Publishing Group, 1974.

MacDonald, Donald. *Detroit 1985: An Irreverent Look at the Auto-Makers, the Dealers, the Government and You*. Garden City, N.Y.: Doubleday, 1980.

MacFarlane, Peter Clark. "Beginnings of the Automobile." *Colliers*, vol. 54, 9 January 1915, supp. pp. 42–59.

Mahoney, Tom. *The Story of George Romney*. New York: Harper & Brothers, 1960.

Man, Automobile and Road. Stowe, Vt.: Mercedes-Benz of North America; Safety Seminar, July 1974.

Mandel, Leon. *Driven: The American Four-Wheeled Love Affair*. New York: Stein & Day, 1977.

——— and Peter Revson. *Speed With Style: The Autobiography of Peter Revson*. Garden City, N.Y.: Doubleday, 1974.

———. *William Fisk Harrah: The Life and Times of a Gambling Magnate*. Garden City, N.Y.: Doubleday, 1982.

"1981 Market Data Book Issue." *Automotive News*, April 1981.

"Manufacturing Lesson; Shift to New Materials." *Business Week*, 26 January 1935, pp. 8–9.

Martin, Edward S. "The Motor Craze." *Outlook*, vol. 96, 19 November 1910, pp. 627–31.

"Materials They Use in New Cars." *Business Week*, 4 September 1937, p. 17.

"The Motor More Deadly Than War." *Literary Digest*, vol. 94, 27 August 1927, p. 12.

Montbrial, Thierry de. *Energy: The Countdown: A Report to the Club of Rome*. Elmsford N.Y.: Pergamon, 1979.

"Motor League Favored." *The Motor World*, 6 February 1902.

Motor Vehicle Manufacturers Association Vehicle Fact and Figures, 1978. Detroit, Mich.: MVMA, 1981.

Nader, Ralph. *Unsafe at Any Speed*. New York: Grossman, 1965.

"The National 55 mph Speed Limit." *Fact Sheet*, Washington, D.C.: U.S. Department of Transportation, Office of Public Affairs, May 1976.

Nelson, Walter Henry. *Small Wonder: The Amazing Story of the Volkswagen*. Boston: Little, Brown, 1965.

Nicholson, T. R. "The Duesenberg J and SJ." *Classic Cars in Profile*, vol 4. Edited by Anthony Harding. Garden City: Doubleday, 1968.

Norback, Craig T., ed. *Chilton's Complete Book of Automotive Facts*. Radnor, Penn.: Chilton, 1981.

"Oldsmobile 3,000-Mile Tour in England." *The Automobile*, 19 November 1904.

Olson, Steve. "Prospects for the Automobile: Sputtering

Toward the Twenty-First Century." *The Futurist*, February 1980.

Page, Logan Waller. "Our Highways and the Motor Car." *Collier's*, vol. 48, 6 January 1912, sup. p. 38.

Parker, Maude. "Is There an American Aristocracy?" *Saturday Evening Post*, vol. 204, 4 June 1932, p. 21.

Penman, H. C. "Motoring and Nerves." *Harper's Weekly*, vol. 62, 15 April 1916, p. 413.

Perry, Harry Wilkin. "The Automobile and the Full Dinner Pail." *Collier's*, vol. 48, 6 January 1912, sup. p. 50.

Perry, John. "New Products for Postwar America." *Harper's*, vol. 186, 2 February 1943, pp. 330–32.

Porter, William Harley. "How the Automobile Affects Other Industries." *Harper's Weekly*, vol. 54, 20 August 1910, p. 25.

"The Private Automobile Stable." *The Automobile*, 5 July 1902.

Rae, John B. *American Automobile Manufacturers: The First Forty Years*. Radnor, Penn.: Chilton, 1959.

———. *The Road and the Car in American Life*. Cambridge, Mass.: MIT Press, 1971.

"The Regulation of Automobiles." *Outlook*, vol. 82, 24 February 1906, p. 388.

The Report by the Federal Task Force on Motor Vehicle Goals Beyond 1980, Draft, Executive Summary. Washington, D.C.: U.S. Government Printing Office, September 1976.

Rollins, M. "Women and Motor Cars." *Outlook*, vol. 92, 7 August 1909, pp. 859–60.

Rose, Albert C. *Historic American Roads*. New York: Crown, 1976.

Rothschild, Emma. *Paradise Lost: The Decline of the Auto-Industrial Age*. New York: Random House, 1973.

Rowland, J. B. "Coaching College Runners from a Motor-car." *Harper's*, vol. 51, March 1907, p. 372.

Schorr, Alvin L. "Families on Wheels." *Harper's*, vol. 216, January 1958, pp. 71–75.

Scott-Montagu, John. "Automobile Legislation: A Criticism and Review." *North American Review*, vol. 179, August 1904, pp. 168–77.

Setright, L. J. K. *The Pirelli History of Motor Sport*. London: Frederick Muller, 1981.

Shippey, Lee. "Building a National Turnpike." *Collier's*, vol. 48, 6 January 1912, sup. p. 31.

"Show Room 20—Longevity of Passenger Cars in Sweden." Rockleigh, N.J.: Volvo of America.

"Six Econo-Racers." *Car and Driver*, January 1969.

Sloan, Alfred P., Jr. *My Years With General Motors*. Garden City, N.Y.: Doubleday, 1964.

Smith R. P. *Consumer Demand for Cars in the USA*. University of Cambridge, Department of Applied Economics, Occasional Paper 44. Cambridge, England: Cambridge University Press, 1975.

Special Subcommittee on the Federal-Aid Highway Program of the Committee on Public Works, House of Representatives, 90th Congress, 2nd Session. *Highway Safety, Design and Operations, Freeway Signing and Related Geometrics*. May 7–9, July 9–11, 16 and 18, 1968. Available from Superintendent of Documents.

Speed, John Gilmer. "The Modern Chariot." *Cosmopolitan*, vol. 29, June 1900, pp. 139–52.

Stern, Jane and Stern, Michael. *Auto Ads*. New York: David Obst, 1978.

Stickley, Gustav. "New Romance of the Road." *Craftsman*, vol. 17 (1909), p. 46.

Stobaugh, Robert and Daniel Yergin, eds. *Energy Future: Report of the Energy Project at the Harvard Business School*. New York: Random House, 1979.

Strong, Sidney. "Looking Backward." *Collier's*, vol. 50, 11 January 1913, sup. 21.

Teahen, John K., Jr. "Deepening Auto Recession Is Story of Year for 1981." *Automotive News*, 4 January 1982.

"They Drive a Lot ... but Don't Buy Much." *The Motor*, September 1929.

Thomas, E. R. "The Development of the American Automobile. *Harper's Weekly*, vol. 51, 16 March 1907, p. 386b.

Trager, James, ed. *The People's Chronology: A Year-by-Year Record of Human Events from Prehistory to the Present*. New York: Holt, Rinehart and Winston, 1979.

Transportation in America's Future: Potentials for the Next Half Century. Part I: Societal Context; Part 2: Transportation Forecasts. Menlo Park, Calif.: Stanford Research Institute, 1977.

Turner, Frederick Jackson. *The Significance of the Frontier in American History*. Edited by Harold P. Simonson. New York: Ungar, 1963.

"Union Pot-Boiler." *Business Week*, 9 March 1935, p. 8.

"What the Public Wants in the 1934 Models." *Business Week*, 19 August 1933, p. 14.

"Where the Car Has Helped the Church." *Literary Digest*, vol. 70, 16 July 1921, pp. 52–53.

Whitman, Roger B. "The Automobile in New Roles." *Country Life*, vol. 15, November 1908, p. 53.

Widick, B. J., ed. *Auto Work and Its Discontents*. Baltimore: Johns Hopkins University Press, 1976.

Winther, Oscar O. *The Transportation Frontier, 1865–1890.* New York: Holt, Rinehart and Winston, 1964.

Wolfe, Tom. *The Kandy-Kolored Tangerine-Flake Streamline Baby.* New York: Farrar, Straus & Giroux, 1965.

Wright, J. Patrick. *On a Clear Day You Can See General Motors: John Z. DeLorean's Look Inside the Automotive Giant.* Grosse Point, Mich.: Wright Enterprises, 1979.

Yates, Brock. "Street Racing." *Car and Driver,* September 1967.

———."The View from Ground Zero." *Car and Driver,* March 1969.

———."Roadtesting the Roadtesters." *Car and Driver,* June 1969.

———."America's Two-Dimensional Sweetheart." *Car and Driver,* March 1971.

"55 Years of Progress: Old Skin Game." *Newsweek,* vol. 32, 29 November 1948, p. 62.

Index

Index to Photographs

The text was set in Sabon by TGA Graphics, Inc.,
New York, New York.
The book was printed on 150 gsm. Solex paper
by Amilcare Pizzi s.p.a.-arti grafiche, Milan, Italy.
Bound in Italy by Amilcare Pizzi.